B 829.5 .F8513 1987

Funke, Gerhard.

Phenomenology, metaphysics
 or method?

W9-CZZ-468

WITHDRAWN

PHENOMENOLOGY–
Metaphysics or Method?

SERIES IN CONTINENTAL THOUGHT

EDITORIAL BOARD

Lester Embree, Chairman,
Center President
Duquesne University

Algis Mickunas
Secretary
Ohio University

Edward G. Ballard
Tulane University

José Huertas-Jourda
Wilfred-Laurier University

Joseph K. Kockelmans
Pennsylvania State University

William McKenna
Miami University

J. N. Mohanty
Temple University

Thomas M. Seebohm
Johannes Gutenberg—
Universität Mainz

Richard Zaner
Vanderbilt University

INTERNATIONAL ADVISORY BOARD

Suzanne Bachelard
Université de Paris

Rudolf Boehm
Rijksuniversiteit-Gent

Albert Borgmann
University of Montana

Amedeo P. Giorgi
Duquesne University

Richard Grathoff
Universität Bielefeld

Samuel Ijsseling
Husserl-Archief te Leuven

Alphonso Lingis
Pennsylvania State University

Werner Marx
Albert-Ludwigs-Universität

David Rasmussen
Boston College

John Sallis
Loyola University, Chicago

John Scanlon
Duquesne University

Hugh J. Silverman
State University of New York,
Stony Brook

Carlo Sini
Università di Milano

Elisabeth Ströker
Universität Köln

Jacques Taminiaux
Louvain-la-Neuve

D. Lawrence Wieder
University of Oklahoma

Dallas Willard
University of Southern
California

Sponsored by the Center for Advanced Research in Phenomenology, Inc.

PHENOMENOLOGY–
Metaphysics or Method?

o by
   Gerhard Funke

o with a Foreword by
   Thomas M. Seebohm

o translated by
   David J. Parent

Ohio University Press
Athens

Translation © copyright 1987 by Ohio University Press.

Originally published as *Phänomenologie—Metaphysik oder Methode?* by H. Bouvier & Co., Bonn, 1966.

Printed in the United States of America.
All rights reserved.

Translation was funded in part by grants from Inter Nationes and Illinois State University.

Library of Congress Cataloging-in-Publication Data

Funke, Gerhard.
  Phenomenology, metaphysics or method?

  (Series in continental thought ; 13)
  Translation of: Phänomenologie, Metaphysik oder Methode?
  1. Phenomenology.   2. Metaphysics.   3. Methodology.
I. Title.   II. Series.
B829.5.F8513   1987   142'.7   87-15220
ISBN 0-8214-0719-8

Contents

Foreword

by Thomas M. Seebohm

Phenomenology—Metaphysics or Method? develops a programmatic conception of phenomenology together with vivid criticisms of not only the post-Husserlian phase of the "phenomenological movement," but also of the *Zeitgeist* in general. Seen in its context—namely, philosophical discussion in Germany in the first decades after World War II—the book speaks for itself and does not need a foreword to explain its intentions. In principle the reader of this translation could reconstruct the context, for numerous references to other authors and positions are made. Still, the American reader seeking orientation would find it very cumbersome to carry out such a reconstruction without assistance. Thus some explanations might be useful, especially because the version of phenomenology which Funke and then his school represents is not as well known in North America as in the Spanish-speaking world or Japan. To be sure, there is a brief remark about him and his followers in the latest edition of Herbert Spiegelberg's *The Phenomenological Movement*, and some of his writings are available in English.[1] However, the larger American works on Husserl have in most cases neglected his position as a possible alternative.

Before looking into the context of the following work, this neglect itself merits some comment. It is characteristic of the development of "phenomenology and existentialism" that—setting aside some very significant exceptions which will be considered immediately—Husserl was of interest as a forerunner of Sartre, Merleau-Ponty, and, above all, Heidegger. Precisely this way of understanding and criticizing Husserl is the target of arguments in Funke's book. It represents what has been called the "Husserlite" position and is a position which was not acceptable to the mainstream representatives of the "phenomenological movement." Of

course, there also have been and are in the United States former students
and followers of Husserl who did not agree with the mainstream judgment
of his phenomenology as only a preparatory step. But even most of
them—like many other phenomenologists in Europe—criticized Husserl's move towards a transcendental phenomenology and the idealism
which they saw as its consequence. Very few took the transcendental
turn.

In this connection Funke can be interestingly contrasted with Aron
Gurwitsch, the most significant "transcendentalist" in the United States.
From a historical point of view such a contrast is not merely arbitrary: out
of their interaction Gurwitsch was guest professor at the University of
Mainz and Funke was later Theodor Heuss professor at the New School
for Social Research. From the moment he began to formulate his own
theory of consciousness, Gurwitsch criticized Husserl for the positive
function of a transcendental subject which, as a spontaneity, synthesizes
a matter that is intrinsically devoid of structure. By contrast, for Funke
the concept of transcendental subjectity (*Subjektität*) and its activity—its
Leisten and *Leistung*—are of crucial significance for transcendental
phenomenology. Furthermore, Gurwitsch still represents the general
phenomenological distrust of the regressive construction of hypothetical
presuppositions, while for Funke "hypothesis" has always remained a key
term. Thus it is tempting to understand Funke's interpretation of
phenomenology as the final point of that appraisal and critique of Husserl
which begins with Natorp's reviews and ends with Hans Wagner's
profound considerations of Husserl's late philosophy.[2] However, even if
one were to regard Funke's as the most positive of the neo-Kantian
interpretations of Husserl, the label "Kantian" could all too easily be used
to dismiss the program developed by Funke as not "relevant" to the
development of the "phenomenological movement." In what follows I will
offer a biographical and then systematic discussion to show why the
neo-Kantian label *cannot* be pinned on Funke.

Phenomenology—Metaphysics or Method? very often presupposes
philological arguments, but it is not a philological investigation of what
Husserl "really" had in mind. Its main intention is not to show that
Husserl's critics are wrong merely because they misinterpreted his texts.
Seen from the viewpoint of strict Husserl philology one might even argue
that in some cases there is in Husserl's writings no positive evidence for
Funke's theses about phenomenology. Funke himself says that in some
cases Husserl did not give the proper answer, or left open questions he
should have answered. Nor is the book a phenomenological investigation.
To be sure, it often presupposes phenomenological investigations and
their results. For example, in some cases it is left to the reader to follow

the references and to verify the details of Husserl's phenomenological investigations concerning, e.g., eidetic intuition or intersubjectivity. Rather, the book presents an argument determining what phenomenology can and ought to be in the context of the present development of philosophy and of humanity in general: *philosophy as a rigorous science in a very specific sense*. At the same time, the argument shows that the phenomenological movement after Husserl failed to fulfill this task and so fell back to the level of a dogmatic metaphysics which forgot the method of discovering its own conditions, and thereby compromised its own claims to have shown some last absolute ground.

The book thus has the character of a manifesto. It should be kept in mind, however, that this manifesto is not an empty claim lacking more concrete corroboration. Funke himself has published extensive Husserl interpretations and phenomenological investigations, first of all his *Zur transzendentalen Phänomenologie* of 1957, but also other books in Spanish and Japanese. Numerous other articles on phenomenological topics and on hermeneutics and history belong to the background of this manifesto. And he can refer to four published dissertations by his students from this period, which can count as a partial fulfillment of the program.[3] In the series *Mainzer philosophische Forschungen* and *Conscientia* many other books have been published which belong to the same context. It would be wrong, however, to assume that there is something like a school in the sense of a group of philosophers devoted to the exegesis of the writings of the master and filling in the lacunae in his system. The reader of *Phenomenology—Metaphysics or Method?* can easily verify that the existence of a school in this sense would contradict the basic intention and maxims developed therein to guide transcendental reflection.

With regard to Kantianism and neo-Kantianism it should be noted that Funke and his followers considered the critique of the neo-Kantianism of, e.g., Hönigswald and Wolfgang Cramer, as a central task, and in the following work Funke himself criticizes Wagner.[4] By contrast, Funke also obviously has positive connections to different representatives of transcendental philosophy as evidenced by his favorable references to P. K. Schneider and R. Lauth.[5] In any case, Funke was from his student days familiar with the various neo-Kantian and Fichtean positions; one of his teachers was the neo-Kantian Bruno Bauch. However, the following work shows clearly that another of his teachers, Erich Rothacker, is at least as important as "Kantianism" for the development of Funke's position.[6] Rothacker represents historical consciousness and historism, the thesis that every position is context-bound and dogmatically presupposes its principles. Looking into this combination of names and positions, it becomes clear that Husserl's transcendental phenomenology is presented here as a possible synthesis of radicalized historical consciousness with the idea of a universal transcendental critique. This critique stems in part from Kant—although transcendental philosophy and Kantian philosophy are not synonyms—but it is realized as science only in phenomenology. Husserl and phenomenology in general are not regarded as being fully understandable only by adding a Kantian transcendental subject, a thesis which would indeed be neo-Kantian. But Husserl is also not understood merely as an "improved" Kant, i.e., as the discoverer of the only method whereby philosophy can be rigorous science. Transcendental phenomenology is, rather, understood as the method wherein radical rational critique and radicalized historical consciousness can come together.

Having offered these more biographical remarks, let us briefly characterize the basic intentions of the book. The thesis that phenomenology had forgotten the question of being, i.e., the question which alone can lead to the ultimate foundations, was accepted by most representatives of the "phenomenological movement" in Germany in the middle of the century. The opinion that phenomenology has value only in conjunction with metaphysics was reflected in the title of a famous book, *Phenomenology and Metaphysics*. Others searched for a final grounding of phenomenology in speculative thinking.[7] The interpretation of Husserl's last work, the *Crisis*, as a renunciation of his Cartesianism and of the ideal of philosophy as a rigorous science by turning to the life-world as the phenomenological Absolute can be considered as an attempt by the "phenomenological movement" to save the master's philosophical honor by showing that he finally came to his senses.

The problems connected with this interpretation of the *Crisis* and the concept of the life-world are of central significance in the last chapters of *Phenomenology—Metaphysics or Method?* The main thrust of the argument has two aspects. The first is the simple philological proof that this interpretation of the *Crisis* and of the development of phenomenology in the late Husserl is in every respect untenable. It is worth mentioning that H.-G. Gadamer—who of course does not at all share Funke's philosophical position—independently offered a similar philological refutation. The publication of the letters of Husserl to Ingarden prove that both Gadamer and Funke are correct in their evaluation of the situation.[8] The second and central aspect of the argument in the following work answers the question: "How is it possible to have philosophy as a rigorous science, given that the analyses of the *Crisis* and other investigations show the historical character of reason?"

The question "What is philosophy?" is the topic of the first chapter of the book. Funke offers nine theses which determine the essentials of scientific philosophy, and it is later shown that phenomenology and only phenomenology can fulfill the requirements offered. The theses cannot be discussed here, but what catches the eye of the reader there and in the later chapters is the use of Kantian terms such as "critical," "dogmatic," "presupposition," and "hypothetical." It is especially the last term, which plays a significant role in Natorp's philosophy, that can lead the reader to assume that Funke offers a neo-Kantian revision of Husserl. Yet without entering into an exegesis of Husserl's criticisms of Kant and the neo-Kantians—which Funke intentionally omits from his book—we can still mention one criticism that is essential to Funke's project. Husserl rejects their *regressive-constructive* method, which introduces entities "by hypothesis," i.e., entities which are *ex definitione* not empirical and so not phenomena. Such entities—the *thing-in-itself* as well as the *transcendental subject*—are presupposed as the highest conditions of the possibility of experience. According to Husserl, to presuppose them entails a "reduplication" of the world. The third thesis in the first chapter of Funke's book also disallows such a reduplication in a scientific philosophy. Husserl's phenomenology avoids such a mistake because it broadens and radicalizes the concept of phenomenon. Everything is what it is only as a phenomenon, i.e., as a correlate of consciousness. This holds for "things-in-themselves" as objects of a certain type of thinking as well as for transcendental subjectivity, consciousness itself. The task of scientific philosophy is to discover by means of critical reflection the conditions under which objects are given as this or that type of object.

Since consciousness is also given to itself as a phenomenon, it is obvious from a formal point of view that phenomenology—the scientific philosophy—will end in an infinite regress. This means that critical reflection will never end by finding a last absolute ground. Phenomenology is not foundationalism in this sense. Furthermore, this infinity is a bad infinity in Hegel's sense: phenomenology or scientific philosophy will not be able to develop a good infinity, the whole which represents the Absolute.

This conclusion is supported not only by formal considerations about the regress, but also by the phenomenological observation that consciousness and also reason are radically historical. That is, each is infinitely open to the constitution of new realms of objects—at the levels of life-world, science, and metaphysics—and all validity is context-bound, topical, and connected with a certain dogmatism which can be uncovered in phenomenological reflection on a case by case basis. Just as Funke employs Husserl to radicalize and broaden Kant's concept of "phenomenon," he also employs Rothacker's discussion of the "problem of historism"[9] to do the same for Kant's concept of "dogmatism."

From the viewpoint of the majority of Husserl interpretations, the thesis that for Husserl reason is historical comes as something of a surprise. However, with a sufficient amount of material from *Ideas* II (Hua IV), the two volumes of *First Philosophy* (Hua VII and VIII), the Fourth and Fifth *Cartesian Meditations* (Hua I), the *Crisis* (Hua VI), and *Experience and Judgment*, Funke shows that such an interpretation is viable. What could be added is Husserl's discussion of Dilthey and the human sciences in *Phenomenological Psychology*. From this material there can be no doubt that for Husserl, a universal human science (*universale Geisteswissenschaft*) as envisioned by Dilthey and Rothacker must be considered as a specific path to the transcendental phenomenological reduction. Such a science is thus identical with transcendental phenomenology. This relation between the human sciences and phenomenology is discovered in the fields of genetic phenomenology and the phenomenological analysis of intersubjectivity, fields to which Funke devotes many of his own phenomenological investigations in a narrow technical sense.

Phenomenology—Metaphysics or Method? is as a whole a critique of metaphysics, and is thus of interest to the present phase of the "phenomenological movement" in which the "end of metaphysics" and even the "end of philosophy" are discussed.[10] While metaphysics claims that it is capable of reaching ultimate foundations and is thus a science, Funke's critique rejects this claim. The method of this phenomenological critique is scientific because it asks in a specific way for the conditions of something pregiven. However, it is not foundationalist or metaphysical, because in its investigations it discovers that "ultimate conditions" can never be reached. Hence metaphysics as *prima philosophia* has come to an end, and only phenomenology can be scientific philosophy.

This does not mean that there will be no metaphysics in the future. There is no realm of object which is not given under the dogmatic presupposition of certain conditions. This is true for contexts belonging to the life-world or to science. A metaphysics is in general a doctrine which determines such conditions and presents them as (a) ultimate foundations, and (b) unhistorical and unchangeable. The task of phenomenology in its critical regress is to reject such claims on a case by case basis. However, this also involves justifying that the conditions in question belong to just this realm of objects, i.e., to the context for which they determine standards of validity.

Any attempt at a destruction of metaphysics which still presupposes general structures of the historicity of being-there (*Dasein*) still belongs to the realm of metaphysical thinking. It must also be seen that every attempt to discover some *telos* in history—or some viewpoint in a history of Being—through which it can be grasped as a whole is valid only in its historically bound context. For phenomenology, there is no whole, nothing universal without qualification, nothing eternally present, and thus nothing in which metaphysics can get a foothold from a theoretical point of view. Regarding Husserl's *Crisis*, Funke claims that the concept of *telos* occurring there is only relevant from a practical point of view. He also proposes that if Being is not the beginning, one might instead begin with what ought to be, and he points out that Husserl leaves such questions unanswered.

In this connection Funke—as the author of a later book, *Von der Aktualität Kants*[11]—does not criticize Kant's transcendental philosophy as insufficient from the viewpoint of transcendental phenomenology but rather criticizes Husserl from a Kantian point of view. This criticism—which is only hinted at in *Phenomenology—Metaphysics or Method?*—is made explicit in an essay available in English.[12] Funke claims that while Husserl in the beginning denied the primacy of the practical, he came close to affirming it in the end, although, unlike Kant, he never explicitly stated that the demand for philosophy as rigorous science and as rational critique must itself be subject to critical questions. For Funke, answers to such questions cannot be given theoretically. Rather, if these questions are answerable at all, their answers must be given by practical reason.

Notes

1. Herbert Spiegelberg, *The Phenomenological Movement: A Historical Introduction*, 3rd ed. (The Hague: Martinus Nijhoff, 1982). Essays of Funke available in English are: "Consciousness and Conscience from the Viewpoint of the Theory of Civilization," in *The Journal of the Indian Academy of Philosophy* 9 (1970), pp. 1–10; "The Object of Philosophy," in *Visva-Bharati Journal of Philosophy* 7 (1971), pp. 8–22; "Good Conscience, False Consciousness, Judging Reason," in *Proceedings of the 3rd International Kant-Congress. Held at the University of Rochester 1970* (Dordrecht: Reidel, 1972), pp. 63–89; "Phenomenology and History," in *Phenomenology and the Social Sciences*, Vol. 2 (Evanston: Northwestern University Press, 1973), pp. 3–101; "A crucial Question in Transcendental Phenomenology: What is Appearance in its Appearing?" in *Journal of the British Society for Phenomenology* 4 (1973), pp. 47–60; "What is an Object, if any, of Philosophy?" in *Pathway to God. A Journal of Spiritual Life* 8 (1973), pp. 37–52; "Husserl's Phenomenology as the Foundational Science," in *Southwestern Journal of Philosophy* 5 (1974) pp. 187–201;

"Concerning Eternal Peace—Ethics and Politics," in Witt and Werkmeister, ed., *Reflections on Kant's Philosophy* (Tallahassee: University Press of Florida, 1975), pp. 91–107; "A Transcendental-Phenomenological Investigation Concerning Universal Idealism, Intentional Analysis and the Genesis of Habitus," in W. McKenna, R. M. Harlan and L Winters, eds., *A Priori and World. European Contributions to Husserlian Phenomenology* (The Hague: Martinus Nijhoff, 1981); "A Transcendental-Phenomenological Investigation concerning Universal Idealism, Intentional Analysis and the Genesis of *Habitus*: Arche, Phansis, Hexis, Logos," in W. McKenna et al., ed., *Apriori and World: European Contributions to Husserlian Phenomenology* (The Hague: Martinus Nijhoff, 1981), pp. 71–113; "Anonymous Presuppositions in Spinoza's Philosophy," in The Israel Academy of Sciences and Humanities, ed., *Spinoza—his Thought and Work* (Jerusalem, 1983), pp. 53–70; "Practical Reason in Kant and Husserl," in T. M. Seebohm and J. J. Kockelmans, ed., *Kant and Phenomenology* (Washington, D.C.: Center for Advanced Research in Phenomenology and University Press of America, 1984) pp. 1–29.

2. For the primary and secondary sources connected with the dispute between Husserl and the neo-Kantians, see the bibliographical essay (vi–vii) and the bibliography (pp. 203–14) in *Kant and Phenomenology* (see n. 1, above).

3. For references to writings by immediate disciples, see *Phenomenology—Metaphysics or Method?* (hereafter PMM), chap. 2, n. 56, 84; chap. 3, n. 58; chap. 4, n. 23, 25, 26, 29, 76; chap. 7, n. 47; chap. 8, n. 11, 39, 61; chap. 9, n. 16. A bibliography by Gisela Müller of Funke's other writings up to 1974 has been published in A. J. Bucher, H. Drüe and T. M. Seebohm, ed., *Bewusst sein—Gerhard Funke zu eigen* (Bonn: Bouvier, 1975), pp. 427–43.

4. *PMM*, chap. 3, n. 20, 35; chap. 7 n. 37.

5. *PMM*, chap. 3, n. 19, 37, 38; chap. 7, n. 60; chap. 8, n 36.

6. *PMM*, p. 35.

7. The book is by Ludwig Landgrebe; cf. *PMM*, chap. 2, n. 5, and later. The idea of speculative phenomenology was developed by Eugen Fink; cf. *PMM*, chap. 3, n. 61, and later.

8. Hans-Georg Gadamer, *Philosophical Hermeneutics*, trans. and ed. D. E. Linge (Berkeley, Los Angeles, London: University of California Press, 1976), esp. pp. 151, 158–59. The original German version was written in 1963. Cf. also Edmund Husserl, *Briefe an Roman Ingarden*, ed. Roman Ingarden (The Hague: Nijhoff, 1968), esp. pp. 92–93 (letter LXXVII). The title of Rothacker's book quoted in *PMM*, p. 35 is *Die dogmatische Denkform in den Geisteswissenschaften und das Problem*

des Historismus. For Rothacker the necessity of treating forms of thought as always guided by certain dogmas in the human sciences and the problem of historism belong inseparably together.

9. Although the "phenomenological movement" has a certain unity seen from a historical point of view, we cannot here discuss whether or not the name "phenomenological" is still applicable to this movement in its later phases.

10. Gerhard Funke, *Von der Aktualität Kants* (Bonn: Bouvier, 1979).

11. "Practical Reason in Kant and Husserl" (see n. 1, above).

Introduction

The Grounding of Knowledge in the Twentieth Century[1]

In the aftermath of Kantianism and German Idealism, the twentieth century has witnessed, in succession, the alleged or final collapse of the systematic philosophical schools, the emergence of vitalist irrationalisms, and the so-called "resurrection" of metaphysics; it has experienced the celebration of crisis in all fields as avant-gardism; and it has accepted the victorious advance of hectically welcomed religions-in-disguise, the crypto-scientifically garbed proclamation of totalitarian ideologies, and the demand for sheer *engagement* for its own sake. This present age, philosophically fertile like scarcely any other, has not been favorable to a universal and critical, i.e., philosophical, investigation of grounds, carried out as science.

Unbiased devotion to the facts—an attitude taken for granted in all the specialized sciences—is not the mark of popularizers in matters of "world view" and "ideology," palmed off as philosophy. The confusion of world-view profundity and partisan doctrinary acumen with strict theory's irrevocable claim to convey conceptual clarity and well-articulated reasoning is widespread in the field of philosophy (or of what is considered to be philosophy by pragmatically oriented consumers of systems of thought, satisfying at best a desire for prestige). Irrationalism, which accounts for nothing, together with its retinue, decisionism and existentialism, weighs heavily on philosophy. Pseudo-soteriological systems for explaining the world, with their naively and brutally asserted claims to be the final authority, severely compromise the process of the gradual elucidation of the pregiven, situatively articulated reality.

Philosophy treated as a science does not find favor with public opinion in the form of the illustrious "man in the street," though this decisive authority is seldom ready and able to present even the most modest proof for his adamantly held attitudes and opinions. It is certainly not a commonly held view of our age to admit that certain prerequisites must always be met before a right to have a say can be asserted. Science, on the other hand, lives from the striving for an ever deepened grounding and explanation of the pregiven objects which are in consciousness as phenomena. And so there is an obvious contrast between those confident and uncritically charismatic individuals who feel called upon to make all possible decisions and others who seek, in the service of objectivity, to broaden the circle of knowledge one step at a time.

To want to know what reality looks like in its ultimate basis is, however, at least as legitimate as to dispense altogether with any effort at grounding science. Consequently, a science of grounds too may legitimately ask for toleration.

The sector of reality which will always draw attention is the one that manages to appear in consciousness, becoming a phenomenon in the broadest sense of the word. A philosophy whose aim is to place such phenomena within foundational contexts which are to be disclosed without bias and controlled by critique may well be called "phenomenology." Since this kind of philosophy, although itself never without assumptions and always only conditionally free of bias, seeks to dissolve prejudices and to clarify presuppositions, it will be the discipline which deals, in principle, with the conditions for the possibility of something as something. Thus it may claim the venerable title of a "transcendental phenomenology," which is located within the domain of logical and epistemological theory and treats all questions of being as problems of sense. For it, metaphysical positions taken from an "existential" vantage point are not sacrosanct, but questionable, as is everything else. This phenomenological philosophy does not constitute a system of didactic treatises. In reiterative regresses back to the conditions that make possible any object which happens to be under discussion—regresses carried ever further through continued reflection—it develops foundational connections whereby philosophy is presented as "philosophizing," as an ongoing critical and rational grounding process. It takes as its theme the context of metaphysical postulates which are presuppositions and the methodical clarification of systematic conclusions.

Compared with the flickering twilight in "world views," with lyrical daydreams in "Being," with the sacrifice of reason implied by ideology's glorification of the "friend-foe" category, and finally with life in faith and pseudo-life in superstition, phenomenology seeks not professions of faith, but knowledge. It is theory—with all the subtle demands that this implies. With its program, first initiated by Husserl as transcendental-phenomenological reflection upon grounds and designed to be "strict science," it is the subject of the following investigations which are to introduce and typify the *Mainz Philosophical Studies*.[2] Knowledge of the historical preconditions for this book will make it easier to understand its subject matter; to adapt a remark inscribed by Hegel under a picture of himself, "Whoever knows me will recognize me here."[3]

Chapter One

What is Philosophy?

The question asked is "What is philosophy?"[1] not "What does philosophy mean to us?"[2] It is a matter of a particular *thing*, not an ever-changing individual estimation of such a thing. In an unstratified, pragmatically oriented society, agreement on the role of philosophy can probably be achieved quickly: philosophy is considered to be absolutely "impractical" (and hence superfluous), the "science of what is not really worth knowing," an "art of thinking" whose significance is at best restricted to aesthetics or to one's personal life, "vague speculation" with an astonishingly long-lived claim to be taken seriously, a "world-view theory" of secularizing provincials, finally the "aggregate of more or less incoherent opinions" such as every individual forms of God and the whole world, or in conclusion the "revolt of sixty-year-olds" against life.

On the contrary, it must be kept in mind that philosophy is a science. It remains theory and does not become practical, nor poietic.[3] If it is theory, then of course it is theory about very determinate objects reserved for it as its specific domain. The polemical objection that philosophy's only problem is philosophy itself is probably intended to discredit it totally. The same objection is expressed in a different form when the history of philosophy is assigned to philosophy as its most proper field of work and activity. For such an assignment means nothing else but that philosophy has created the problems it deals with.

These charges, which are formulated provocatively and sometimes unobjectively, can, however, easily be reversed into something positive and objective. Since the Socratic-Platonic initiative, the main task of philosophy seems to have been to draw a distinction between *doxa* and *epistēmē*,[4] i.e., to separate subjective opinions and convictions from objective knowledge of the facts. Philosophy, then, has nothing to do with mythical images, religious belief, gnomic wisdom-sayings, or poetic pronouncements as such. As a science or as the striving for knowledge, when it studies relations of being, it can never give instructions for a determinate conduct. As a theoretical discipline it may become the basis for normative applications,[5] but even then it is not itself worldly wisdom or prudence, not a set of guidelines or a blueprint for life.

The individual sciences each have their specific subject matter (for instance, botany studies plants; medicine, sick and debilitated bodies; philology, languages). But philosophy's task is not, in this context, to study a previously forgotten and omitted sector of pregiven reality, bringing it up to date and completing it. It does not conclude the long series of natural and human sciences. Philosophy itself belongs to neither of the two sets of sciences.

As a matter of fact, philosophy is the science that treats of the problems which it, and only it, raises.[6] To find them, however, the complacent matter-of-courseness of living along in particular natural-scientific or human-scientific problem-contexts must be abandoned. Such matter-of-courseness is perfectly adequate for any technical and scientific work in the strict sense. For the visible "world" is actually assigned entirely to the individual sciences, and work in them follows guidelines that remain within a determinate taken-for-granted horizon. One thing philosophy does not do is to obtain these results of specialized sciences over again in a summarizing process. Nor does it find its task in merely rearranging, simplifying, and disseminating findings of other research. Finally, it can especially not claim to reachieve by its methods what the technical disciplines accomplish with the greatest refinement in their domains. Philosophy thus does not map out a "royal road" to things; it is not a summary of accomplishments attained elsewhere; and it is absolutely not a totalizing universal science.

Every science which is as such well established in the natural-scientific, the human-scientific, or any other field starts with certain presuppositions that serve as its foundations and are themselves not its topic of discussion. The conditioned is open to view, but the conditioning factors at first remain hidden. Hence in the concrete course of development of the sciences, the most obtrusive, i.e., the refractory and most conspicuous, problems become the subject matter of the earliest desire for knowledge. And the most remarkable thing of all may well be that a mysterious bond seems to unite all things—that a dark, hidden force determines them, that they are the eloquent exterior of a silent interior. If *before* the development of the genuine sciences the mind was set upon attaining knowledge, perhaps even arcane knowledge, surely the sciences proper, *after* they have been applied to their task, must not completely lose sight of this aspect.

In fact, the existing scientific disciplines, which ultimately developed into academic fields of study, likewise always strive to penetrate behind and to explain, indeed to ground, the merely pregiven stock of objects within their domain. This ongoing process shows one thing to be permanent—namely, that the boundaries of the unexplained are always being pushed back further and further. But the investigation always rises from a particular foundation which has a specific location. It is always topically fixed. The foundations from which the natural and the human sciences carry out their specialized investigations into problems which open up precisely from there are not problematic for these sciences themselves. To this extent, it is correct to say that all these sciences— however critical and even sceptical they are with respect to the particular connections of objects within *their* field—are necessarily naive as to the initial level from which they commence their work.[7] To clear up a technical question of astronomy, one does not first discuss the theoretical possibility of knowledge in general, or the relation between thought and being or between knowledge and the object, or, as the case may be, between nature and history. It goes without saying that all these factors, even when not discussed, are implicit in the point of departure. It is taken for granted at least, for instance, that in principle there is such a thing as knowledge, that the object of research is an entity, that as a natural object it has its own specific essence in contrast to everything historical. In addition to such general presuppositions, there are specific ones which follow from the peculiar nature of each discipline. That in a given case *x* is grasped exactly *as* it is represented depends on a great many more conditions than are elucidated by the technical research appropriate in the particular case.[8]

In this sense, it must be said that philosophy actually does itself bring up and *create* the problems it deals with. It does not, of course, study all kinds of objects in the world in order to describe and classify them; however, it also does not discover its objects in a dreamworld, a speculatively invented never-never land. The problem it centers on is what is taken for granted in the particular sciences as the very basis of their ability to function. Philosophy discovers the problematic at this level too. Characteristically it seeks to explain what is allegedly "self-evident" as only apparently "self-evident," to ground and understand it in terms of its specific presuppositions. The natural-scientific and the human-scientific disciplines study the world as it is presented in common-sense experience and in the practice of the sciences. Philosophy acquires its own method, its own problem, and its own subject matter by bringing to light the presuppositions and conditions which the sciences left unquestioned and stripping them of their matter-of-courseness. It must begin with "meditations on possible methods."[9] This subject matter, namely the covertly assumed precondition for the world-object grasped in naive and scientific experience, is itself *not* of this world. In brief, the "object of philosophy" will be precisely what every specialized science has used as "evidence which is accepted without proof."[10] Several consequences follow from this.

1. Philosophy is not a natural or a human science, since it takes as its theme the total complex of conditions and presuppositions which in practice first make possible the natural and the human sciences as sciences.

2. Philosophy is a grounding science, since it does not phantasize or speculate on the conditions and presuppositions at the basis of the natural and the human sciences, but it discovers *"if-then"* connections which explain that an object or a world must appear as it does if precisely these or those premises are supposed.

3. Philosophy is a topical and not a utopian enterprise, for it does not *invent* its objects ("reduplicating the world"), but discovers them by starting from the given facts of the individual sciences as the conditioning grounds for their possibility.

4. Philosophy is, moreover, absolutely never oriented by so-called eternal, ever-recurring problems, but only by those which come to view in naive or in practical experience: crossing over beyond what is given, it ascertains the conditions of possibility for such an actually given reality.

5. Philosophy is, then, not just topically fixed, but also historically conditioned. Insofar as real or purported knowledge is grasped on its own foundations, namely the specific ones which came about historically, philosophy becomes eminently "relevant."

6. Philosophy is, then, not dogmatic, but critical; it does not preach or proclaim, but clings to what is given in order to understand it in terms of its presuppositions: it thereby dissolves calm satisfaction with what is present on hand and becomes a permanent unrest in research into grounds.

7. Philosophy becomes systematic philosophy only when the reality whose foundations it is investigating is itself a logically coherent system, or when this consciousness which constitutes reality is itself systematic. However, it can give no information about this at the beginning, but only at the end of the research process, once it has accomplished the work of grounding.

8. Philosophy is, finally, never again what it ever was: by continuous regression to "presuppositions" located further and further back, the *same*

thing can never again come into view as it did in an earlier effort; and so philosophy, as it continuously reflects further back on the foundations that make possible the given reality, becomes ever "more subtle," "world-remote," "unnatural," "esoteric," indeed "incomprehensible," to the so-called "man in the street."

9. Philosophy is thus, in the end, never popular and close to life, never a matter of "common sense," coextensive with the pregiven,[11] because it seeks a foundation for the pregiven and doubts what common sense considers to be the most matter-of-course thing in the world: it is concerned not with what is most matter-of-course, but with the ground even of what is taken for granted as a matter-of-course.

It has often been denied, of course, that philosophy has any particular subject matter of its own, and asserted that philosophy is always merely its own subject matter.[12] Obviously, such a statement must be wrong. For "much to the annoyance of all those who can bear no uncertainty, radical doubt must remain a vital element of philosophy."[13] If in the twentieth century philosophy should indeed no longer really be a vital power— though it certainly was so, for instance, at the height of German Idealism and during the Age of Reason—then here too one could ask regressively about the conditions for the possibility of such an estimate. And that in turn would be a philosophical question, a task for philosophy.

If, by regressing to the foundations of a particular opinion or purported knowledge, philosophy indeed dissolves familiar contexts, it becomes understandable why it is felt to be disquieting. Challenging the claim to validity of everything that is naively accepted, dogmatically asserted, or taken for granted as a matter-of-course, philosophy is the critique, control, and corrective of things considered "matter-of-course" in the life-world, in belief, and in science.[14] It does not design anything new, but clears up old matters. It does not predict future conditions from the present state, but it *grounds* the given situation and the situative-contextual conditions from their peculiar presuppositions.[15] It lives in "*if-then*" connections and not in absolutely fixed decisive projects. Critical reflection and not dogmatic decisionism is its business. It thus remains a factor of constant unrest, because definitive statements to calm future-oriented minds can never be expected of it. This critical philosophy is soberly interested in the given reality and its presuppositions; it does not appeal to feelings, to the power of the will, or to hidden, neglected interiority. It discovers connections and does not call for action.

To be sure, if security, embeddedness in the life-world, the glorification of inherited guidance systems, and stabilization in one's own shell are regarded as the most important things, then to such a tendency a philosophy that raises "*why?*"-questions will seem "untimely." When uncertainty becomes unbearable and the longing for security is grandiosely intensified, philosophy, with its surmounting of what is so reassuringly matter-of-course, must seem to be absolutely the worst enemy, i.e., the disturber of the peace.

Scientific theory and world-view dogmatisms, ideological and religious dogmatisms, have therefore always taken offense at philosophical critique's reiterative-reflective procedure. Dogmatic metaphysics—which always stands behind the standpoints of the various doctrines of faith, the numerous secularized world views, and the ideologized scientific systems (claiming to explain and redeem the world)—has been subjected by philosophy in the eighteenth, nineteenth, and twentieth centuries to an investigation which probes further and further back. But the very fact of the investigation proves that the matter-of-course positions must have already lost their unquestioned credibility, otherwise such an investigation aiming to clarify their presuppositions could not have begun—an investigation which no longer accepts as "ultimate" the dogmatic and ideological, the supposedly "ultimate groundings" of those universal explanatory systems.

Such a critical, purely rational questioning of their positions was as highly suspect for the vulgarized scientific "world view" of the nineteenth century and the politicizing scholasticism of twentieth-century ideologies as it had been for the ecclesiastical orthodoxy of the eighteenth. If philosophy now holds firmly to its rational-critical task and constantly reduces whatever is "sanctioned" by faith, world view, or science to the preconditions for its validity, it thereby becomes the intellectual conscience *par excellence*.[16]

It sees tasks for possible enlightenment even where a positional metaphysics so conducive to an unreflective living-along, or religious dogmatism, scientistic doctrine, or party ideology, has stopped asking questions.[17] For that very reason, these sheltering standpoints regard philosophy as the disruptive agency which comes up with surprising results and causes unrest. Twentieth-century ideologies based on race or class perspectives are typical of a reaction in which free philosophical endeavors are routinely hereticized.

In an age which has, out of a need for security, made its theoretical peace with the "facts" of the dominant ideologies, philosophy must be "untimely" to a consciousness oriented in this way. This seems to be the case in the mid-twentieth century. The spirit of the times endorses the current ideological state and assures itself that there is no place for any philosophy that reaches out beyond the current time conditions and back to the prior foundational conditions. But the fact remains that philosophy finds its sole field of work in such reflective regresses to the conditions for the possibility of something given here and now—regardless of whether the tasks which arise in such a field are taken up and solved in every age. This is where philosophy *is* legitimated, even if it does not actually fulfill its legitimate task. On this point, as always, a strict distinction must be made between what should be and what is.

Prescientific endeavors were bent upon comprehending the mysterious magical relations behind visible things; philosophical inquiry sees its goal as one of disclosing the hidden natural and nature-conditioning factors behind the appearances. In either case, it is a matter of a deepened knowledge which penetrates through the surface conditions and does not simply accept them as they are. Thus philosophy's task is constantly to revise the familiarized bases of conviction, and its intent remains reiteratively critical.

Only by carrying out such ongoing radical investigations into grounds does it become possible in a given case to unmask prior convictions as illusions which are effective in life, but illusions nonetheless.[18] Where the matter-of-course convictions of the natural or quasi-natural conception of the world have been discovered to be merely provisionally adequate, philosophy proves to be a detector of illusions. Abolishing the familiarity of unreflective living-along in more or less legitimate convictions and doctrines, refusing to accept and adopt the current naively expected explanations of the world and of things, and hence not stopping with what was always already anticipated, philosophy is dis-illusioning.

The person living along in a current understanding is disillusioned when his expectations, always at home within certain matter-of-course horizons, are not confirmed. And in precisely this more subtle sense philosophy is constantly "disillusioning." It constantly abolishes the established and traditional explanations of connections by reiteratively reaching back further and making what was apparently very familiar become weird. That is, philosophy is the interminable process of the disillusionment of favored absolutized expectations. And precisely because twentieth-century man cherishes nothing more highly than old expectations and purportedly "progressive" dreams, which philosophy then—analyzing more deeply—cannot confirm and corroborate, this same man now, inversely, finds philosophy disillusioning, enough so at any rate for him to turn away from it and give up the critical (because "dis-illusioning") attitude in favor of a decisionist turn to *engagement*, i.e., to allegiance to dogmatic, metaphysical absolutes by an arbitrary choice.[19]

Just as philosophy, if it understands itself rightly, can never become "dogmatic," so too it can never show inclinations toward scepticism. It always starts with dogmatically assumed data and naive, matter-of-course convictions. But it does not stop there; it abolishes the illusion that the accustomed ultimate explanations are really definitive foundations. In this way it is always a process of "philosophizing"—which is what the old adage means when it says that one cannot teach and learn "philosophy," but only how to philosophize.[20] Such an interpretation of philosophy cannot be relativized by being traced back and ascribed to a typological difference between philosophers. Static thinking about timeless conditions of being (that of the Greeks, for instance) is occasionally contrasted with the so-called dynamism of a thinking oriented by eternal becoming (that of the Germans, for example). However, the present exposition is not concerned at all with the anthropological essence of some philosophical thinkers or others, but with an explanation of the problem as such— i.e., whether the venture of a global comprehension may be broken off at any point and dogmatically declared to be terminated, or whether in principle every objective legitimation (*Sachausweisung*) remains related back to deeper-lying foundational conditions, which remained hidden until this moment and which philosophy then takes as its "object."[21]

In such a critical questioning and theoretical revision of the matter-of-course grounds absolutely necessary to sustain life and orient one in the world, philosophy plays the role of a stimulus for inquisitive thought. This does not, however, mean that by repeatedly dissolving dogmatisms, it itself becomes "sceptical."[22] Its procedure involves a methodical scepticism, not scepticism as a "thesis."

Absolute, radical sceptics on principle can and must be given the same answer that critical philosophers have always given them: i.e., "thinkers who are no less critical will always contradict" the sceptics "by appealing to the fact that the very possibility of seriously doubting already presupposes that one has reliable criteria to see into the justification for doubt."[23] Thus philosophy, in its critical effort to clarify the conditions of reality, will indeed start from "theses," from dogmatic ultimate explanations which it finds present in the "average consciousness" of "normal contemporaries," but it will also find their naively assumed matter-of-courseness to be problematic and will treat it as a problem. It shares the basic starting point for its investigations with naive as well as with more precise scientific consciousness, but it does not posit metaphysical, doctrinary accents of final validity. It is thus, in principle, revision of metaphysics. From Plato to Kant and Husserl, philosophizing means the capacity and need to question even where everything is supposed to be matter-of-course. This very attitude makes philosophy seem disillusioning. Of course, the abolition of the familiar views on the ultimate conditions does not follow arbitrarily and in any way whatever, but results in view of and starting from the specific relations in each case. Even philosophy does not explain everything, and not all at once; it remains bound by the data as they appear. So it does not speak about things anywhere and nowhere, but about what happens to make its appearance at the present time: it remains topically oriented and does not chase after utopian contexts.[24]

There can hardly be any doubt that philosophy, if it is continuously a critique of metaphysical standpoints that were assumed to be matter-of-course, contests only their claim to ultimacy, and not their necessity for life and action. It lets stand as "provisionally" right what they claimed was absolutely final. But the fact that this is always its stance explains the reproach that philosophy never *really* explains anything, but again and again replaces all statements by other statements, and thus not only never actually reaches the course of a strict science,[25] but could not become an exact science even theoretically. However, this historical objection, constantly repeated especially by representatives of the specialized sciences, itself also contains a very specific, unacknowledged metaphysical thesis—namely, that the individual sciences have already performed the entire critical task of explaining reality and contain nothing that could still seem dubious or worthy of further inquiry.

Scientific consciousness can, under certain circumstances, no less than the so-called "naive" consciousness, fall prey to delusions. Both the life-worldly and the scientific conceptions of so-called common sense do not as such represent any fixed magnitude, but are variables, the "average result of philosophical doctrines which have become popular." That the philosophically uncritical mind settles for such a development does not mean that it is impossible to break the illusion that this is an authority which provides ultimate information. That is, philosophy—so understood—is and remains the indispensible corrective for so-called "common sense" with its one-sided dogmatizing. It shows the latter's historicity and mere tentativeness.

An age such as ours, which each and every day practices belief in a genuine and supposed scientific and technical progress and hence lends its approval to every novelty for novelty's sake—i.e., an age which races uncritically from one avant-gardism to another—is at the same time extremely reactionary when it repeatedly draws back to "common sense" as a touchstone of reality. Actually, common sense is a "magnitude" that originated historically and always represents merely the rear guard of thought. The crossing beyond what is familiar and comprehensible to common sense is not done by the person entangled in it. As a "resultant" he can never have access to the "determinants" which condition the new.

It would certainly be right to say that "life is faster than reflection, which is supposed to master it mentally."[26] But it seems to be just as correct to state that "common sense" is slower than the "critical mind" which sets the determinants of tomorrow's common sense. Philosophy, by abolishing what is supposedly "self-evident," always achieves more than common sense. It starts from its level and appropriates what can be grasped from there, so it does not lag behind it. At the same time, however, it rises above this initial situation, insofar as it does not remain caught up in the views of finality which accompany "common sense" in its ordinariness.[27] The acquisition of a new, higher perspective from which what was previously matter-of-course becomes questionable is possible only when the previous dogmatisms lose their cogency. Philosophy is the process that makes this development transparent.

So there is not just *one* privileged point of departure for the philosophical endeavor of thought and knowledge. What thought relied on in the course of its historical development and what served in each case as the frame of reference for philosophical-critical retrospection has changed in its situation. Natural experience, which is verified by practice, is no more a "self-evident" magnitude than is concrete reason, without whose case by case application it is even impossible to have good grounds to doubt. The accepted stock of knowledge of "confidently advancing" sciences is no less problematic than experiences from history. In brief, whatever is assumed to be matter-of-course does not depend on philosophy. It is proclaimed, defended, absolutized in open or secret metaphysics.[28] Philosophy finds it and uses it as the point of departure for reiterative reflections on the conditions of its own possibility. That is why new ideas as to what philosophy itself is and how, according to its essence, it should be defined arise again and again, and are taken for granted in each case—only to be stripped of their claim to absolute validity from a higher level of consciousness and reduced to the conditions for their formulation.

Since philosophy is not expected to provide definitive "metaphysical" tenets, its concept can also be clarified once its progressive methodical process is understood. In contrast with all established theses which claim absolute validity, philosophy employs a hypothetical procedure in which it seeks, for everything given, the corresponding preconditions as *imposed*. In contrast with every dogmatism and contentually rigid doctrine, it defends the right to criticize and to pose further-reaching *"why?"*-questions.[29] Although the content of such a historically conditioned philosophy may change materially, philosophy remains formally the activity of philosophizing, i.e., critique of grounds.

It becomes possible, in addition, to differentiate absolutely all dogmatic positions against the background of continual critical efforts and to reduce them to typical cases. When it is a matter of exploring reality and making ultimate statements about it, one can first draw back to the pronouncements of persons who have at some time or in some way formed an opinion on this subject. The doxographical historical procedure then accords validity to whatever has been said on a subject and creates a lexical philosophy which can merely cite *doxa* after *doxa*. But if the content does not consist merely of opinions presented more or less without commitment, but rather proclamations and predictions are propounded and beliefs professed, what we are dealing with is the dogmatism of prophetic charismatics claiming to know the absolute truth about the sense and structure of the world, for which they engage themselves. This is the position of philosophical orthodoxy in the broadest sense. Where the same basic stance, then, involves less allegiance to such a position and more its description and mere exposition, philosophy will emerge theoretically and thetically. But the dogmatic content of positions need not always consist in a "doctrine about things"; it can consist in the demand that a particular "royal road" to these things be recognized. Philosophy would then be methodically and technically oriented, making apodictic judgments on the procedure to be used. Examples can be found among the dialecticians, the linguistic analysts, the proponents of etymological depth research, and the *sic-et-non* encyclopedists, who all represent patterns of methodological intolerance. Where it is claimed that one can progress from the given to what is in principle not given, and that what is fundamentally transcendent would "somehow" have to be apprehended in the manner of immanent conditions, philosophy's procedure will be analogical-paradoxical. The "Completely Other" would then in a certain sense again belong "to this world," in terms of which it is understood. On the contrary, philosophy which sticks completely to the pregiven will have either a "naturalistically" oriented character or one that is oriented by "objective mind." It is physicalist and analytical when it seeks to abstract a unitary explanation from the facts of nature and when whatever does not fit within its system is included within an *epoché* and declared absurd. Conversely, when it becomes a philological hermeneutics it strives to interpret, out of the total context conceived as a meaningful unity, the pregiven sense which it suspects to be in a structure. In either case, however, a thesis is dogmatically presupposed— namely, that the phenomena of nature or the objectified sense-formations of the mind can be understood on their own terms and have a "meaning-in-itself." In the first instance, the individual sciences do the work of bringing into experience whatever can be said about nature, and philosophy becomes superfluous; in the second, absolutely all sense-formations are interpreted as products and projects of the mind, whereby every individual science, together with everything it does and achieves, becomes philosophy.[30]

In contrast with all these positions which absolutize a particular thesis, whether of content or of method, in contrast with these "philosophical dogmatists" about whom and about whose claims interminable disputes are possible,[31] "critical, hypothetical philosophizing" posits no new thesis which would in its turn have a fixed content. It simply shows that philosophizing is a formal procedure which consists in seeking foundational contexts even where the naive attitude, the ideological world view, or the doctrines of a special science are based upon evidences accepted without proof.

Insofar as knowledge is supposed to result, such philosophizing too cannot do without the most primary "matter-of-course" assumptions, which in turn enable this knowledge to come about—i.e., the transcendental presuppositions under which stands absolutely everything that ever manifests itself in consciousness.

That a "metaphysics of knowledge" has always been present in knowledge since time immemorial,[32] is a thesis which explains as much or as little as does any other definitively asserted metaphysical thesis. Or that mind, reason, knowledge, consciousness, *has* reality in the present objects, which are "apprehended" in a particular way, in the same way as if these objects were *not* known, is a postulate whose correctness remains unprovable. To prove it, the apprehending faculty would have to overleap itself and its only possible way of mediating an object and provide a comparison between reality-in-itself and apprehended reality, which would not be possible without apprehension by this very consciousness then functioning in a certain way.

These conditions for the possibility of the knowledge of objects are founded in the very structure of consciousness. They can be encountered by an oblique inward turning, i.e., by reflection.[33] The thesis of the depiction of reality in knowledge is, then, a mere thesis, unless this reality can be taken as a correlate of consciousness itself. What it is supposed to be beyond what it means as correlate of the modes of advertence leaves open all conceivable metaphysical interpretations. This is not philosophy's place. It asks, rather, about the conditions for the possibility of being only in the sense that it investigates what must be posited in order to explain this or that existing ("apprehended") fact. Thus consciousness as something actually given can also become a problem for itself.

Philosophizing, then, begins with the actually given, which can be a thing, a segment of the world, a mental entity, or an intended sense of whatever kind. Critical philosophizing asks about the conditions why and how this *phenomenon*, which proves accessible in a determinate sense, looks the way it does. Depending on the circumstances, a phenomenon can be an affair, a thing, a body, an object, a subject matter, a unity of sense and meaning in the broadest sense. And what it shows itself as depends on its kind of showing. If all these things are conditioned, then the conditioning factor is obviously not of the same nature—it can then also not be called "phenomenon," or affair, thing, body, object, subject matter, unity of sense or meaning, and precisely therefore it is grasped terminologically as a precondition and condition for all that, i.e., as the non-objective, and hence as consciousness, mind, reason, etc. That is the meaning of the transcendental attitude of consciousness. Whenever—as in the above discussion—consciousness, mind, or reason are mentioned, and these unities of meaning are without a doubt "phenomenalized," the operation which makes these reflective legitimations (*Ausweisungen*) possible, and which is the correlatively appropriate condition for their possibility to exist, is precisely not a phenomenon (i.e., something manifested).

Philosophy has to do, all in all, with transcendental connections, wherever these are at work.[34] Thus whenever there is a question of the transcendent and the immanent, i.e., whenever something shows itself *as* something, certain transcendental preconditions without which the given could not be given are fulfilled.

That which stands out as an object within a certain horizon of experience is and remains the goal of research of a specialized science. But the horizon of assumptions which makes it possible to place the object to begin with is made understandable by philosophically asking back from the implicitly present preconditions. Critique proposes a determinate hypothesis to test whether or not something previously merely assumed *de facto* can be explained in terms of that hypothesis.

If twentieth-century philosophizing is, then, characterized by an "experimental style,"[35] one may let this pass. No critique aiming at research into grounds can do without hypotheses. But if it is said that "the philosophy of our century is characterized generally by a consuming and experimental character," that is very problematic in the present context, especially when one continues that "it feverishly processes the influence of almost all previous systems, methods, standpoints, and judgments, and prospers in a medium of incessant disputes."[36]

It may be that an encyclopedic, Alexandrian philosophy in our time too proceeds just as derivatively, i.e., annotating and labeling, and syncretically. When it does this, it actually calls upon itself the reproach of being "unserious" and "theatrical." And the reproach means that anything is tried in order to obtain an original point of view, but not to solve an actually existing task. Such a philosophy can be said to be in a state of "most extreme dispersion." On the contrary, the kind of critical philosophizing which focuses on underlying preconditions makes possible the most extreme concentration. Starting with the given, it scans the whole horizon of enabling conditions. Not every random thing, however, is of interest in this process; and philosophy is not, then, the science of "God, the world, man, and absolutely all things" (as Christian Wolff claims), but is historically bound to the place and state of experience, whose precisely fixed matter-of-course presuppositions it pushes back.

Thus it is essential to this task that philosophy is always new. It cannot be blamed for becoming, not easier and easier to comprehend, but more and more complicated and subtle. Finally, that it thereby tends to be disappointing confirms the importance of its task. Why philosophy exists at all, however, was explained by Bernard Bolzano, the logician, who achieved late reknown in the twentieth century, when he said: "Philosophy is the science of the objective configurations of all those truths into whose ultimate grounds we have made it our task to penetrate, in order to become wiser and better."[37] Philosophy, however, necessarily becomes phenomenology and phenomenological critique, for it is a matter "of giving phenomenology the form of development required by the idea of a First Philosophy, focused on beginnings, which creates itself in the most radical philosophical self-consciousness, in absolute methodical necessity."[38] Starting with what is registered in consciousness in any sense, i.e., with the phenomenon, regressive steps of critical grounding disclose the conditions for the possibility of a particular given; and in this process of regressive reflections, philosophy is realized.[39] Philosophy is rationalism.

Chapter Two

Dogmatic Knowledge and Critical Science of Foundations[1]

Although the so-called philosophy of the modern age in Europe since Nicholas of Cusa, Luis Vives, Giordano Bruno, Francis Bacon, René Descartes, and Gottfried Wilhelm Leibniz has always seen rationalist and irrationalist tendencies blossoming side by side; although there have always been systematic-scientistic and aphoristic-artistic movements, theoretical-logical and practical-political interests; and finally, although standards were always set simultaneously by abstract and concrete, religious and secular, academic and popular viewpoints, it has nevertheless become commonplace in contemplating the cultural history of the period between the seventeenth and the twentieth centuries in Europe to postulate something like a continuous particular development. A direct line is supposed to lead from the predominance of the scientific mentality, via the emergence of unimpeded life, to the discovery of existence in its unanticipatable self-determination.[2] Mind, Life, and Existence would thus be the chapter headings for the philosophically determined cultural history of the last three centuries in the West and in Western-oriented thinking worldwide.

This same development from mind to life and then to existence can supposedly also be traced in the development of a particular philosophical school of the present, namely phenomenology. Within this line of development, Husserl purportedly defends the primacy of mind and of strict science, Scheler discovers the particular strata of life, and Heidegger steps forth as the hermeneuticist of *Dasein* and the thinker of being.[3] This development is thereby understood as a historical process, as the development of thinking in the sense that the old abstract, academic philosophy of science, continuing to function in the form of transcendental phenomenology, was increasingly replaced by a philosophy of life interested in the concrete problems of man's reality, while this vitalist and personalist phenomenology then in turn had to yield to a hermeneutics of facticity and analytics of *Dasein*, i.e., phenomenological ontology. In this connection, a concretization of the problematic seems to be detectable.[4] Neither an abstract universal "subject as such," nor an ideal unreal "personal being," but only "*Dasein* condemned to freedom" would in the end serve as point of departure for the decisive philosophical discussions. Regarded as decisive is the question of the "being of consciousness," the being of the subject, of the person, of the center of the self, or finally the being of *Dasein* as *Dasein*. Thus philosophy turned out in the last analysis to be interested only in the nature of existence.[5]

This view raises numerous problems. Its underlying dogmatic position cannot be left unexamined.

This first conviction, which has become almost common knowledge, is joined by a second, no less problematic one. The last third of the nineteenth century, with its essentially positivist orientation, had already insisted that philosophy's task is primarily "realistic," namely to obtain a "world-concept" free of religious and metaphysical interpretations.[6] In the aftermath of Turgot and Hume, Comte and Mill, Mach and Avenarius, the goal was thus the unbiased elaboration of a "natural world-concept." The positively experienced world was supposed to include only segments of the world, i.e., things which have become known in empirical data.[7] The twentieth century then heard Husserl's call for *Philosophy as Rigorous Science* (1911), the call "to the things themselves."[8] However, the difference between the positivist and the phenomenological attitude is clear. Franz Brentano had raised the question of the stratification of reality in 1862 in his book *On the Multiple Meaning of Being according to Aristotle*; and he had thus steered research toward the clarification of differences of meaning within the concepts "being" and "reality." In 1899, Alexius Meinong could present in his "theory of objects" a carefully elaborated theory of the various classes of objects.[9] He operated to a considerable extent with the principle of correlativity, so that each particular kind of objects was constitutively associated with its own corresponding ways of being brought to experience. Husserl, in his *Ideas Pertaining to a Pure Phenomenology and to a Phenomenological Philosophy* (1913), formulated "the principle of all principles"[10] to the effect that *every* originary presentive (*gebende*) intuition is a legitimizing source of knowledge. This means, however, that the exclusive right of *one* kind of experience, namely sensory perception, is contested, thus invalidating the positivist and neopositivist principle of relying only on the senses. Empiricist monism is replaced by the pluralism of *cogitationes* and of the numerous classes of most varied *cogitationes*. What matters is this: that something manifests itself *as* something. Thereafter the call "to the things themselves," which Husserl raises and which Heidegger later takes up and expands in his fashion,[11] means simply this: whatever falls within the horizon of consciousness through any legitimating mental performances can be the object of possible inquiry and must be taken seriously. This marks an escape from the spell of purely realistic and positivistic, i.e., "naturalistic" philosophy: to do justice to phenomena, as they are manifested, with precisely the appropriate attitude, and to omit no field of meaning—this represents an extraordinary expansion of the field of work.

The "thing" as perceptible sensory unity and the thing as a nonsensory unity of signification and validity are essentially different.

Now in the twentieth century such a so-called "return to the things themselves" has repeatedly been associated with a "turn to the object,"[12] indeed even more with the view that it was a matter of a "resurrection of metaphysics."[13] But obviously, metaphysics, as something about which knowledge still exists even in the highly modern, new sense, must itself fall back within the phenomenological domain. Since Husserl's expansion of the Kantian concept of phenomenon, "metaphysics as the science of the Completely Other" has become impossible.[14] Phenomenology, as the science of grounds within the domain of appearances, always deals with phenomena of every kind and with the conditions of their phenomenality. Accordingly, it interrogates every naive metaphysics stemming from a "natural attitude," asking about the conditions and presuppositions implicitly at work within it. In short, it will never be able to be anything other than the "critical conscience" of every dogmatically posited metaphysical position, which is always indispensible as a jumping-off point; and at some point or other, the starting basis of the so-called "exact" sciences, as well as of the "interpretative" sciences, will always be a dogmatic position. Even toward itself, phenomenology remains unchangeably the theme of a continually repeated critical questioning.[15] This can be seen from the concept of phenomenon as such, which says that every something, every x, can be what it is only on the basis of correlatively appertinent conditions of legitimation. This connection between a consciousness in which something is evident and that which has become evident is not simply left standing by phenomenology, but is analyzed. The result is necessarily an "absolutism of consciousness." For each of these performances of first a direct, then a reflective, then a doubly reflective advertence to the pregiven object remains a performance of consciousness and is dependent on the possibilities of this very consciousness.[16] But it would be absurd to speak in anticipation of all possibilities of consciousness whatsoever: they arise historically and first make their appearance in reiterative reflection insofar as they become transparent there.

Even what the "being" of this same "consciousness" might well be can be learned, in turn, only by new performances of consciousness. Thus no ontology whatsoever—neither the dictate of the perennial traditional ontology nor the primacy of the destructive modern fundamental ontology—can have priority over the philosophy of consciousness. If ontology is understood correctly, and fundamental ontology estimated precisely according to its own historical origin, it will be meaningful only as transcendental philosophy, as transcendental phenomenology. Its truth is "*veritas transcendentalis.*"[17]

Husserl's "principle of all principles" made possible a plurality of methods and of legitimations which can recognize not only intuition and perception, not only cognitive acts, but also, for example, emotional-cognitive acts.[18] Insofar as something presents itself at all to be known or understood *as* something, consciousness is present. And even in so-called non-intentional experiences it is always *this* and not *that* that is experienced in one way or another. It is a question, for example, of "anxiety" and not of "fear," to cite Heidegger's examples. Even when "*Dasein* in its being is concerned with this being itself,"[19] precisely that about which the statement is made is a phenomenon—a phenomenon as it makes itself known in consciousness in the appropriate mode.

Any information about consciousness, being, or existence is attainable only by means of appropriate apprehensions. A "being as such" and an "existence in its complete specificity" (*Eigenheit*) is, even in such a statement, an understood being, an understood existence, about which information is communicated in each case *as* that which it means there.

Phenomenology deals with the "communicable," "demonstrable" phenomena. It knows of the being of an entity, of existence in its existing, in principle only insofar as this being, this existence, has become transparent, i.e., when pure being and *Dasein* have reached consciousness. A being that becomes clearer as well as a *Dasein* that understands itself will have to contain in its outset what the word "consciousness" (*Bewusst-sein*, i.e., being-conscious) says. The meaning of consciousness is abridged if, contrary to Husserl and contrary to the "principle of all principles," it is restricted to a determinate "naturalistically" distorted variant. But the meaning of the object in phenomenology is also abridged if it is apprehended ("realistically," "positivistically") "as a segment of the world." For it is an object only as the sense-correlate of an act of meaning

(*Vermeinung*). Even in Heidegger's "understanding-ful dealing with"—
for instance, while hammering—something is always known and conscious, namely the ability to hammer, although perhaps the hammer as
such still remains undiscovered, and the object too is not grasped as an
"objective" part of the world accessible to all. To say something about
"intelligent handling" of any implement is, all the more so, a determinate
new meaning (*Vermeinung*). All this falls within the realm of consciousness.[20]

First, the "hunger for reality,"[21] which—it is said—characterized the
men of the first decades of this century, then a decreased receptivity for
all merely epistemological and analytic-critical considerations, and finally
the impressive objectivity of the new science resulted in the application
of the Husserlian principle of self-validation to obtain a new metaphysics
(contrary to the mind of the founder of phenomenology).[22] Self-
bestowing, the direct grasping of something in its essential quiddity, and
the recognition of all disclosures of world and reality of the most various
kind—all these factors, in turn, led to enthusiasm for a new intuitive and
straight path to metaphysical truths; and phenomenology would be, above
all, such an enthusiasm.

Kant, in his small work *On a Recently Elevated Tone in Philosophy*
(1796), rejected all teachings and strivings which relied on sheer feeling,
on the most personal intuitive insight, on special illumination, subjective
inspiration, and enthusiastic quickening. And Husserl, with his theory of
"ideating abstraction," which is so imprecisely defined as a "seeing of
essences," actually did not intend to map out a "royal road to the things
themselves" that could be followed as the result of an inner "chosenness."
Essences, essential forms, and essential relations are and remain correlates of consciousness as it toilsomely works its way forward, and they
have nothing to do with a transcendent world in the old metaphysical
sense—to which the privileged person finds access. Rather, the grasping
of essence is a work of description and comparison made possible by
changes of attitude.

Everything, then, even metaphysics and metaphysical claims, will have
to validate itself in consciousness according to this claim and thereby
confirm one of the possibilities of this consciousness. Even metaphysics is
accessible only as a "phenomenon" in such a sense, or it does not exist.[23]
And as a phenomenon it is subject to all analytical investigations and
critical discussions of the conditions for its possibility, just as any other
phenomenon is.

To establish the transcendent in the "absolute" sense thus remains an
impossibility. It is different with the so-called "transcendency within
immanency" of consciousness.[24] This slogan implies the following: the

thing does not coincide with the performance; or, in other words, the act and what is constituted in the act—even when they appear together—are still two different things. Phenomenon, then, means: to be a unity of sense; and this unity of sense and validity must be regarded as a correlate to the appertinent mediatory performance. Traditional metaphysics, however, wants to make transcendency accessible in an absolute sense. It would thus cross the boundaries of the phenomena in their phenomenality; it would want to grasp them without remaining bound to the modes of grasping.

These three viewpoints all need to be examined: (1) whether such a general "development"—from the predominance of mind and consciousness, via the emergence of life striving to assert itself, to the manifestation of decisionistic existence—can be meaningfully affirmed;[25] (2) whether the "turn to the things themselves" actually grounds an "objectivism" which then immediately maintains a connection with a more or less uncritical realism;[26] and finally, (3) whether the urge for totally concrete experience, the "hunger for reality,"[27] may be interpreted as if thought developed quasi-necessarily by overcoming Husserlian and Schelerian positions until finally the Heideggerian approach creates the possibility of escaping from the thinking of the philosophy of consciousness and of obtaining a "genuine," unrevisable "metaphysics." The following consideration belongs at the beginning of such an investigation.

The intended "destruction" of philosophy[28] is proof of unhistorical thinking—at any rate, of thinking that believes it owes nothing to the real, concrete course of this very thinking and declares an "absolute" beginning to be possible. On the other hand, a topical "philosophy of science" that is always bound to its place holds firmly that all thinking, together with its innovative disclosures, is and remains historical through and through. What this means is this: every later form of thinking can say something about earlier forms of the same thinking beyond what these earlier forms themselves can say about themselves. The discoveries of pre-Socratic thinking, for instance, appear differently to the pre-Socratics than to the thinker who is in a position to compare the achievements of these pre-Socratics with later efforts elsewhere, and thus to draw a distinction between them.

To call philosophy of knowledge, philosophy of the self, philosophy of consciousness, or in short any academic philosophy by the label "philosophy of problem-forgetting,"[29] furthermore, itself means to engage in some consciousness-philosophy. Effervescent life can always recognize only itself; it has forgotten nothing; and, allowing itself everything, it understands absolutely nothing else. Existence, in its existing, knows nothing of the forgottenness of being and of problems; nor does it rise to the grasping of such a thing as the "structure of existence," i.e., to the *existentials*. Only re-flection brings the *intentio recta* face to face with something new.

The attempt must, therefore, be made again and again to understand philosophy through and through as "philosophy of consciousness." As philosophy, it does not want to provide rhapsodic experiences, but systematic knowledge—which it obtains historically from the matter-of-course metaphysical grounds of belief. In regard to the ascertainment of the so-called transcendent, this philosophy can be only *philosophia transcendentalis*, and this means that it can then also strive only for *veritas transcendentalis*. Finally, it will remain completely restricted to the appearances and to the sense in which these appearances become graspable. And it will be the science of these appearances by seeking to ground them. Of course, the attempt to clarify the constitution of the phenomena in consciousness also requires its own special mode of communicating knowledge, which can begin only here. In contrast to any merely registering description, it must obviously be sought in simple and intensified "reflection" which justifies a correctly understood "universal idealism."[30]

Phenomenology, in its striving for grounding knowledge, has neither a royal road at its disposal nor arcane lore for the initiated.[31] In principle it says farewell to all gnosticism and esotericism. In the process of its strivings, it is completely caught up in what Hegel disparagingly called "bad infinity."[32] It settles for that, because the other infinity is utopian. Whereas the Hegelian Absolute, the Spirit, is supposed to contain infinity in a simple manner—so that the opposites are directly preserved (*aufgehoben*) within itself[33] and the particularities of actual development are nevertheless still supposed to follow from and be derived from it itself—phenomenology has nothing to do with such an Absolute. Hegel's fixation of the Absolute in "self-reflection" must, after all, leave this Absolute standing without beginning or end, since as Absolute it can in no way be encompassed, since that would always be restrictive. But Hegel (like Fichte and Schelling) then nevertheless again and again puts restrictions on this Absolute in order to explain how this entire concrete present reality is derived from it.[34] Precisely thereby, the Absolute is again missed from the very outset, because in every self-limitation of whatever kind within the Absolute, something happens which seems understandable "after the fact"—in terms of the "world which has become"—but which cannot be explained in terms of the Absolute *as* Absolute.

Consistent phenomenology knows only "bad infinity," i.e., the one which Hegel calls "empirical external infinity," which has "the other of its self always outside itself." Phenomenological consciousness goes after this other in a constantly renewed regressive reflection. It is bound topically to situations and contexts, and it is historical through and through. Every position (every validation) thereby becomes the occasion for the critical dismantling into the constitutive conditions of possibility. The unfinished and unfinishable process of this critical analysis, which takes place in a flow of *cogitationes* exceeding anticipation, is the phenomenological absolute beyond which there can be no further regress: namely, the life of consciousness, which lifts the starting positions—quite legitimately posited and accepted in a naive-dogmatic sense—through the transition to super-positions, and which precisely then is critique, metacritique, critique of metacritique.[35]

The sense and being of consciousness, of being a person, of being a subject, of existence, remains a constant theme of the philosophy of consciousness insofar as it does not involve mental operations, moods, or states-of-mind *as such*, nor, for instance, categories and existentials *as such*; rather, all these factors are evidenced as what they mean and achieve. Philosophy is an effort to disclose the mediations that produce knowledge. Unreflective living-along in certain attitudes of everyday life, existing as existing, says absolutely nothing about this existing as life and *as* existing. But insofar as something is indeed said here, a mediation through the apprehending consciousness is present. This is what phenomenology as scientific philosophy is concerned with. The turn which it brings can be ascribed only to the consequences of implementing such an apprehension.[36]

Nowhere can it contain a "subject-object dichotomy." For it is always determinate disclosures of meaning that depend on consciousness's ways of coming to appearance in this way or that. There is no such thing as an empty grasping, understanding, or comprehending, and an empty and hence "relationless having of knowledge" (Rehmke),[37] just as there is no consciousness that is not consciousness of something or consciousness with a particular quality (Latin = *quale*). The much-discussed "intentionality of consciousness" can have no gaps. Even when non-intentional experiences are cited—for instance, anxiety or care—anxiety or care itself is not nothing, but precisely the disclosure of the corresponding quality. Above all, however, anxiety or care is never already an "ontology of anxiety or care," but must always still rely on the grasping which happens to achieve such an ontology. And the elaboration of a categorial system of being needs objectifying fixation as well as the depiction of the context of existential structures.

Anxiety and care are really taken for anxiety and care *only* because they are evidenced *as* anxiety or *as* care. They say nothing of existentiality and the composition of being; they have nothing to report about *Dasein*, which "in its being is concerned with this being itself."[38] Or if they do report something of this, then they are intentional after all, in a more comprehensive sense than was first postulated. From this a rule follows: the intentional references must actually be investigated in the corresponding attitudes of consciousness. If this is done, then consciousness discovers factors which certain moods or states of mind by themselves do not at all reveal.

When Nicolai Hartmann first calls thought and knowledge a "relation of being,"[39] and, on this ascertainment, then considers an "ontology," or rather a "metaphysics of knowledge," to be possible, the ascertainment of the being-relation still remains dependent upon the possibilities of cognition to raise this very ascertainment to consciousness. Even in such an understanding of consciousness, which accepts thought and knowledge as a relation of being and considers them valid, the entire aprioristic structure of this transcendental composition of consciousness is implicitly co-posited.

On the one hand, in the twentieth century an extraordinary faith in science has certainly gained ascendency; but just as undeniably, on the other hand, doubts concerning the validity of this scientifically oriented world view were heard again and again. On the one hand, one is tempted to speak of a "new Enlightenment";[40] on the other, the tendencies are growing stronger to go back behind the image of the world distilled out by the sciences.[41]

This is where the reiterative character of modern phenomenological, consistently critical philosophizing stands out most clearly. No one can be unaware that a fundamental problem is present, and not one that would merely characterize a particular situation, say Europe in the mid-twentieth century. If—like other world views before it—the scientific world view likewise does not portray "the world in itself," if one would like to go back behind the scientific interpretation of the world in order to reach a "natural view of the world," this desire reveals either a fundamentally utopian or else an underlying historical tendency. It is "utopian" to believe one could attain a "natural world view" merely by excluding scientific theorizations, substructions and constructions. "Being-in-itself," prior to all interpretation, the "natural" world, cannot be reached in that way. After rejecting the scientific interpretation of the world one can perhaps arrive at a "mythical" or a "gnomic" world-experience, etc. But it certainly is never possible to overleap interpretation as interpretation, i.e., the transcendental structure in its respective determination. The Absolute is nowhere; it remains utopian.

The altercation in which consciousness is engaged shows the traces of the inner structure of this very consciousness everywhere. So perhaps an analysis of the real circumstances can describe how the "scientific world view" is a "processed world view."[42] Once it is shown, the new prescientific world view, which is uncovered at a lower stratum, is anything but "natural." It is not scientific, but it too is the constituted correlate of appertinent (other) performances of consciousness, in which it stands as "this-there" (*dieses da*).

To believe that disclosing the "scienticized" world-interpretation is all that would be needed to reach a genuine ("absolute") natural world is proof of completely unhistorical thinking. Phenomenology admits of no such genuine world, for every appearance emerges solely as the correlate of modes of consciousness which make it possible. And the world of appearance never ceases to be a counterpart to precisely this consciousness which apprehends it. Thus it is never "natural," not even upon continued retrogression behind the interpretations. No stopping at any phase of development of consciousness guarantees the discovery of the natural world—neither the point of departure from the overinterpreted Descartes,[43] nor the one from the overtaxed pre-Socratics.[44] It thus is utopian to absolutize any phase in the development of conscious life—the place where the Absolute could be located cannot be found.

Historically, the problem is apprehended as soon as it is admitted that every world-disclosure is and remains, as such, "interpretation." This includes that every consciousness of a phenomenon is likewise interpretation: it shows the world as the aggregate of appearances which belong correlatively to this state of consciousness and this project of consciousness. It is unhistorical to choose, for example, the Cartesian position of the *cogito-sum* point of departure as the absolute starting point;[45] it will have to be called unhistorical to demand the same for a certain "poetic legend."[46] If phenomenology claims to be reiterative reflection, that is because it seeks again and again to *unmask* precisely the (anti-historical) absolutizations *as metaphysical opinions in time*. The "metaphysics of myth" looks different from the "metaphysics of natural science,"[47] but it would be illogical to believe that one is more natural than the other. For if one actually wanted to hold this belief, it would presuppose that "the world as such" could again become a phenomenon with which then one interpretation, called "provisional," and the other, called "less provisional," could be compared. On the basis of such a comparison, one of the two interpretations could then be qualified as "more natural." The entire crux of unhistorical thinking is revealed in this dilemma.

The retrogression from one world-design to another world-design which is transcendentally just as dependent does not yield a world-in-itself, does not release a completely "natural world." Historical thinking is fully aware that even nature, or what is understood thereby, is a "cultural construct"—i.e., something apprehended and understood that remains completely determined by the transcendental conditions of precisely this apprehension and understanding, as well as by work, performance, desire, and need, i.e., by the praxis of theory. And this holds good not just for the removal of scientific structures; it holds good equally for every other prescientific world-design of a merely supposedly "natural" thinking.[48]

Rousseauism in metaphysics and ontology is indeed very seductive, but in view of the transcendental formation of every phenomenon-cognition, it remains a mere dogma. Moreover, every absolutization, of whatever kind, contradicts the phenomenological principle of inquiring into grounds.

Constitutional research has to analyze the presuppositions and conditions under which something comes to appearance *as* something and the way it acquires this or that sense. Certainly, it is not supposed to take a stand on what appears in the sense of simply declaring the discovered connections to be the ultimate ones and omitting any further regressive inquiry. For it thus itself becomes metaphysics, and indeed a metaphysics of indescribable naiveté.

It is neither right to say that the Cartesian point of departure with the *cogito* has once and for all moved the ego as empirical subject to the center or to the absolute beginning—for the *Cartesian Meditations* show that this subject cannot guarantee itself the "duration of its existence"[49]— nor is it true, for instance, that the "audible Greek word" puts us "directly in the presence of the thing itself, not first in the presence of a mere word sign."[50] Husserl revised the first, subjective-dogmatic starting point; the second, Heideggerian dogmatism, still needs to be dissolved by a fundamentally critical and not "ontological" or etymologically fixated phenomenology. There is such a thing as epistemological demythologization.

In sum, where everything that can be the possible object of meaningful investigation presents itself as a "phenomenon"—and this means, where it makes itself known together with its sense and significance as the correlate of the appertinent acts of consciousness—"metaphysics" is always possible only as "transcendental philosophy." Consciousness, however, as superordinated title for all transcendentally determinative performances, can clarify itself over and over again only by subjecting even what is said about "this consciousness' own being" to an ever-repeated examination.[51]

Everything that seems definitively known about mind, life, and existence results from particular ways of treatment by this consciousness.

In Kant, "transcendental reflections" are what give information about "categorial constitution" and the "*a priori* forms." In Husserl's phenomenology, which broadens the Kantian concept of phenomenon so much that all unities of sense and significance fall within it, every form of transcendental constitution, as well as what is constituted "naturally," can itself become a "phenomenon"—only never at the same time. The performance now working constitutively is not conscious of its constitutive character during the execution, but this does not mean that this quality would have to remain completely hidden. It can be brought to light in the form of the "bad infinity"—so badly slandered by Hegel—of an ever repeated regression to the preconditions of what is present here and now. Heidegger's "fundamental ontology" is established from the first as a "transcendental philosophy"; however, it rejects reflection as an adequate source of information.[52] But even when it does this, it remains within the general framework of a philosophy of consciousness which starts in principle with correlations.

This is not at all changed by the fact that consciousness is not mentioned or that the philosophy of consciousness is expressly accused of adhering to the traditional "subject-object dichotomy." Even "existence, in its existing," is what it is only in correlation with what is witnessed by it—but it does not know that it is precisely this. On this point, existentialism goes beyond "existence" by detecting the existentials which are valid for *Dasein* as *Dasein*, but at first remain completely hidden to this *Dasein* itself. To stop with a "secret metaphysics" of a *Dasein* that always understands only for itself (*vor sich hin*) is still not a philosophical position at all, i.e., one aiming at grounds. This metaphysics is actually also clarified in fundamental ontology and in existential philosophy, for *Dasein*, as the being which in its being is concerned with this being itself, is traced back to the factors that must be presupposed and recognized *as* transcendental existential relations. This is a new achievement of consciousness, which here at least is not so absorbed in self-interested *Dasein* that it would no longer be capable of disclosing existential forms of that kind or of *Dasein* in general.[53] In the disclosure of existentials, one's own immediate interest is always overleaped and the regression to something ascertainable is begun. Like life irrationally streaming along as life, immediately decided existence in its existing is not something that points beyond itself. Every grasping of a life-form, of an existential structure, demonstrates on the contrary a transcending in the sense that precisely the immediate performance of a mental process (*Erleben*) or of a self-interested existence is left behind—in favor of the grasping of such a form, structure, mode of being, etc.

In no sense, then, can there be any question here of a definitive "resurrection of metaphysics,"[54] as long as the constitutive relations that apply to any phenomenon are kept in mind—even if this phenomenon is called "mind," "life," or "existence." The "turn to the object" is certainly a turning to the entire manifoldness of the existent—but the existent is, according to its sense, always constituted by sense, and what is constituted by sense points to the kinds of constitution. This shows that a first possibility of cognitive consciousness is the general description of the existent that appears in the most varied aspects, i.e., of the phenomena in their totally different determinacy of sense and being. But that is just a first possibility. The uncovering of the quiddity (*quale*) as such, i.e., of what was formerly called essence or *eidos*, will remain indispensable; still, it has little to do with "philosophical science." Philosophy is neither purely fact-determinative nor merely *qualia*-descriptive; it seeks rather to know why something is as it is. And this means why it occurs as a phenomenon in the way it presents itself in the pertinent attitude, and why it appears binding.[55]

Transcendental phenomenology will, accordingly, always have to be regressive, since precisely the *object* that comes to light is understood as the correlate of subjective ("object-bestowing") performances. Thus the purported "turn to the object" is of necessity disclosed to be a repeatedly required return to transcendental subjectity (*Subjektität*) and to the active-passive constitutive performances of consciousness.[56]

It is quite futile to speak of hypostatizations of the human mind when forms of objects, appearances, i.e., phenomena, can be grasped only based on certain modes of apprehension and attitude. For all this too is not nothing, that the worlds change with a changing approach (*Zugriff*) on which they depend.

It should not, for instance, be attempted in a new metaphysical turn (e.g. in Marx) "to extract the core out of the glorified forms" while leaving the starting plane dogmatic.[57] But of course the following should be done: the supposedly "natural" and the artificial "glorified" appearances should all be interpreted as forms that are apprehended and dependent on apprehension. This means that the question of the transcendental structuring of the given is a *universal* question. Man in his Marxist particularity as the "creature that produces" himself and his world[58] is here too already the product of a self-apprehension and absolutely not something "in-itself." This is always forgotten in an orthodox interpretation of Marx. It is precisely in an orthodox-naturalist interpretation of man as a natural being that specific possibilities of being are denied to this man in each case, and exactly this lack is then supposedly identified as the essence of man, so understood.[59] But what has really happened is this: the interpretation of man's essence in such a fashion originates simply from the

function of a determinate potential understanding within the interpretation alone. Phenomenology now fulfills its task by pointing to the
indissoluble connection between the transcendental structure of understanding and what is understood, while refraining from any dogmatic
recognition of one of the legitimated (*ausgewiesene*) positions (whether it
be historically the first or the last). If in so doing it uses the terms
borrowed from Descartes—*cogitatio, cogito, cogitatum*, etc.—that does
not mean that this philosophy of consciousness would and should be a
Cartesian philosophy of consciousness.

Descartes' metaphysical meditations are, in the last analysis, themselves dogmatic, since the assumption of a God who preserves everything
remains indispensable for the implementation of the methodical doubt.
The doubting ego experiences itself as being only as long (*quamdiu*) and
as often (*quoties*) as this doubt takes place; and from this instantiform,
momentary certainty it gains no certainty in general, i.e., no guarantee of
its permanent existence. The subject which is certain of itself in this
instant dethrones no one.[60] It is moreover certainly false to attribute to
Descartes that he understood man in principle as an isolated subject in
contrast with an equally isolated object. For Descartes, too, doubt is
possible only if there is "something" to doubt; the self without consciousness of an "object" is no longer a self. This means that the self does not
stand at all self-sufficiently opposite a world or a cosmos of objects, which
are likewise self-sufficient, but insofar as the self is, it is consciousness of
an *object—or it does not exist*. To be sure, Descartes considers it quite
immaterial whether this thing or that one is conscious, or whether this
thing or that one is true or not true. But it does violence to the
interpretation if one fails to note that this interrogated consciousness
always remains, in the displaying *cogitatio*, consciousness of the object,
perhaps an illusory, erroneous, hallucinatory consciousness of an object,
yet definitely always connected with the object as a mediated object.[61]

It is not as if consciousness, the *cogito*, first of all is something and then
would have to confront itself with a universe of objects. Descartes never
propounded such a "philosophy of subjectivity." Descartes seeks certainty; he wants to reach solid ground via the self, and, rightly or wrongly,
he starts with the conviction that for this purpose he can make no further
use of this factor: that consciousness is always consciousness of an object.
But this does not change the fact as such at all. Only on the occasion of an
actually present consciousness of an object is the showing of existence
possible. Nowhere is the content of consciousness crossed out *as* content;
only the question is not raised of the particular content and whether it
would have to be assumed as certainly existing and being (not merely as
imagined, assumed, hallucinated, fictional). Nor is this a "failure to ask"

something that should be asked.[62] On the contrary, one could say: Descartes can carry on his demonstration of existence only after just one thing has become absolutely indubitable—namely, that consciousness always presents itself as consciousness of objects (which is simply not "problematic").

Interpretation of Descartes falls short of the mark if one wants to rediscover in the *First* and *Second Meditations* the dogmatism of the "subject-object dichotomy." On the contrary, the Cartesian statement of the question implicitly recognizes the "subject-object connection." And in his investigations Descartes actually arrives, strictly speaking, only at the statement of the *cogito-sum*, i.e., at a designation of synonyms. Cartesian reflection achieves no more than this; it says merely: thinking is present. To call this thinking, insofar as it is present, an existent thinking may be traditionally feasible, but it actually does not lead beyond what is disclosed (*das Ausgewiesene*).

Another reason why Descartes may not be accused of forgetting the problem is that the only task he had set for himself was to find an absolutely certain point of departure for philosophizing. He did not want to develop the question of the sense of being, nor that of the sense of the being of thought (of *cogitationes*). Historical thought must be eminently objective, accurately grasping its object; it must deal with the very questions and statements of the problem which dawned upon consciousness in a concrete situation, and only with these. And it serves no purpose to ascribe to forgetfulness problems which are not brought up otherwise. There is not the problem of being-in-itself, *or* the problem of knowledge, *or* the problem of life in general, but there are the problems which have become relevant in the historical life of consciousness—otherwise nothing.[63]

Only from a final standpoint of a transcendental philosophy that has become absolutized or attained conclusive positions could it be said which problems have contributed greatly to promoting the elaboration of such a transcendental philosophy that solves all problems. Until then there is only a critical historiography that takes the viewpoint of transcendental philosophy into account in historical temporalizations. A historical reason will have to take all disclosures of consciousness seriously as disclosures of consciousness and discuss its problems in them, but it must not want to find problems discussed where they did not arise at all and become relevant.

If Nietzsche spoke of "forgetting the world" and Heidegger of "forgetting being," it would be possible in the mid-twentieth century also to speak of "forgetting history." For today in a completely unhistorical view it is supposed that reality is such that it knows only one really important problem,[64] and that problem, illustrated by Heideggeran dogmatism, is: *why is there anything at all and not nothing?* If fundamental ontology argues thus and criticizes a former skipping over and overlooking of the "question of being," from a dogmatic standpoint that is right. Consciousness and reason, however, develop in "concrete" situations, historically, and what thereby emerges correlatively is the discovered world.[65] The historicity of thought is, then, just a mere name that means nothing, if on the other hand there are supposed to be, and always to have been, absolute problems such as the problem of being, which alone are important in the stricter sense, and if thus the entire fullness of the problems which have historically actually become relevant is removed from the pertinent situations and compared with what really always should and had to have been a problem.

If man is "thrown back upon the naked 'that-ness,' the naked 'facticity' of his existence as the ultimate starting point of every philosophic reflection,"[66] then this reduction to an absolute beginning of his existence, as it comes to consciousness here and now, is also a historical appearance through and through. The problems of academic philosophy or the problems of the metaphysics of life are, then, like those of fundamental ontology, historically temporalized problems, and as such are anything but absolute or absolutely—namely, always already—relevant.

Scheler's metaphysics of life and person, Heidegger's metaphysics of *Dasein* and being are something completely historical, and their historicity does not remain hidden from reiterative regressive inquiry into the origin of their positions. For this, of course, the attitude of regressive inquiry must be preserved. Where something is called simply a position, everything is matter-of-course—including the canon of really important problems. Philosophy of consciousness can do what thetic metaphysical positions cannot: it can reach beyond the pregiven *as* interpreted in this or that way to the conditions for its possibility. The entire metaphysics of being also represents such a phenomenal pregivenness, and it is subject to the fundamental phenomenological clarification of sense, as is everything else that is pregiven. It is transcendable in its respective specifications.

Yet, quite obviously, all correlative relations establish a dogmatic connection between any concrete consciousness and the space opened up by it.[67] Every "finite" circle of understanding is characterized by positions taken and defended dogmatically. And if Kant in his *Critique of Pure Reason* speaks of the dogmatic method, namely "to give a priori strict proofs from principles that are certain,"[68] then this means that it is presumed that such principles that are certain can indeed be found.

Actually, of course, every attitude of life and knowledge is based upon the fact that anything determinate is matter-of-coursely in such or such a way. And the specialized questions of the various sciences and life-world attitudes result from such foundation.

In a classical description, *The Dogmatic Form of Thought in the Human Sciences and the Problem of Historicism,* Erich Rothacker portrayed all this as the only really universal form of concrete thinking.[69] For "the core phenomenon of the basic attitude prevalent here is that in all these cases a firm conviction is expressed, claiming to be true and seeking scientific grounds for itself. An additional primary feature of this basic attitude is that this philosophical faith pursues the ideal intention of serving life and its presence—or mankind—proclaiming wholesome truths, giving recipes for renewal and healing. A secondary aspect is whether these truths express, in many transitions, the convictions of individual prophets, saviors, founders of religions, or lawgivers, or whether they explicate the sense of existing 'institutions' which have already attained power and been elaborated, but ultimately also lay claim to truth."[70]

Phenomenologically, what is here called "solid convictions" are the matter-of-course assumptions which everywhere stand at the beginning, and within which understanding—and hence life, action, and inaction—are located. Every system of understanding played through, every emotional-cognitive life-context, every knowledge-structure is first of all simply for itself the truth. The moment one no longer speaks of "natural science" but of "classical natural science," what now happens to be called "classical physics" (i.e., the position of Galileo, Kepler, Descartes, and Newton) has become a dogmatic position, i.e., one seen from another standpoint to be dogmatic and hence obsolete. [71] Furthermore, "as soon as the modern psychotherapist speaks of the mechanistic and naturalist tendencies of contemporary medicine, he no longer accepts it as 'medicine' itself, but as 'medical dogmatism.'"[72] Much can be learned from Rothacker's examples.

Every system of understanding, sense, and life as such lives under the same assumption that it is portraying the truth. Not until one seeks and finds one's standpoint outside the system itself does the previously matter-of-course circle of consciousness and apprehension appear as dogmatism. To anyone who undertakes investigations on the basis of German legal history, the Roman legal system no longer appears to be universally valid, but rather appears to be a component of Romance culture,[73] i.e., a dogmatically assumed position no longer shared by the observer in question. "Dogmatism" then means simply "the systematic explication of a particular attitude, a particular style, a particular way of seeing."[74] Observed from *within,* i.e., if one happens to share the bases of understanding taken for granted as "self-evident," the form of life portrayed is always *the* form of life; the developed conception of law is *the* law, the manifested understanding is *the* understanding as such. In such a sense, then, for instance in *Being and Time*, there is mention of a "circle of understanding" in the sense that it is not a matter of avoiding it, but that, on the contrary, the difficulty and the problem is to get into the circle at all.[75] Here it becomes clear that one must enter the circle in which the matter-of-course assumptions hold true; and one must share them, must have adopted them as self-evident. Then and only then do the situation of consciousness and the correlate of consciousness, the understanding and what is understood, stand in a circular self-clarifying connection. Whoever does not avoid such a "circle of understanding" but stands within it, on the basis of particular assumptions which he considers valid, thereby belongs at the same time to a "circle of understanders," a circle of like-minded individuals, a school of the initiated, down to the rules of every kind and origin; he belongs to the circle of augurs.[76] Vice versa, for the person who remains outside the circle of understanding, the matter-of-course grounds of positions of understanding cease quite matter-of-coursely to give the truth. For him each of the states of consciousness that can be found in history is characterized by a systematic and typological label and hence transformed into a dogmatic position. [77]

Whoever speaks of the "life-world" has thereby stripped the familiar, scientifically interpreted world of physicalistic objectivism of its claim to absoluteness and unmasked its concepts as dogmatic—certainly understandable, but no longer matter-of-course.

There can now be no doubt that the various positions which present something new are absolutely all developed on the basis of such unquestioned assumptions and unexamined proofs. They are all "dogmatic" because of an assumed "metaphysics." Just when the position is no longer binding, the person who is giving it up gives it a characteristic, delimiting title, and thus it is made outwardly knowable as "dogmatism."

This very thing is, in principle, the case when "critical phenomenological reduction" begins and is practiced universally. For phenomenological reflection says first just the following: one must go back to the correlates of a particular context of understanding in order to make this understanding, which is present at this moment, understandable. Starting from the self and its determinate mode of apprehension, the intentionally appertinent world must be brought into grasp; and inversely, it holds true that consciousness, this at first not understood empty concept, can be elucidated only in terms of what is intentionally understood and by virtue of performances done within the *intentio recta*. The same applies to the terms *noesis* and *noema, cogito* and *cogitatum,* but also to that entity which in its being is concerned with this being itself, namely *Dasein.* To "determine" the appertinences, however, means to rise above them, to move beyond them. This is where critical reduction proper begins.

The phenomenological reduction will, then, repeatedly lead back to the specific here and now states of consciousness and to the appertinent connections of understanding which are opened up from here, but it will at the same time convert them all back into dogmatically assumed positions. Of course, this does not mean that the finite systematic context of the particular circle of understanding is destroyed by laying bare the structures of understanding and their performances. It continues to exist in itself, as it always was. Only the understanding is additionally illuminated in this manner. But one more thing has, of course, happened—namely, that the matter-of-course claim to give and reveal the truth becomes clear *as* a mere claim (belonging to this position and to no other). And so it can no longer be overlooked that the position one has can henceforth be considered only as a dogmatically chosen position—as a position that stands under some conditions or other, although the validity of the conditions as universal and matter-of-course has long since been abandoned with the rising above to the constitutive presupposi-tions. This is where transcendental idealism is right, in Husserl's view.[78]

In this light, the phenomenological philosophy of consciousness is not a metaphysics of this or that state of consciousness, but philosophy in the sense of an ever repeated reduction to the understanding which functions according to the situation, whose different variations of historical expres-sion have been discovered and which therefore can no longer be absolutized or metaphysicized. By this method of tracing back to the conditions of possibility of a particular understanding, every understand-ing that is produced naively and matter-of-coursely is transcended as "dogmatic." This is and remains the only transcendency of phenomeno-logical consciousness which is maintained in all retrogressive steps and in all reflections on the constitutive factors.[79]

All phenomenological critique is directed primarily not at the "intrinsic credibility" within a context of consciousness, life, or understanding, but only at the "abolition of belief in the self-evidence of naively practiced attitudes of conviction."[80]

The method of phenomenological reduction to consciousness thus constantly needs particular pregivens. These pregivens are the ever concretely ("situatively," "contextually") assumed states of understand-ing, interpretation, and attitude, at whose basis lie quite originary convictions, to which the historically manifest system of understanding, interpretation, and attitude then corresponds. This is all the case even absolutely "pretheoretically," and it holds true in the realm of the scientific conception of the world, in which even the most highly complicated scientific procedures are based on presuppositions assumed to be absolutely matter-of-course, and are supported, and function, through them alone. The metaphysics of these positions is revealed when the position is no longer merely taken, but grounded (i.e., reduced to the constitutive relations)—or at least when the attempt to do so is made. When faith in the universal validity and matter-of-courseness of certain convictions is no longer present, the position previously "considered natural" is now just a "position"—and whereas it wanted simply to be true or claimed to be true, now, observed from the outside, it receives the character of a "dogmatism," i.e., of a position that is meaningful and understandable only if the presuppositions and conditions are taken for granted. It is precisely unquestionableness that is repeatedly cast in doubt in the phenomenological reduction to historically particular consciousness, because consciousness-as-such does not exist, but just states of consciousness[81] with the dogmatically appertinent correlates. Science has to do with "*if-then*" relations, and philosophy inherently, as a critical foundational science, all the more so.

This shows how there simply can be "no material metaphysics of consciousness" within the framework of phenomenological discussions. The "method" of regression to states of consciousness expressly prevents the absolutization of any single one of them and makes impossible any "doctrinaire metaphysics" of consciousness from within.[82] Just as understanding and what is understood in the broadest sense, just as also the state of consciousness and the horizon of consciousness always belong correlatively together and make no sense whatsoever one without the other, so it is also certain, above all, that one side can never become the other.

By the method of reduction, dogmatic metaphysics—which otherwise prevails in the matter-of-course assumptions of the contexts of understanding—becomes graspable as dogmatism and as metaphysics; and conversely, the regressive-reflective method of reduction can only be what it is if it is located on the solid ground of a particular position and investigates the correlations from this plane of what is considered objective there.[83] Any kind whatsoever of phenomenological consciousness-in-itself, i.e., beyond this critical-methodical rising above the pregiven relational laws, is an absurd concept. It would be "unobjective"—namely, located outside a relation without which mediations are not possible. But consciousness is, precisely, the place of mediation *par excellence*. A critical rising above the dogmatically taken positions is then the method of intensification of this very consciousness.[84] It takes place historically in reiterating initiatives. If there is a rational system it is revealed here. The philosophy of consciousness begins "topically" somewhere; however, it does not reach the completely Absolute, Nowhere, Utopia. Constantly revising its positions, it will prove to be "atopical."

Chapter Three

Reflective Consciousness and Reiterative Regression to Conditions of Possibility

As a universal transcendental philosophy, pure phenomenology seeks to determine what the constitutive conditions for phenomena are, each in its own specific kind, i.e., conditioned situatively and contextually. That is the only way it can legitimate itself as the science of grounds, as philosophy.[1] It seeks the reason and condition why something makes its appearance *as* something and exactly as it shows itself.

Such a point of departure necessarily involves, from the outset, a consciousness through whose transcendental form the structure of phenomena and finally also the structure of something like a world in general is conditioned.[2] No philosophy must or can go beyond this originary relation such that every observable phenomenon, everything whatsoever which is apprehended in any sense, must correspond to a determinate formal structure in its very possibility of being grasped. It may be that the constitutive function of the transcendental structure of every apprehending consciousness remains hidden from this consciousness itself as it performs its function. In that case, these apprehending performances take place purely thetically, naively, or they are taken for granted metaphysically-dogmatically. Then they are anonymous.

But since science recognizes its only goal as leaving "nothing" standing and taking nothing for granted as "self-evidently" given,[3] the scientific attitude in philosophy will therefore focus on the positional assumptions of the originary and natural attitude toward life, when they can be "discovered."

Since philosophy as a whole is not a specialized science among other specialized sciences with the task, like theirs, of defining and delimiting, for example, power, life, right, language, or matter, and since it does not reprocess and sum up the totality of the relevant factors in each case, and finally since it also does not make the goal of its research any single determinate world-object—i.e., an object which those other specialized sciences had previously just omitted—the basis of philosophy's "universal claim" must be clarified from the first. For when philosophy steps forth as a science of grounds, this indubitably is a universal claim.

To the scientific attitude, in principle everything that previously came to consciousness as a matter-of-course can become a phenomenon, i.e., an object of meaningful inquiry. There are many of these matter-of-course assumptions.[4] They cannot be enumerated, for the discovery that they are assumptions requires a certain "critical" maturity of consciousness which cannot be anticipated, and which discovers itself and determines *the whole series* only in the course of its development.

Although philosophy always has certain problems that need clarification, what these problems are cannot be stated once and for all. What is matter-of-course generally enters consciousness only when its matter-of-courseness ceases to exist. But when something ceases to remain unnoticed as matter-of-course, this is a historical event in the development of a reason oriented toward establishing grounding connections.

So philosophy, precisely as phenomenology, will at first paradoxically have nothing to do with a sector of the totality of phenomena which is already before man's eyes within the natural attitude, but will again and again in historical variation come across things that once were matter-of-course, which it suddenly, to its astonishment, finds dubious. Thus it is the fundamentally "historical" discipline pure and simple.[5] Philosophy, which in each case focuses on its phenomenon—first just to describe it, then to ground it—has no static, fixed subject matter; it incessantly *discovers* new subject matter in that which, in an otherwise scientifically compartmentalized world of experience, is a remnant of the matter-of-course.

All individual sciences start with prescientific experiences, which they theoretize but on which they remain metaphysically dependent in this regard: they simply assume a certain field of objects which is relevant to the naive attitude as a field of objects and proceed to investigate it. All sciences thus contain a metaphysics in that component of them which is an unexamined object given quasi-"self-evidently." At the moment when these metaphysically presupposed but scientifically uninvestigated objects (matter, energy, number, life, etc.) which serve as the basis for specialized research, in turn do not remain matter-of-course segments of the world, data to be recognized and accepted without question, a new problem has already manifested itself. Philosophy could then be defined formally as that scientific discipline which treats of the newly discovered problems—i.e., those problems which fall out of the framework of the previously well-founded individual sciences and find no place in them. It is thus a problem-science *par excellence*[6]—the science of the problems which it alone finds and raises.

The phenomena treated in philosophy are in an eminent way finitely historical phenomena, for it is a historical fact of an exceptional kind when anything whatever that was previously taken for granted *loses its matter-of-course character*. So what we have is not a sectorial phenomenology in the sense that here a segment of the world merely forgotten till now is subjected to investigation, whereby the cosmos of the sciences finally would be completed. Phenomenological philosophy is not a "complementary science," any more than it formerly would have been a matter of an elaborative or summative science.

The objects of phenomenological philosophy are the matter-of-course assumptions at the moment when they are discovered to be such. Thus phenomenology becomes, essentially, the "controlling" science of all metaphysical positions that ever emerge.[7] For the matter-of-course convictions always are, contain, and defend metaphysical positions. When consciousness, with its radical will to know, comes upon things which are taken for granted, it simultaneously discovers metaphysical positions at work in them.

As phenomenology now seeks to find the conditions, presuppositions, and bases for what is considered matter-of-course, it at the same time dissolves and abolishes the matter-of-course *as* matter-of-course. Phenomenology, as transcendental philosophy, is philosophy of constitution—but phenomenology as philosophy of constitution is also continually "critique"—namely, the grounding dissolution of whatever metaphysical positions become conscious. Hence phenomenology is possible only as control over metaphysics, but not as itself metaphysics.

The claim to "universality" of this phenomenology, so defined, is based on the fact that the attitudes of dogmatic everyday life and of scientific theorizing can absolutely all be thematized once it has been discovered that they are only "considered" matter-of-course. But no life as life, no existence as existence, no school as a school is without some matter-of-course assumptions allowing something which was not a phenomenon in the naive-natural attitude or in the scientific-secondary attitude, namely the natural or quasi-natural convictions, to become a phenomenon at all. This is the course of development of a consciousness that attains clarification. And this consciousness itself, in which the former matter-of-course convictions turn out to be problematic, is no exception to the task of continuously carrying through such checking out of matter-of-course convictions. Consciousness, understanding, the scrutinizing mind itself is an object—a peculiar kind of object; for the matter-of-course convictions concerning consciousness, understanding, and mind are really just the first case where that general and fundamental control is applied.[8] That is, even the matter-of-course transcendental structures are not just data to be recorded statically and respected naively. They too are subject to the control of consciousness; they too, then, are in the given case phenomenalized and made questionable, i.e., transcendentally reduced.[9]

This does not mark a "crisis of consciousness," since what would have to be called so is always, and could only be, discovered by this very consciousness, whereby precisely the power of this consciousness comes to renewed discovery. As a consequence, phenomenology is also "not a metaphysics of consciousness"; rather, it provides the key to the reiterative attempt to dissolve the matter-of-course by grounding it. The dogmatic position taken under critical review and itself in turn quite concretely assumed is thus always the position of the moment. In a new regressive turning back it too can be made knowable as a position with an appertinent metaphysics. Phenomenology, so understood, leaves behind all absolutist dogmatism of mind, being, and soul, by unmasking it as a metaphysics, a metaphysics that is "taken for granted" for a time.

So again and again in the course of historical variations, different positions have been stripped of their matter-of-courseness. And in that very operation the consciousness that reached clarification made itself noticeable. This entire process is historical. The transcendental connection remains a relational connection that comes to be known only historically. And it is a result that has come about historically, to be able to discuss, for instance, life instead of the living, being instead of the existent, and finally consciousness instead of knowledge. It is a difference whether *veritas transcendentalis* "is valid" or becomes conscious and recognized *as veritas transcendentalis*.

Phenomenology develops no universal image of the world and of world history in the sense of offering, or even trying to offer, a historically proceeding characterization of the mind on the basis of universal, all-encompassing essential descriptions. It does not start with the so-called earliest history in order to advance in dialectical steps to the logical connection of all phenomena that have ever appeared. Its procedure is quite the reverse. It starts with something that is matter-of-course here and now but is just on the verge of becoming questionable, and so it is constantly historical.[10] For this fact—that something appears questionable here and now—remains totally underivable at the moment and forms the (dogmatic) basis of research valid at this moment. So ultimately phenomenology turns out, in a very eminent sense, to be "the science of the present."

What is now discovered to be a mere assumption is its subject matter; thus that is what it questions and seeks to understand by analyses of constitution. In other words, phenomenology is science of the present insofar as it expressly does not unconcernedly let stand but investigates the metaphysical assumptions underlying the current view. That it stumbles upon them at all cannot yet be further derived at the moment of problematization, but without a doubt points the way to further possible controls for what is taken for granted, which controls can be added reiteratively to the current one.

Finally, it must be kept in mind that the method by which such a transcendental and constitutive phenomenology must work in analyzing what is taken for granted must ultimately be that of "reflection" and continued regression, for only in phenomenological consciousness are those assumptions "manifested" and only in critical consciousness are they "dissolved." [11]

The universality of phenomenological philosophy's questioning is based upon the knowledge that of course some dogmatically taken positions or other always make a beginning possible, and accordingly are the source of all intellectual, contentually articulated knowledge—but the dogmatic position never recognizes itself as dogmatic, nor does it want to. Phenomenology, by dissolving all assumptions, is the questioning of every metaphysics present in consciousness, including the metaphysics of consciousness itself. It is nothing else but the discipline that finds and invents the points of view which are suited not to allow what is taken for granted to stand dogmatically, but to show it to be meaningful by applying the appropriate points of view (which simply have to be found).

One thing, then, is clear: this phenomenology knows no clearly demarcated circle of objects which always belong specifically to it, since whatever can enter into appearance as its object depends upon the consciousness which legitimates itself historically and upon the transcendental structures functioning within it. Phenomenology is thus not the science that could anticipate today what will be possible for consciousness tomorrow. It is consciousness of phenomena in the form of the abolition of matter-of-courseness.[12] So this phenomenology does not share the world with other sciences: they, rather, always let certain assumptions stand as necessary for their work; phenomenology, however, explicitly makes absolutely all of them, as questionable, its object, and thus constantly broadens the circle of the existing phenomena.[13] To this extent, and only to this extent, it becomes a science of the whole (which it again and again purports to be). It does not, like physics, have as its object the laws governing matter; nor, like biology, unfathomable life; nor, like the philologies and the historical sciences, the mind, which inventively embodies itself in particular sense—i.e., it does not in its turn have a specialized object, called "the whole," as its special theme. There is for phenomenology no object, *the whole*, under which more than an abbreviation could be thought. Even phenomenology cannot bring such an absolute into its grasp contentually.

The world of objects, then, does not draw the phenomenological philosopher's attention to itself in any privileged sector; rather, it is the thinkable as thinkable, the appearance as appearance, the meaningful as meaningful that does this. The question then is: why is this or that thinkable, why is it appearance, why is it meaningful?[14] This question is universal, for it can be appended to everything that is the object of observation in any specialized science. To be able to discover matter-of-course assumptions of every kind, an "anticipation" of consciousness that leads beyond the matter-of-course is of course necessary. Consciousness, subjectity, is, then, the title of the authority that causes the new to become visible. The universality of phenomenological thinking obviously does not consist in reaching forward beyond the findings of the well-established individual sciences to a kind of hypothetical image of the universe of the thinkable. Nor does phenomenological philosophy anticipate the individual-scientific process of a world-mastery that still leaves quantitative gaps, and achieve by a bold move what the specialized sciences had to work at only slowly and laboriously. No philosophy has such an ability. But it can, indeed, investigate the foundations from which all those objective, detailed, ever more subtle investigations are carried out in the domain of world and object.

It is, then, the science of the world frameworks opened up by the structures of consciousness and by the (metaphysical) positions used positively in each case.[15] In short, phenomenological philosophy as universal science is anything but an "extensively" exhaustive and supplementary knowledge of objects in the mundane realm.

If a striving for universal knowledge arises anywhere, the goal of this striving can only be to call attention to the "transcendental-constitutive modes of consciousness" present in all objective knowledge.[16] Together with the things they take for granted, these modes of consciousness are what give the objective structure the character, the form, in which it stands for the phenomenological "life-worldly" and "scientific" consciousness. The theme would then be that consciousness, in this or that phase of its development, allows one thing or another to be taken for granted. But it always remains the consciousness in which something shows itself as something. Thus a universal phenomenologizing philosophy would have to be referred back to this consciousness itself.[17]

That this or that metaphysical position was simply a position invented, approved, held, and defended by non-reflective consciousness, and why it was so, becomes the object of a universal discipline which occupies itself successively with pregiven assumptions that must be dissolved. But there must be no misunderstanding on this point: not a word said here should postulate the thesis that it is "the task of a philosophy of consciousness" to abolish metaphysical systems and cause them to disappear! The opposite is the case: an immediate desire to know (taken for granted and as such perhaps not philosophically clarified) first finds what was previously matter-of-course to be again and again actually questionable. So a process indeed unfolds; but nowhere is it said that an inner goal is fulfilled in these processes as a whole.[18] Such a statement would, rather, itself be disclosed as a reducible, naive, metaphysical, dogmatic position, when critical consciousness on this point awakens. In this regard, therefore, the process consists in a continually deepened acquisition of consciousness. But the enterprise of grounding and hence understanding something simply given strips that given of its claim to absoluteness (namely, of being independent), abolishing its claim and devaluing it metaphysically.

In this entire philosophical endeavor, it is not just a broadening of the "circle of objects" that comes about; rather, a new "problematic dimension" becomes visible. It is a question of the performances of consciousness and subjectity[19] which are responsible for each and every world view. When they have actually been discovered in any one case, it is not a "new segment of the world," not an additional sector of the boundless field of objects that has been made accessible, but the condition for such sectorial seeing and object-determination that has been discerned and communicated.

Every world of objects that is approached in a particular way in the individual sciences, *which rightly proceed dogmatically*, constantly requires consciousness in a counterrhythm and as a counterpart—a consciousness which in turn has its own object precisely in this: that it becomes a problem to itself in the manner of object-grounding.

Since the dissolving of the matter-of-course assumptions always occurs as a historical process, and since the grounding and abolition of postulated and assumed metaphysical positions appears as a historical process, the reflection of consciousness upon itself and its performances is likewise a historical event through and through. Reflection is, then, itself not at all something matter-of-course, but something that results "historically." Phenomenological philosophy, which studies what is taken for granted as valid in the life-world and the world of science by making it questionable, is, hence, necessarily a philosophy of reflection. It must remain a philosophy of reflection, because the thematized assumptions belong to consciousness itself.[20]

The thinking of the individual sciences, which is bound to the world-objects, and natural and quasi-natural historical consciousness, are so preoccupied with the world-phenomena—and so absorbed in describing, arranging, and comparing them—that thought and consciousness, with their own transcendentally functioning structure, do not come into view. Work is done on the object and not on consciousness. Reflection on the consciousness of phenomena is something extremely "unnatural" and does not designate a natural given in itself. This reflection is a means for dissolving what was originally most matter-of-course. It thus becomes the "most unnatural" thing in the world.

To have a phenomenon become a problem is possible even in the realm of individual sciences only if new and different points of view are added to the object itself by an act of consciousness, which points of view cause the given to appear problematic. A new problematic dimension results at the moment when the object of a cognitive act is the operation of this very same consciousness: it is the dimension of reflective thought turned back upon itself. It is not the objects as such that comprise the whole of possible observation; rather, "consciousness," which causes the objects to appear in certain ways of construing them, "is the universal."[21]

Of course, any thinking that rightly proceeds dogmatically also deals with a greater or lesser circle of objects which are its problem. These objects, in the way they are grasped and problematized, absolutely all refer back to a consciousness in which all this happens. Thus philosophical thought, no matter how universal the claims it raises, is referred back to this very thinking itself, to consciousness, in which everything that belongs to the world happens.[22]

Consciousness, in its desire for knowledge, is characterized, even with regard to itself, by the trait of eliminating and dissolving the matter-of-course assumptions by grounding them. Consciousness thus strives to illuminate itself down to its very foundations. Phenomenological reflection is a turning-inward of thought away from the objects which are the first goal of its clarifying effort, insofar as it grasps itself according to its essence, origin, performance, and capacity.[23]

Reflection is, then, in a first sense, a look back at object-bound thinking, at its possibilities and its results. Reflection will, in a second sense, be the inward turning toward this thinking itself. That is, object-directed thinking, no less than the immediate consciousness of objects, is not the only thing that can be reached by reflection. A philosophical contemplation of the conditions of thinking itself, a phenomenological investigation of the possibilities for the constitution of the object, is not matter-of-course, but it is also not incomprehensible; it will have to be called "object-oriented" in a different sense than thinking about biological, legal, linguistic, or other phenomena.

Certainly, here too something becomes transparent in consciousness, but in its own kind of "second-level reflection." Thinking about the thinking of objects, consciousness of the consciousness of objects is "oblique" thinking, "oblique" consciousness. "The thinking of an object," "reflection on the thinking of an object," and "reflection on the reflection" thus represent the three dimensions of phenomena which consciousness can encounter.[24] The first heading, "the thinking of an object," sums up everything that becomes directly evident in any *cogitatio* at all—the *cogitatio* can be something rational, but it may just as well include emotion, volition, or sensation, insofar as it has been noted and (consciously) grasped. All intentional and all non-intentional elements of consciousness belong here. This too is a cogitative phenomenon: that an existent of *Dasein*'s kind is anxiously concerned about itself. Precisely insofar as not something senseless, not nothing, is experienced here, but rather the questioning of *Dasein* is "anxiety," a particular phenomenon has indeed attained disclosure.

Thinking in the immediate, direct attitude, being-present with things, quite possibly goes hand in hand with the complete self-forgetting of consciousness. To abolish this self-forgetting of consciousness in observation, experience, and entanglement in phenomena of every kind is itself an accomplishment of consciousness, a late and unanticipatable event. This is even more the case when reflection does not focus on consciousness of an object, but rather when the reflection focusing on consciousness of an object itself becomes the theme of reflection. Theodor Litt called this the "reflection of reflection," a second degree of reflection. He states pointedly, for instance: "We who have here reflected upon objectively oriented thinking should consciously take account of the essence and content of this reflection of ours by a second inward turning. We want to know what we are doing, and for this purpose we must ask ourselves what we are doing, or what we have done. Only so does the self-examination really penetrate to the depths."[25] No doubt, a phenomenology that is supposed to describe the process of the self-clarification of consciousness will also not neglect this reflection of reflection. It points directly to consciousness as consciousness, to consciousness in the form in which it is structured. But in the other direction, immediate knowledge of thing and object can never remain completely unaffected by knowledge on this point—quite the contrary.[26] Matter-of-course assumptions caught within directly objective thinking focused upon thing and object find their explanation in the various ways of thinking and possibilities of cognizance which must now also be clarified.

All this is, of course, a phenomenon in the broadest sense of the word; it is and remains something that is presented in the consciousness in some comprehensible sense or other, namely as this thing here. That is true of the phenomenon as direct correlate of acts and experiences, as well as for understood moods and states-of-mind—it is true in addition of the phenomenon which emerges as the correlate of reflections of the first degree (i.e., with respect to acts, experiences, and states-of-mind)—and this must also be kept in mind concerning those phenomena which are valences of sense-meaning (*potenziertes Sinnvermeintes*), which can be noted in reflections on reflection.

In all this it is important to see that a determinate matter-of-course assumption of consciousness prevails "at every stage."[27] The consciousness that is devoted to things, immersed in moods, and marked by states-of-mind, is deprived precisely of the awareness of being present *as* being present. Even reflection upon an accomplishment and attitude performed in the *intentio recta* does not have "itself" as theme: reflection as the ability to reflect remains completely unexamined here. Finally, in reflection about reflection, the last performance—the current reflection itself—again becomes a subsequent phenomenon and displays its innermost possibilities in the present evidence. At this point, consciousness has reached absolutely its maximum phenomonologizing possibility.

All statements about mundane appearances, all communications about any existent whatsoever, take place within the first attitude. All statements that any kind of appearances and existing data are legitimated in thus and such a way, and come into view in this way or that, are not given with a direct look at this type of appearance or this existent, but open themselves up to a particular form of advertence: namely, reflection. Wherever "forms of apprehension" are noted—i.e., where the concrete, contentually relevant lived experience does not stand in view by itself, but rather is transcended toward a universal structure—reflection is already involved. Living, existing, thinking is one thing—but to know that one lives, exists, and thinks is another. And it would be a third thing if one had exact knowledge of the form and universal structure of this living, thinking, and existing. Only in reflection on what happens in "living, existing, and thinking" can what it is as a phenomenon be ascertained in each case. As long as it does not become a phenomenon, it also does not let itself be discussed—and it is then not a philosophical object at all.

What is matter-of-course has no knowledge of itself. Thus an immediate *cogitatio*, a capacity to deal with things, can implicitly demonstrate a determinate understanding—all it lacks is that it understand itself as understanding. What is lacking here comes about only in "transcendental reflection." But reflection is possible even about transcendental reflections and what they help to clarify. And this is the very first stage at which such a thing as transcendental philosophy becomes transparent.[28]

The line of argument expounded here proves that consciousness, which at first seems interested only in things and devoted to the world, actually must and can have only itself as its last and universally decisive object. Thus consciousness comes into view at any given time in its historically documented form as the source of the correlatively appertinent experiences of the world and of objects. Instead of a "turn to the object," the demand is made for a "return to subjectivity."

Consciousness, which thus in the second form of reflection tries to clarify itself and dissolves the inherent pregivens *as* matter-of-course assumptions, thereby accomplishes what Hegel demands: "it is such philosophical consciousness as grasps time in thoughts."[29] For on this now established form of consciousness depends precisely what possible understanding appears in the thereby correspondingly opened up world of life, existence, and knowledge. Here something is not merely "expressed," but is brought into a concept.

It is perfectly accurate to say that philosophy does not "have" problems, but that it always is a problem to itself in this way (one that is always historically renewed): and it is a problem to itself insofar as, in uninterrupted sequence, it examines the attitudes taken in consciousness dogmatically, thetically, and positionally, trying to ground them, whereby it first understands and "grasps them in thoughts." The possibilities of establishing grounding connections, however, do not lie ontically or statically somewhere—as if one needed merely to penetrate more deeply into a Platonic realm of Ideas, more strongly into the Augustinian complex of creative thoughts in God, or more perfectly into the totality of Leibnizian possibilities.

Phenomenological consciousness knows no phenomena-in-themselves except those which are shown for consciousness. To speak of Ideas, creative thoughts, absolute possibilities, indeed even of "things-in-themselves" which do not actually present themselves to the understanding in consciousness, is absurd. This consciousness too knows no possibilities for grounding what was previously taken for granted, unless it encounters it in these reflections and thereby begins to make it questionable. This comprises the historicity of this position.[30]

Further, that current matter-of-course convictions become problematic confirms the expressed "historicity" of rational consciousness. All structures of life, existence, and knowledge are what they are in any "doctrine" or "theory" on the basis of legitimating reflective performances of consciousness. A life drifting along in care (*Sorge*) does not make known the "existential structure" of care; a thinking according to the statement "*ego cogito cogitatum*" says nothing about the transcendental-constitutive connection of consciousness and what is grasped by consciousness. That man's life is, according to Scheler, a personal existence, that for Heidegger *Dasein* as *Dasein* is concerned with its *Dasein*, and finally that reality for Husserl is *ratio* in the constant movement of self-clarification—all this is not given in direct living, existing, and thinking, but in a clarifying turning back to what is happening in each case. The movement of consciousness as historical movement thus ends in a constantly renewed self-inquiry of consciousness. And philosophy can therefore never again be what it ever was before.[31]

Veritas transcendentalis, then, exists only in the philosophical performance of the structure of consciousness which posits world and object.[32] An object-determined thinking or else one that is absorbed in cognitive analysis of time, is perhaps the first stage of historical development. The act of first-level reflection relates to this, i.e., to this very thinking and understanding in its directness. That will be the basis for the second level.

The act of "second-level reflection" focuses, inversely, on thinking that is not directly absorbed in understanding, thinking that is not directly dedicated to the object; rather, it proceeds from the reflective attitude. That would be the third level. Certainly, new reflections can always be done; numerically, there is no set limit. Everything taken for granted that becomes questionable becomes the theme of a new reflection. In principle, nonetheless, there are only the three stances which were characterized here: first, the *intentio recta* and direct understanding, second, the first turning-inward to what is happening in the *intentio recta*, and third, the second-degree turning-inward which observes reflection and describes its result, i.e., "reflection upon reflection."[33]

Clearly, any phenomenon-containing philosophy must begin by investigating what is given in unreflective living-along. Its position is absolutely fixed. But the more of life becomes questionable, the more the transition from this state of consciousness to the reflective one will ensue. Litt called attention to this with unsurpassable clarity.[34]

The disclosure of the transcendental structures which belong correlatively to the apprehended phenomena is not—as has been objected with a polemic twist—a doubling of worlds.[35] Rather, it makes clear that dogmatism of any kind can provide merely a provisional platform for thinking. In its desire for knowledge, consciousness does not ask whether the results of a cognitive endeavor are compendious or not, ideologically relevant or not, personally interesting or not. It wants to "know," and it is satisfied with "knowing." It would settle for just a scanty increase in knowledge if the raising of reflection to a higher power produced nothing more. Actually, the results of reflective regressions are not slight.

So the idea is abolished once and for all that any consciousness which might merely not be the current one has to do with a "reality-in-itself."[36] And it becomes clear: consciousness always, rather, finds itself—and the structures of its own specific consciousness which make something possible—facing the appertinent horizon-formations. To be sure, the historical and the absolute character of knowledge are decisively inter-connected in this polarity.

This happens as follows: if every transcendental constitution has a determinate object which is constituted by it, then the entire horizon so-constituted is a unity behind which no one can regress starting from the given presuppositions of consciousness. Within the realm thus posited and determined (i.e., "inside the walls" of this life-world, of this reality), very specific truths hold good, and they hold good absolutely: they relate completely to the transcendental structure of the present consciousness as it apprehends reality. When a historical development of this rational consciousness occurs and new transcendental forms take effect, new structuring realities arise, which are indissolubly connected with them.[37]

Here too, as on the previous level, specific connections corresponding to the now existing constitution of reality are considered true. Actually, they are true, if the grounding relation is seen. From the first level to the second level, however, a change of the constitutional conditions has occurred, i.e., a historicization of reason. A concurrent result is that the transcendentally constituted correlate-worlds are different. Accordingly, it becomes necessary, in applying the "absolute" concept of truth, to speak precisely of truths which have become *historically* possible. The truth in question is the only one considered valid in each correlation-context, where it knows no restriction. And yet there are, thus, steps in the development of the absolutely true.[38]

Further, when the transcendental presuppositions change, the field of reality that is opened up and the entire complex of truths that are to be located there also shifts. Constitutive phenomenology, by encountering these factors, renders the dogmatism of a thinking in terms of "worlds-in-themselves" impossible. It replaces them by a starting point from a "life-world considered natural" in each concrete situation, which life-world it would then, in the course of its regressive reflections, like to repeatedly prove to have been, after all, also recently grounded. On the whole, this phenomenology is, in its performance, nothing else but the process of the constant abolition of naivetés.[39] From this perspective, for instance, a highly complex, scientific world view which has become matter-of-course is, then, in the conventionally customary reception, just as naive as any prescientific world-conception which has developed naturally.[40]

What matters is not whether such a world view arose earlier or later in the objective course of history; rather, only this is important: that the supporting evidence accepted without proof and assumed without proof in each of these positions is the starting basis for understanding and thinking which remain in the direct attitude.[41] The dogmatic Marxism of the twentieth century is, in this respect, just as unproven a *metaphysics* as any "early myth."

Every such position commands a horizon of understanding based upon unexamined and tacitly recognized presuppositions. Immanent physics depicts what is possible within its framework, i.e., in the midst of the world-context which opens up here; what determines this framework itself is the actual "metaphysical presupposition" for this very horizon and its contents.

Thus the result of phenomenological reflection is that *there is no world-in-itself*. That truth always remains bound to correlation-contexts would be its second result. That rational consciousness ("rational" in the sense of developing rational points of view) is historical, since it temporalizes itself, would be a third finding provided by this investigation. Finally, that truth cannot be discovered by any "return to the mothers" of whatever kind, but that it always emerges now, today, here, when farewell is said to the things reason takes for granted—this seems in the end to be the most important outcome.[42]

These brief deliberations give the following results. Phenomenology, in its regressive reflections undertaken from a historical position and in regard to what is taken for granted in each particular case, has nothing to do with supplementing the task of the sciences or critiquing their work within any transcendentally constituted world and historical horizon, which is their inherent domain. It does not devote itself to the fields of objects pregiven there for their own sake, as if, for instance, one of them had perhaps been forgotten or neglected by the individual sciences and the task now fell to philosophical research to close the gap.[43]

Transcendental and constitutive phenomenology always has to do with what makes something possible (*Ermöglichungen*). But what is possible within a world of life, existence, and knowledge depends wholly on the correlatively appertinent structures of consciousness and understanding. It is, in its turn, opened up and made visible as the ground for the possibility of concrete experiences by way of first- and second-level reflection. To this extent, philosophy is here a problem for itself, through and through. [44] It turns *to itself*, i.e., it turns back to the transcendentally structured consciousness, which validates the only attainable truth, the *veritas transcendentalis*.

It would be futile at this point to begin a dispute about whether the horizons of world and of history are formed by active or passive performances of consciousness, whether the constitutions ought to be called intentional or non-intentional: if consciousness is taken in the broad sense which underlies these considerations, it can be seen that every form of realized understanding constitutes something in consciousness, for it brings some sense or other into appearance: the sense of a segment of the world as well as that of the structure of the world and existence, the sense of category as well as that of the existential, the sense of *cogitatio* as well as that of states of mind.

All these things which were once taken for granted—the flux of the *cogitationes* and the understanding ability to deal with things, the disinterested observer and interested *Dasein*, being-a-person in performance and the natural attitude toward the world—are first grasped in reflection *as* what they are and as what they here function as. [45] Philosophy is, then, not a description of reality that revels in sublime evidences; rather, philosophy of this kind remains analytical-hypothetical. The *regressive reflections* of transcendental phenomenology simply reproduce the invention made by reason in full consciousness of the pregiven situation with respect to things previously taken for granted. And reason made that invention merely by crossing beyond the mere description of the immanent contents of lived experience. By rising above mere reproduction, it opened up the field for all kinds of expansions of horizons.

Philosophizing generally does not have to do primarily with the attempt to master extensive material. It does not wish, as one specialized science among others, to carve out as its object of study a particular sector of what is given within a world and a horizon, whereby the question would constantly remain as to whether what is given within a world would, then, provide the ultimately adequate philosophical object. It wants, rather, to choose as its theme the "convictions taken for granted" in all inner-worldly lines of investigation (and indeed at the beginning of any order that is regarded as intrinsically valid). Thus philosophy, in its aims, never overlaps with the natural or human sciences, which always retain their inner-worldly orientation. Nevertheless, it does not become metaphysics. [46]

This means, however, that the ever fragmentary knowledge obtained by the individual sciences still remains fragmentary after the application of such a philosophy. Philosophy has no secret means of quantitatively and extensively promoting the inner-horizonal strivings for possible complete knowledge. It can, however, in its regressive reflections, always prove the dogmas of the respectively taken position to be dogmas, and thus raise overall understanding to a new level. It does not carry on the totalization of knowledge within a specific correlational context, but rather tries to show that every research position that is taken for granted as "self-evident" is "metaphysical" and can also be proven to be "metaphysical." It thereby contributes to the self-clarification of reason by awakening the new consciousness: here no static worlds-in-themselves exist, but rather here a historical reason makes its appearance in transcendental steps of self-ascertainment.[47]

To encircle and restrict the extensive infinity of all world contents by investigation is, then, not a specifically philosophical task. This is where the individual science in its whole manifoldness sets to work. Philosophical striving aims, rather, to be intensive: its endeavor seeks a self-opening of consciousness that goes back to its "ultimate ground." And in so doing, it is and remains a philosophy of reflection. This does not exclude its having an eternal task before it; nor does it at all mean that it is, by any chance, not objective.[48]

It seems appropriate to point out that the reflection which in such a way aims at the existing transcendental constituents must not wait until the "content" of a world constituted of such transcendentals has been fully exhausted "extensively." If this were a precondition, then a reflection on the grounds by which things are possible could never begin—extensively complete knowledge of the world and horizon perhaps does not exist for man with respect to any "correlative system."[49]

The most fundamental problems are opened up in another way, namely in a determinate radical mode of inquiry. The method of inquiry that must be used is reflection upon the conditioning foundations. When Scheler speaks of "person," when Heidegger presents an analysis of "*Dasein* which in its being is concerned with this being itself," and finally when Husserl designates as man's ultimate self-understanding, "his self-understanding as being in being called to a life of apodicticity,"[50] something is said, in each case, about the form of being a person, *Dasein*, and being-oneself, on which depends "how" man then can concretely make his appearance.

In all three cases, reflection in the genuine sense is present.[51]

This reflection does not need to wait—temporally—until the metaphysically posited frameworks of understanding are completely exploited extensively in knowledge of particulars. Reflection can leave the *intentio recta* at any time. Thus it can, in Heidegger, always go beyond the "moods" and "states-of-mind"; in Scheler, beyond "act" and "person"; in Husserl, beyond "cogitative consciousness" and "intersubjectivity," once the matter-of-course stance of merely letting these factors stand has become problematic. Actually, not everything is possible at all times; and to that extent, critically examining, regressive-reflective reason is also a historical reason through and through. Only in a concrete situation do its questionable aspects show up; they do not always exist. And so there is no such thing as the "eternal" philosophical problems typical of static philosophizing.

It can be determined exactly when something has become "questionable" and ceased to be the taken-for-granted ground of thought, conduct, and being. That does not mean, however, that upon "raising a question," i.e., with the loss of any prior matter-of-course recognition of determinate "contents," a clearly accepted answer to the problems raised is given or would even be possible.[52] But, indeed, this much is true: once something has lost the character of being taken for granted before rational consciousness, it can never regain it. Naiveté remains "irretrievable."

Rational consciousness's self-reflection upon itself and its attempt at self-clarification is therefore a historical problem of *this* consciousness now, not of a consciousness that has always existed. The crisis of the matter-of-course assumptions is the "confirmation" of critical consciousness. Reflection can never proceed otherwise than in such a way that it repeatedly draws up the transcendentally posited horizon that has to be clarified and studies it for the structures of consciousness at work in each case. In short, at the second level of reflection, consciousness may well observe itself; this also happens, though it is not admitted, when the forms of understanding or ways of being are explicated and portrayed as correspondences of form of act and form of being, viz., correlations of *cogitatio* and *cogitatum*, as is the case in Heidegger, Scheler, and Husserl.[53]

Consciousness, which is its own world and dwells in its own world, can thus under certain circumstances abolish the direct attitudes and turn back in reflection to itself as the transcendental ground that makes the particular ways of understanding possible. That is possible only on occasion. But that also means: it always reaches back from an apprehension considered "natural"—i.e., taken for granted as valid and activated without further reflection—to forms of understanding. The word "natural" in this context never means what lies back in gray prehistory and was merely distorted by progressive scientific theorizing—"natural" is, rather, for man, simply what has "come to be" taken-for-granted. It includes "everything" natural and historical, especially the sheltering world-interpretation. And since man himself is not in the least a natural being, but continually completes his innate nature with historically developed structures of a quasi-natural kind, precisely this nature, modified into culture, is for him what is "considered natural in each case within his historical horizon."[54] That is what Husserl means when in the first sentences of *Ideas* I he says: "Natural cognition begins with experience and remains within experience. In the theoretical attitude which we call the 'natural' [one], the collective horizon of possible investigations is therefore designated with one word: It is the world."[55] It is easy to see that there is no question here of "dehistoricizing" the natural attitude and the natural world. Husserl begins with his investigations at a "determinate point in time" (in his present, namely the one in which the scientization of all world-conceptions has become matter-of-course) in order then reflectively to dissolve this position, which is historically explainable and genetically developed, and yet has become an immediate natural possession as well as a taken-for-granted foundation of understanding.

For phenomenological reflection, then, the natural conception is, at any one time, something different. From this it follows that the development of a natural understanding of the world, the production of a natural world conception, can have nothing, absolutely nothing, to do with the elimination of the scientific world-attitude. This is perhaps the problem in a particular situation—say, in the situation of the twentieth century—but it is not *the* problem of man, simply speaking.[56] The interpretation of the world by scientific substructions always remains just one interpretation, namely the interpretation which has at present become matter-of-course for transcendental consciousness. Here too, therefore, the elaboration of the natural conception of the world cannot mean the discarding of what has been made possible *until today* by history—i.e., in the twentieth century it cannot mean the discarding of all scientizations in order to return quickly to an archaic, Pelasgian original condition (for that would be merely an uncritical return to an old familiar metaphysics); rather, it means purely and simply that here, from this model, "founding circumstances," "structuring connections," which all stem from consciousness, can be shown. Indeed, the scientifically dogmatic world view is abrogated as being really that which captures the things themselves. But the abrogation of Galileo's "metaphysics"[57] which is prevalent here does not in the least mean at the same time the reinstallation of things taken for granted prescientifically, which simply happened to have been overcome by the positings of the scientific framework.[58]

Phenomenology, from which one always expects a definitive answer to the question of whether it is a method or a metaphysics,[59] can become metaphysics solely if it gives up certain matter-of-course assumptions from the current understanding of reality only to revert uncritically to matter-of-course assumptions of a historically earlier time. It then neglects, indeed betrays, its task of checking the currently unquestioned assumptions, since it itself affirms some positions or other as positions and posits them as absolute, i.e., it provides them with an accent of finality. This happens in the much-cited "return to the mothers" just as much as in "speculative anticipation." In either case, it abandons the attitude of regressive reflection and gives up the "healthy bathos" of experience.

A "speculative" phenomenology would, then, just as much as an etymological ontology, itself be a metaphysics.[60] Such metaphysics have actually arisen because of the turn which Heidegger gave to the Husserlian approach. What must be done in regard to them, in a countermove that applies the consistently followed up transcendental-reflective approach, is to expose the dogmatic positings which also play a role precisely here.

There can be no doubt that a "metaphysics of being" (in Heidegger) and "speculative phenomenology" (as represented by Fink) no longer have anything to do with the method of phenomenology and with the goal of fundamentally "reasoned," "grounding," and "critical" self-clarification. On the contrary, in interpretations based directly on Husserl, which take as their guide the idea of phenomenology and not the ideas of a mysticism of being that is itself merely positional, phenomenology is understood completely as "critical" phenomenology.[61] It always produces out of itself the controlling points of view which guide its intention in this critique, and nowhere does it find them already offered in the given context. To this extent phenomenology finds its object in the performance. When the phenomenologizing rational consciousness, in the second level of reflection, grasps the transcendental structures of the achievements originally performed naively (observing itself as it does so), this means, as Theodor Litt expressed it, that "it really does not so much observe" this entire complex of relations of thought-operations "as rather bring it to knowledge of itself in the performance. . . . "[62]

That this reflective attitude is anything but obvious or natural, and also anything but matter-of-course, makes it the phenomenologically indispensable attitude *par excellence*: it is neither itself taken for granted, nor does it want to let anything else that is performed and released in direct consciousness be taken for granted. Its last impulse is "self-supervision," which it can perform only when it has abandoned naiveté and become completely critical, and remains critical—for which its only source of information is reflection that reaches back again step by step.

Chapter Four

The Historical Development of Systems of Apprehension

Attempts have often been made to divide up phenomenology, as it exists in the form created by Husserl, into "partial phenomenologies," each with different tendencies and conceptions. And subsequently no effort was spared to break up the phenomenological procedure internally and to portray partial phenomenologies linked with various names and forming controversial systems of apprehension.[1]

At an early date, with reference to Husserl, there was mention of a *Göttingen* and a *Freiburg* phenomenology—the first with purely "descriptive," the second with "transcendental" intentions, so it is said.[2] And in the Göttingen circle one then thinks of Adolf Reinach, Alexandre Koyré, Hedwig Conrad-Martius, of Theodor Conrad and Johannes Daubert, of Jean Hering and Herbert Leyendecker, of Roman Ingarden and Kurt Stavenhagen, of Ernst W. Hocking, Wilhelm Schapp, and Moritz Geiger.[3] Husserl's Freiburg phenomenology, however, would show as its representatives Edith Stein, Fritz Kaufmann, Oskar Becker, and Marvin Farber; also Szilasi, Landgrebe, and Fink, as well as Heidegger. But, in addition, three separate other phenomenological schools would have to be recognized—namely those which do not follow the Husserlian tendencies unconditionally. Numbered among these would be the *Munich* circle around Alexander Pfänder,[4] with its descriptive-psychology orientation, to which Aloys Fischer and Gerda Walther, Moritz Geiger (in one phase of his development), and August Gallinger, Dietrich von Hildebrand, and Herbert Spiegelberg would have to be assigned. Further, there is the so-called *Cologne* phenomenology of Max Scheler, who himself had come into contact with the circle of phenomenologists in Munich and Göttingen and who had passed on his contribution to Hendrick Gerardus Stoker and Heinrich Lützeler, to Paul Ludwig Landsberg, and also to Nicolai Hartmann.[5] Finally, one would have to name Heidegger's *Marburg* circle, which is generally passed over, but after the fact—in a most recent development—has shown its great circle-forming significance. If the *Cologne* phenomenology, under Scheler's influence, was essentially a "phenomenology of values," Heidegger's *Marburg* phenomenology was between 1923 and 1928 to a considerable extent a "hermeneutic phenomenology," which acquired a close connection with Paul Tillich's—and in Marburg especially with Rudolf Bultmann's—Protestant theology, and among whose adherents should be numbered Hans-Georg Gadamer, Gerhard Krüger, Karl Löwith, and Helmuth Kuhn, while the narrower Heidegger circle then, moreover beyond Marburg, displays the names Franz Josef Brecht, Karl-Heinz Volkmann-Schluck, and Walter Bröcker.[6]

Surveying these various tendencies, it seems questionable whether and to what extent all this could rightly be called phenomenology; for after all, the naive realism of the Munich group is miles away from the transcendental idealism of the Freiburg group, and the value-objectivism of the Cologne group is worlds apart from the Marburg/Freiburg Heidegger-school's "hermeneutics of being," which is uninterested in any "entity" as such.[7]

Naturally, it is always possible in a larger, more comprehensive whole for works to specialize while keeping the same fundamental research tendency. Yet this is apparently not the case in those various so-called "partial" movements of phenomenology, for the difference between them is not based on the cultivation of different fields of knowledge; obviously, such a fundamental discrepancy results from divergent methodological concepts. This sort of difference, however, would be basically absurd in a philosophical school which, openly and contrary to all metaphysicizing tendencies, understands its own name—phenomenology—as a "methodological concept."[8] For how can a philosophy which derives its name from the application of a particular method then display differences precisely in regard to the methods applied?

One solution to this obvious difficulty could, it seems, succeed only by first calling the whole enterprise "phenomenology of developing reason," then marking off clear phases of this development, perhaps each characterized by specific methods, while all taken together they would be determined in their application by immediate self-possession, so that here and now it would have to be this and no other method.

This interpretation will, accordingly, relate wholly to Husserl's phenomenology, which in principle is expanded into a system of reason, in order from there to gain access to the phenomenological research of the other, comparatively imperfect phenomenologies as a whole. At first there is a tendency to stress simply Husserl's "logical objectivism" and to speak of a "metaphysics of the essence," as does Fritz Heinemann (1929);[9] however, Oscar Becker, in his portrayal of Edmund Husserl's philosophy (1930), already clearly analyzes the double-membered contrast between "phenomenological objectivism," on the one hand, and the "transcendental idealist constitution" of these phenomena, on the other.[10] Wilhelm Szilasi, in his *Introduction to Edmund Husserl's Phenomenology* (1959), then gives a three-phase sequence of "descriptive phenomenology," "transcendental phenomenology," and "transcendental-constitutive phenomenology."[11] Further, Walter Biemel, in his treatise on "The Decisive Phases in the Development of Husserl's Philosophy" (1959),[12] would like to distinguish four stages—namely, those which are representative of (1) *The Philosophy of Arithmetic* (1891); (2) *Logical Investigations* (1900); (3) *Ideas pertaining to a Pure Phenomenology and to a Phenomenological Philosophy* I (1913); and finally (4) *The Crisis of European Sciences and Transcendental Phenomenology* (1935 ff.), whereby it is clear that almost all works conceived down to the *Cartesian Meditations* (1929 f.) belong to the stage characterized by the *Ideas*.

The development of the phenomenology of reason[13] actually seems to be determined by a series of originally philosophical, but also particular objective factors: from the consideration and recognition of the "psychological" factor, the "formal-logic" and "semiasological" factor, the "transcendental-constitutive" factor, the "consciousness-metaphysics" factor, and finally the "historicocritical" factor. But it is obviously always a reason conceived in a specific way that attains legitimation or is posited as transparent.[14]

1. Husserl's writings *On the Concept of Number* (1887) and on the *Philosophy of Arithmetic* (1891) are concerned with the psychological origin of particular ideas—for instance, the ideas of time, space, number, and continuum. Ideas are, however, without a doubt at first simply psychological data of empirical subjects; and certain contents of ideas are what they are on the basis of the simplest psychic thought processes, in which they are formed.[15] In the first step of thought, the process and procedure of thinking gives rise to the phenomena present in the ideas, and this process of thinking has contours typical of the prevalent consciousness. If (in any area) the question of the "fundamental concepts" is asked at all, then this means that after one has worked with these concepts and applied them "naively," they should be investigated to see how they came about. In brief, *the issue is how they were formed*; and on

this very point a study oriented by empirical psychology gives a provisional first answer. The problem then is: how is this or that concept actually built up in consciousness? But the description of the facts is also appropriate to the actual circumstances in the psychic realm. Of course, implicitly and previously, it is always presupposed in all descriptions that what is described shows itself as a unity of "one sense." So what matters is to depict precisely the combinations and ways of combining by which an object becomes distinctly such and such a one which it is or seems to be, this very one. Thus what must be described is not so much the object itself as the object in the "how" of its production. The manner in which certain moments of reality combine and attain unity is not given to the grasp immediately, but is presented only to "reflection."

This reflection on the synthesis-guaranteeing factor which stands at the beginning is, then, what must be studied. Biemel gives an example of this: "When we speak of a continuum we are not concerned with the kind of elements which are involved (for these can vary) but with the manner of composition which is common to all continua."[16] Only if we see this mode of combination do we experience the peculiarity of continua. So if something is described for clarification, it is precisely what is mediated in reflection and not what has become unmediatedly visible.

What holds true in the case of acquiring a unity of sense (*Sinneinheit*)—for instance, that of "plurality"—holds true generally. A spontaneous (transcendentally determined) performance of consciousness typical of the manner of producing a synthetic combination is always involved. Though in a purely empirical attitude it may seem as if the positions taken were at first dependent purely on an arbitrary interest, closer reflection makes it clear that one actually arrives at the unities of sense cast into relief and formed in such attitudes only by adopting the reflective stance. Thus retrospection to the "particular manner of uniting" the various factors into a whole always takes place. One thing is and remains correct: it is a matter of "producing the object as a unity of sense" conceived in this specific way; but here too the investigation remains within the purely psychological-empirical framework. The applied means of determination is the turning back to the concrete, sense-formative processes, i.e. the unifying psychic processes. To this extent Husserl can call numbers (i.e., the mathematical constructs) "mental" creations insofar as they result from activities which we exercise upon concrete contents.[17] If later phenomenology is characterized by the concept of the correlativism between *intentio* and *intentum*, between *noesis* and *noema*, between *cogito* and *cogitatum*, between the "state of consciousness" and the corresponding "horizon of consciousness," the first beginning of that view is found here. There is mention of the relation-concepts which the mathematical constructs are; and that means: these contents are what they are only in their production. They have no "being-in-itself"; they must not be thought of as Platonic, self-existing entities of particular being-modification, but are rather relations within a determinate attitude and only for this attitude.

In the concept of "plurality" and in the explanation of its origin, what matters are *relata*, which there must be—of which, however, what their content happens to be in the individual case remains relatively indifferent; and furthermore, an act of highlighting interest and taking notice is required with respect to these *relata*. Only so is the relation produced; it is nothing in-itself, but it emerges in certain purely psychic processes.

Reflection shows which attitude of interest and taking notice is present. The interest and taking notice itself becomes constitutive for what occurs in this attitude, i.e., the relationally constituted; and the constituted is and remains a "relational concept" and is not inflated to the in-itself. It appears as brought about and produced within a certain attitude. The production of objects, so understood, always contains a reference back to the apprehending consciousness in the "manner of its apprehension." And the reflective disclosure of this retro-relation represents basically a kind of reduction.[18]

That would be the way phenomenology proceeds in analyzing the appearances of, say, colligation—namely, by explaining the psychological connections to which regress is made.

2. The second phase of Husserlian phenomenology is characterized by the discussion of *logical* phenomena; and it turns out that the same manner of "psychological" explanation cannot be chosen for this discussion of logical problems (though they seem very closely related to the mathematical ones). The opposite is the case when one thinks of the struggle against "psychologism" which Husserl carries on precisely in his *Logical Investigations*.

Basically, in the discussion of these *Logical Investigations* (1900/1) a dual expansion of the problem occurs. First, it is no longer, as in the writings on the *Concept of Number* and on the *Philosophy of Arithmetic*, a matter of the concept of number from which the various arithmetical constructs can then be derived by various modes of specialization, but of the fact that an operation takes place (using irrational, negative, or rational numbers). This means, then, that number does not constitute the basis of arithmetic, but that arithmetic basically represents a variegated "system of signs" and, above all, the field of "operation with these signs" (which can also be numbers).[19] Actually, it is now a part of formal logic; and formal logic in turn seems, at least in the first instance, to be a "technique of knowledge." The other expansion can be seen in the fact that reflection upon the psychic processes in which such formal constructs are brought to evidence is no longer attached to the individual case. Not this or that empirical mental process as such is the object of reflection and description; rather, this mental process becomes an object only insofar as it allows a universal to become visible. This means, however, that the mental process as a psychic occurrence is not significant for this reflective investigation; it acquires significance only insofar as on this occasion a universal, the *eidos* of a determinate relation, becomes graspable. The function becomes the decisive factor. The *eidos* in question here is this: in general, "determinate" psychic performances are necessary if determinate contents are to become objects. This holds good in essential universality; and in ideating abstraction an essence of such a kind can be made visible. This is generally known and is a basic phenomenological thought.

Yet here Biemel, to clarify the context, cites a retrospective explanation of Husserl's from the year 1925,[20] from which it becomes clear what the *Logical Investigations* were aiming for when in their later parts they apparently fell back into the psychologism of pure empirical description. There it says: "The individual investigations of the second volume concern the turning of intuition back upon those logical experiences which occur within us when we think but which we do not notice at the time, which we do not have attentively in view when we perform these activities of thought in a natural and original way. We are to grasp this hidden course of the life of thought by means of a subsequent reflection and fix it by means of truly descriptive concepts; in addition, we are to solve this new problem: namely, that of making comprehensible how the formation of all these mental structures takes place within the achievements of this inner logical experience, structures which appear in explicitly judgmental thought as diversely formed concepts, judgments, conclusions, etc., and which find their general expression, their universally objective mental character, in the basic concepts and principles of logic."[21] This discovery of Biemel's is important, and it has further consequences.

The logical structures in question are what they are in a determinate context of thought. If, especially since Bolzano, there is again talk of "statements in themselves" and "truths in themselves,"[22] this cannot mean that such statements and truths have a being for themselves, i.e., are to be interpreted Platonically. They are what they are only in an appertinent determinate thinking and exist only for this "synthesizing" thinking. This is where they have their (relational) being. Within this context, to be sure, they hold good absolutely and without restriction ("in themselves"); but this does not mean that they are any such thing as self-existing realities, i.e., something independent outside the thinking which constitutes them. To this extent, the realm of logic is the "realm of irrealities." But these irrealities always remain independent of the individual apprehending (empirical) thinking: they are the correlate of a determinate attitude of grasping, a "specific mode of grasping." To this extent, they remain valid here and now "*in themselves*" with regard to the individual psychic act and are not dependent on it as "this there"; nor is the individual then in his thinking *glebae adscriptus* (bound to a certain field). However, the acts are not independent of the entire specific, class-like correlative context: they are released only within a certain mode of access (which is then general in kind and not this or that).[23]

These logical structures are certainly the correlates of specific psychic constitutive performances. But this means inversely: it is always only determinate psychic phenomena that open up access to ideal structures— quite in accord with what the sense-structure in question demands by the laws of its constitution. Although the experiences taken singly are indeed individual psychic events, the individual does not constitute the logical structures arbitrarily; he constitutes them by carrying out the corresponding ("appropriate") performances as their preconditions.

The constitution of unities of sense and meaning is never a restoration (in the somewhat Platonizing sense), but constitution of correlates. Reflection can, however, disclose that there is no such thing as the "object-in-itself," which must be made present; it also shows that, inversely, no mental process is empty and no unity of sense is without a mental process. This very fact shows that the question what the one is without the other, i.e., "in itself," is absurd. Reflection discloses this "general genesis of consciousness" and the constitution of the ideal objects as an original production, which, however, aims for correlative structures.[24]

3. All interpretations of the term "constitution" have the disadvantage that they stress altogether too strongly creation and production or restoration and recollection. In the first case, the ideal object seems to remain dependent on the subject; in the second case, subjective consciousness, in the act of grasping, appears to be dependent on the object. Both interpretations must be false, since they each include a "prephenomenological metaphysics." This becomes clear when the investigation is extended beyond, first, the arithmetical and, second, the logical structures to absolutely all possible objects of consciousness. This means: if in a determinate *intentio* only a determinate appertinent *intentum* can be expected, then conversely a determinate *intentum* too must always rely upon the corresponding *intentio*. Here we have neither subjective creation nor objective being-in-itself, but rather "interrela-

tion," which can be descriptively clarified "once reflection has discovered it." For naturally these intentional connections do not discover themselves, but are first seen as what they are in a reiterative reaching back of reflection.[25] That this is possible is a sign of the life and continuing development of consciousness, of heightened states of consciousness.

In writings from the third phase of Husserl's philosophizing, the correspondences present here are understood as transcendental determinations of consciousness. The general formulation of the problem of constitution as a problem of "transcendental idealism" is presented as early as the *Lectures on the Phenomenology of Inner Time-Consciousness* (1904/5, 1928), *The Idea of Phenomenology* (1907/1952), and the *Ideas pertaining to a Pure Phenomenology and to a Phenomenological Philosophy* (1913; 1952).

Again two factors first make their appearance. First, *all* objects for which determinate classes of mental processes and accordingly also determinate regional ontologies can become responsible are now actually grasped as unities of sense and meaning; and second, consciousness itself no longer appears as a static "magnitude" of some kind or other. A universal constitution of "consciousness" in continuous temporalizations corresponds to the universal, variable constitutional makeup of the "phenomena."[26] Because there are no names for all this, as Husserl says in the *Lectures on the Phenomenology of Inner Time-Consciousness*,[27] the expression "constitution" should be reserved for the intentional presenting of all objective unities of sense and meaning, and, separately from them, the non-intentional formation and expansion of consciousness which occurs *on the occasion* of the performance of intentional acts should be called "genesis."[28]

Not just irreal, not just ideal structures are subject to constitutional analysis, but everything that becomes graspable as a unity of sense and meaning, i.e., everything that is a phenomenon in the phenomenological sense. Phenomenon is thus the most concrete and the most abstract, the nearest and furthest, the most important and the least important, the most objective and the most subjective thing there is, insofar as it is evidenced only in consciousness.

Not objects (as segments of the world), not appearances as such, namely as natural phenomena, are, then, the ultimate basis to start from; nor is it the concrete subject or a consciousness—as this individual as such—that serves as absolute starting point, but it is the *cogitationes* as *cogitationes*. They are so, because the object (in its broadest scope) is given *in* them, in their intentional constitution of the thing; and they are so, because *on the occasion* of this thing-constitution a consciousness first temporalizes itself as the center of unity which claims these constitutive acts as its own and is still able to return to the contents and their formation even after the acts are over and done with.[29]

The *cogitationes* designate what precedes all constitution and all genesis. Hence phenomenology cannot be regional ontology, nor a metaphysics of consciousness: its field remains that of describing, dismantling, and examining the constitutive and genetic connections given together with the *cogitationes*. Neither can a determinately fixed world of objects *as correlate of* determinate appertinent ways of constitution be posited "absolutely," nor must a determinate state of consciousness and a determinate disposition of consciousness claim to be the "ultimate" authority. All this points to the "series" of *cogitationes* temporalizing themselves: the determinate variable consciousness as well as the determinate, variantly conceived world. Phenomenology is, then, always "elucidation of the current cognitive situation" (*Aufklärungsactualismus*).[30]

To this extent even here one can speak of the idea of a universal system of reason which must be conceived of as in motion.[31] Phenomenology brings this reason to bear, with its reflective performance, and that is all. It does not thetically design any new world contexts, and it does not posit any determinate consciousness of whatever kind as absolute, but it counts on already determined worlds and determined states of consciousness which belong together. It analyzes these. So it remains, in the exact sense, the science of the transcendental correspondences. And it is universal, insofar as in principle it permits absolutely no position of one kind or another to remain matter-of-course.

The characteristic feature of this third phase is not just the constitution of the thing (the object in general), but also the discovery of the constitutive, or better, genetic formation of consciousness itself. The "universalism of the transcendental determination of world and consciousness" here comes to full expression and obviates all turns to metaphysics and to dogmatic establishments of a positional kind. For the analysis of the world of experience and consciousness happens to be implicitly critique—critique even with respect to the ego-subject.[32]

The *Logos* essay (1911) on "Philosophy as Rigorous Science" had stated that "during no period of its development has philosophy been capable of living up to [its] claim of being a strict science."[33] Accordingly, in contrast with all previous methodological approaches, a task of its own is imposed on this entire philosophy: it is fundamentally critical. And the question of the ultimately valid point of departure—namely, the Cartesian theme of precautionary and provisory methodological doubt and its removal—is the motive for establishing absolutely clear beginnings. That is one thing. The second is the task of showing again and again that all metaphysically taken positions with respect to the whole of the world and with respect to consciousness are merely positings within a determinate correlation context, beyond which they have ("absolutely") no sense "in themselves." This turn against positional metaphysics is expressed in Husserl's sharp statements about the "philosophy of profundity," which are an essential component of the *Logos* essay. Metaphysics knows of the ultimate and lets it stand as such, or it introduces it because of inspirations of wisdom; science dissolves all pregivens into grounding connections and excludes no position from this. Thus Husserl says: "Genuine science, so far as its real [life] extends, knows no profundity. Every bit of completed science is a whole composed of 'thought steps' each of which is immediately understood, and so not at all profound. Profundity is an affair of wisdom; conceptual distinctness and clarity is an affair of rigorous theory."[34] Wisdom gives positions, which philosophy as a foundational science repeatedly transcends.

Transcendental phenomenology tries, on this foundation and in such immediately given, insightful steps of thought, to describe and ground the constitutive context in which consciousness and world always stand, but without ever crossing the horizons of correlation in such a way that decisions are made and beliefs professed.[35]

4. In the fourth phase, which produces the writings *First Philosophy* (1923/4, 1956/8), *Formal and Transcendental Logic* (1929), and *Cartesian Meditations* (1929, 1931, 1950), it is a matter of apprehending fundamental consciousness, i.e., the consciousness which constitutes everything. This explains, for instance, why the second volume of *First Philosophy* is practically dedicated to the various reductions which have to be performed. It also explains how an experiential consciousness that precedes judgmental consciousness is investigated with its own evidences in *Formal and Transcendental Logic*[36]—which opens up the question of the life-world consciousness. Finally, it explains how in the *Cartesian Meditations* an inquiry into a monadological consciousness[37] could be made and a science based on absolute grounding be attempted.[38]

This phase is characterized by the fact that intersubjectity (*Intersubjektität*) mediated by "eidetic, transcendental, and phenomenological reduction," now appears to be the ultimate and apparently insurmountable point of departure. Here terms are used which could remind one of a "static" metaphysics of consciousness, and which must be mentioned since they are a foil to the ultimate perfect transition to the "historicization" of reason, which otherwise does not become so clear, especially in the *Cartesian Meditations*. When Husserl explains: "The intrinsically first being, the being that precedes and bears every worldly Objectivity, is transcendental intersubjectivity: the universe of monads, which effects its communion in various forms,"[39] this needs to be interpreted. Namely, that other statement must be added which says that only "every naive metaphysics that operates with absurd things in themselves" would have to be excluded, but not "metaphysics as such."[40] This looks like a "turn toward metaphysics," at least like one reminiscent of Kant.

Any metaphysics that skips over the constitutive connection in which, if something is given, it must be given precisely as the transcendental connection makes this possible, must be called naive and absurd. Therefore, even for phenomenology—which seeks absolute foundations and goes back to transcendental consciousness as the source of foundations—self-understanding is, of course, also connected with the current form of this consciousness.[41] It would no doubt be premature to say that what occurs within a determinate foundational context of *intentio* and *intentum*, of *noesis* and *noema*, of *cogitatio* and *cogitatum*, of "consciousness" (as intersubjectivity) and the "totality of appearance," and is meaningfully graspable there in its place (i.e., consciousness on the one hand, and what is contained in consciousness on the other), could be dismissed from the "relational connection" at any single place.

Even what consciousness can bring to bear upon itself in determinate reflections remains transcendentally bound to the corresponding structure of this reflective consciousness, which in the reflections only proves the validity of these structures and their efficacy. This means that the consciousness which—because of its transcendental structuring—has quite rightly dismantled and made obsolete the dubious concept of a world and a reality "*in-itself*," cannot believe, when it is a matter of the "self-conception," that perhaps now it could step out of this structure and grasp more than something merely correlationally valid. Even in self-apprehension, this consciousness does not once and for all dispose over the forms of understanding that apply to what is determinate. It contains no certainties of such a kind as would permit the "derivation of a deductive system."[42] This means, finally, that this consciousness always makes possible just a thinking based on the predesignated circle of experience, not a projective transcending of this circle—for instance by definitively positing one's own position of understanding. As long as philosophy is a science, it probably has to deal with reason and with consciousness as does an authority that establishes theses. But philosophy does not establish these theses definitively and say "yes" to them. Whether this may be required by "life," by "world-view points of view," including philosophical reason, or by consciousness-perspectives in transcendental phenomenology, it is not profound reason but clarified reason that is involved as long as transcendental phenomenology remains methodologically oriented.[43]

Naturally, in the given world, understood provisionally and repeatedly needing further clarification, other connections will constantly emerge. Even new metaphysical, new ethical, and new religious positions can develop and be accepted.[44] Philosophy, conceived as science, does not have to add to these positions a further, equally dogmatic, perhaps systematic, position, by attempting to make pronouncements with an accent of finality about itself as a definitive dogmatism of subjectivity. Rather, even on this point it still remains a critique of problems. At the end of the *Cartesian Meditations*, therefore, the demand is made that "universal philosophy now" would also have to be "all-embracing self-investigation."[45] This means, however, that it is "universal" only when by means of this reflection and the attempt to disclose the grounding circumstances it stops nowhere, not even before itself. Only when it also includes itself completely within this self-investigation is it universal— and only insofar as it attains this universality does it go beyond any metaphysical position as a mere position. Husserl's words at the end of this book must be understood in this sense: "The path leading to a knowledge absolutely grounded in the highest sense . . . is necessarily the path of universal self-knowledge—first of all monadic, and then intermonadic. We can say also that a radical and universal continuation of Cartesian meditations, or . . . a universal self-cognition, is philosophy itself. . . . "[46]

Finally, this means that every state of consciousness, together with the corresponding things which understanding makes possible, is "for the time being" always metaphysical. And this "metaphysicalness" must be seen through if self-knowledge is as universal as philosophy strives for it to be in a real general reflection.

5. From here it is then possible to acquire a "historical concept of reason"—a concept which comes out ever more clearly in the fifth phase of Husserlian thinking. Reference had already been made in *Formal and Transcendental Logic* to "pre-predicative evidence and pre-reflective experience,"[47] i.e., the road had been prepared for access to a prescientific life-world. This theme was then seriously taken up and deepened in *The Crisis of European Sciences and Transcendental Phenomenology* (1935, 1954) and in the studies combined by Landgrebe into *Experience and Judgment* (1939, 1948).

The question of the transcendental shaping and forming of a "life-world" raises the question of the historicity of reason.[48] Prior to all determinations which tend to attribute a general "teleological" character to this reason right away again, the moment of "universal" investigation must be firmly held. Phenomenological philosophy is universal, as was established, when, and only when, it lets nothing be taken for granted even in the domain of grounding. This is in a genuine sense, as was further noted, really the case only when this philosophy itself is actually included in the continual process of investigation. Every single result obtained by this philosophy must be questioned as to the basis from which it was possible to be attained. This entails the moment of the self-temporalizing of reason. The given consciousness is a correlate-consciousness—it knows exactly what can be discovered starting from the existing transcendental grounds of determination, and it inquires into the conditions that apply to such a given. If it discovers these conditions, then a given no longer remains a mere given, but becomes an understood given.

To recall universally this connection between a "transcendental state of consciousness" and "what is transcendentally determined" brings the dynamic moment under investigation.[49] For just as the grounding process is in principle not broken off anywhere, but rather, as in any given grounding process, is carried back to the grounds for possibility (*Ermöglichungen*) which belong precisely here, there can no longer be any static philosophical knowledge, but only "philosophizing as a quest for grounds."

The "reduction to historical reason" makes it clear that no contentual evidence can ever be left standing as evidence which must be accepted dogmatically. The transformation of positional knowledge into a rationally grounded knowledge never comes to an end. What is conceived as a matter-of-course self-possession or as the actual self-givenness of an appearance, and stands quite naturally in view in a specific way, contains within itself (in this very matter-of-courseness) the stimulus for a regressive grounding that points further back. If "evidence" is a "basic kind of experience,"[50] then the obvious goal is to obtain such evidence; but then the matter-of-courseness of this evidence again becomes the new goal, etc. In this regressive process, the self-understanding as being is contained in its being called to a life of apodicticity:[51] what holds good for the positions cannot be *not* binding for one's own.

The "historicization of reason" and the incompleteness of the evidences entails that all systems of understanding understood as all-embracing and assumed to be definitively true, and that all worlds represented as true, are provisional. It may be that the scientific world with all its basic demands originates by a transformation and elaboration of the typical structures of the life-world.[52] This "life-world" is and remains what it represents in a determinate and unchangeable state of consciousness that belongs specifically to it. It is, first of all, quite originarily naive. Critical consciousness, which emerges with reason as it develops historically, always goes beyond both the world of science and the life-world when it sees the world in a "sequence of phases." The regress to the origin of scientific experience in the experiences of the life-world can have absolutely nothing to do with the "return to the mothers," i.e., to "absolutely original and final evidences," because critical reason then repeatedly rises above these again merely supposedly "ultimate" experiences, by grasping them as (supposedly) ultimate and reducing them to a position that is once again still merely "dogmatic and doxic."

Only when constitutive performances which condition the life-worldly evidences also become the object of critical analysis is that carried out which, according to Husserl in the *Crisis*, is the task: to investigate and disclose the historical performances of historical reason in historical steps of regression.[53]

Certainly, if one works with the method of reduction in this way, the return to the origins of all validity must remain the last word. And so traditionally applied logic then also requires a "preliminary logic of experience." But that "the experiential judgment" is the "original judgment"[54] remains, of course, a judgment valid only here and now—a judgment that makes sense only in this critical state of consciousness. In his description of the decisive phases in Husserl's philosophy, Biemel pointed this out.[55] Husserl must also ask back to "the constitutive performances which make the life-world itself possible," for only then do we approach the anonymous achieving of the transcendental ego which, in the *Crisis*, is revealed at the same time to be historical reason. Contrary to all subsequent attempts to absolutize this position in the phenomenological "school," this thesis deserves complete agreement. But just as certainly Husserl himself did not actually carry out this necessary and methodically indispensable "self-abolition of the life-world position" in a higher critical reduction.

Consequently—of course, contrary to the main thrust of phenomenological investigations—the attempt to redogmatize the life-world position as if it were really the conclusive one and contained the ultimate logic called for by Husserl can be observed. This attempt occurs meaningfully where a "metaphysically interpreted phenomenology" would permit approximation to the metaphysical-factical position of "fundamental ontology."[56] Such an approximation, however, succeeds and is meaningful only if one forgets that the *a priori* attainable by phenomenology can always again be only a correlative *a priori*. Nowhere is it presented as salvational knowledge; rather, it is detached critically from the existing noetic-noematic connections, which are always *transcended* in this analysis. The unconditional does not become free, even in phenomenological regresses to an ever more ultimate, ever more original, more subtly subjective primal evidence.[57] Only within the correlation-connections which thus guarantee the objectivity of the critical steps back are evidences possible; thus they would have to be called "relative."

Language fails if one then still wants to communicate an image of the "most ultimate" real evidence. This *a priori* can be only a "limit concept" and not a "fact."[58] When phenomenological research, in its critical analyses of constitutional connections, does not hold firmly to the idea of an infinite task to be done in this regard, and hence does not allow itself to be instructed by Kant, it can claim to be able to release primal experiences *as* primal experiences and to present their content. Only then does it know of primal institutions (*Urstiftungen*) in themselves.[59]

Before one sets out to ascertain the intrinsic content of a sense-context by means of philosophical inquiry, attributing a teleological character to reason, which must start generally and perform regresses, it is quite sufficient to perceive the logical character by which a philosophy in quest of grounding is compelled to make "grounding revisions" which are in principle "unending," whereby it simply must be historical. The grounds of any insight are not transparent to naively executed insight. Any philosophy which makes "universal" claims will have to try to obtain this insight concerning itself, this knowledge of its own preconditions. Only thus is evidence no longer a title simply to be resorted to for the ascertainment of a determinate state of consciousness. Evidence is provided when the grounding connections in general become transparent.

It is not as if philosophy dealt simply with grasping and taking inventory of a particular realm of essential connections and had not finished with this task quasi-quantitatively, while in the individual case it already had a perfect overview and genuine self-evidence. In fact, this evidence is first achieved only when the foundations from which the insight results are also seen through. Thus Husserl, in his Vienna Lecture on "The Crisis of European Mankind and Philosophy" (1935), states that "what is most essential to the theoretical attitude of philosophical man is the peculiar universality of his critical stance, his resolve not to accept unquestioningly any pregiven opinion or tradition so that he can inquire, in respect to the whole traditionally pregiven universe, after what is true in itself, an ideality"![60] One must not allow oneself to be misled on this point. The only thing "true in itself," which must be held firmly here, is the connection between consciousness and the object of consciousness, and it is without fail put to the test ever again with every new knowledge that comes about, for instance, through reflection.[61] All other truth relates to the constitutional connection between this consciousness and that object of consciousness.

It can thus be said: consciousness always proves to be at first a dogmatic consciousness through and through. With its transcendental constitutive forms given in a particular situation it conditions whatever can, from this starting point, enter the grasp of an understanding scrutiny. For such a consciousness, all truths which thus come to view are absolute. To be absolute, then, means that they tolerate no doubt and correspond completely to what must be thought, can be experienced, and is understandable of a consciousness of this or that kind.

Positional consciousness always makes absolute claims. And any naively exercised understanding within a circle of understanding, any experience within a community of persons, any cogitative grasping of a transcendence in immanence carries on its business from a ground of disclosure that is considered absolute and posited as absolute. The correlation context is never exceeded in this understanding, mental process, and grasp, in the sense that this context itself ever becomes a problem retrogressively.[62]

But that is precisely the case when the states of being and states of consciousness, interrelated as relative, are absolutely all historically relativized. That each and every understanding can make a correlation connection evident between the situation of understanding and what is understood prevents from the outset the definitive absolutization of any determinate understanding or of any specifically understood world. It can also no longer be said that the horizon of the "life-world," which can be disclosed, for instance, behind "physicalistic objectivism," is nothing other than the "horizon of world history," as Landgrebe says.[63] For "world history" remains, even from the perspective of the life-world, nothing more than the correlate of a determinate appertinent apprehensional position. It is what it is in terms of that position; and for Landgrebe, history, then, ends with the "life-world." But no surrounding-world nature is alien to reason, and history, with its views of nature, is not alien to mind;[64] thus even what "life-world" is and means has become historical.

Naturally, the proposition "all possible historical variants are variants of the world that is valid for us" remains right.[65] This holds good also for the particular case in which the conditions of possibility, for instance, "of experiencing a life-world as historical, as an early historical world in its historicity" are under discussion. This prescientific life-world, which is experienced and still tacitly accepted as valid even in the scientific age, still remains something historical—and above all it is something "historically surmountable." The scientization of this world and its critical analysis proves in what sense it can be and has been superseded.[66]

The crossing beyond the naively adopted grounds of life, understanding, and knowledge is achieved by historical reason. It always goes beyond positional consciousness, which remains within determinate horizons. Husserl has accordingly demanded that if philosophy which holds firmly to its cognitive task raises claims to absoluteness, then "epistemological theory itself" become "historical retrospective inquiry."[67] For it is only by retrogression to the total "historicity of the correlative manners of being of humanity and the cultural world" that such claims can be maintained.[68] Again, the following must be adhered to: absolute knowledge never means the totalization of the knowledge possible within a transcendental-constitutive position taken by consciousness when it understands. Absolute knowledge, furthermore, does not mean complete knowledge with respect to the sequence of historically resulting states of consciousness. Finally, absolute knowledge does not mean the autarchy of a determinate knowledge and of the state of reason responsible for this knowledge.

Absolute knowledge makes sense only if it is understood as the process of the self-discovery of reason through continual self-limitation. This self-limitation results precisely through the reiterated abrogation of all ultimate statements. To want to grasp the absolute here and now is an absurdity, since in the very grasping it is constantly particularized. Absolute knowledge can thus not want to mean this. If the term still has any meaning, it can refer only to the methodological problem of the phenomenological science of the *a priori*. The last word would thus be a "reduction to historical reason."[69] All static states of consciousness, together with the corresponding horizons of understanding, then appear as what they are within their context of understanding only by *going beyond* the respective initially finite circle of consciousness or by analyzing the circle of understanding. What is ascertained by consciousness within the respective positions is true; but it is not true in the sense of finality, if the consciousness which discovers the truth does not remain once and for all "this-there." Here obviously Hegel has the word: "If epistemology has never been regarded as a peculiarly 'historical task' and if one seeks to turn this into a rebuke of traditional philosophy,"[70] then phenomenology means, for reason which has been discovered to be historical, a transcending of the positions of consciousness. Each state of consciousness's claim to finality is disclosed in the historical-analytical-critical perspective to be just a provisional claim. Not only mankind's concepts of nature, but also the life-world views can then appear only as hypotheses which within the position are dogmas, but outside it merely assumptions. Phenomenology must, then, count on two great problems in the context of the philosophy of reason. The first is this: how can one arrive at a universal, evident *a priori*? And the second goes: can such an *a priori* be portrayed and grasped "exhaustively" as invariable?

The *a priori* is sought as the absolute. But this *a priori* is acquired by a reflection upon the ultimately constitutive ego and its originary evidences as originary experiences. This ". . . 'I' . . . 'cannot be declined' and, in fact, is named 'I' only through an equivocation. This 'nondeclension' . . ."—as Landgrebe explains—"is nothing other than what Heidegger designates as 'ever-mineness' (*Je-meinigkeit*). It signifies a singularity which lies beyond the difference between logical universality acquired through idealization, and individuals subsumed under the universal."[71] This interpretation shows how from a certain point of view an approximation to the Heideggerian position is clearly supposed to be undertaken. For Heidegger's *Dasein* was at first thoroughly an existent—namely, that existent which in its being is concerned with this being itself. But then it was no longer a matter of this individual existent, but only of *Dasein* in its "existentiality," for which the concrete projects were completely irrelevant and so were not taken into account. Nor was *Dasein* to be acquired through "idealizations"; and the particular "*Dasein*" was not to be an individual case of *Dasein*. This problematic conception of the universal and the particular is now applied back to Husserl.

Yet it is unnecessary to take up once more the quite dubious doctrine of "unmediated" experience and read it into Husserl.[72] For Husserl himself, as Landgrebe points out, wanted to regard the *a priori* as invariable but did not consider the *a priori* structures exhausted (or exhaustively known).[73] Whether in absolute reason or in ultimate transcendental subjectity the "dialectic of the one and the many" becomes obsolete—because "in its singularity . . . it implicates the *one* world common to all and, thereby, humanity"[74]—can be decided only by *absolute reason* itself. Finite reason knows no supersedings (*Erübrigungen*) of mediation—not even in regard to the fact that transcendentally ultimate, and completely absolute subjectivity would, in its undeclinableness, not need it.

Phenomenological considerations cannot start from such a reason at all, since it is not a "phenomenon." The critical phenomenology of reason, rather, as an intentional phenomenology, always (and hence here too) remains "objective"; and this means that it always shows itself to be bound to something pregiven. As comprehending reason, it takes up the pregivens and transcends them, which is evidenced by the very fact of applying a new point of view, from which—i.e., from outside the pregiven, hitherto familiar, position—the critically comprehending grasp occurs.

It must be remembered that phenomenological reason cannot provide any reason which would ever somehow have to be fixated (or *reified*). The *a priori* grasped by reason itself signifies that it stands in an incessant historical process of "self-clarification" and "self-demonstration." What this self-limitation looks like cannot be anticipated by any word. The factical-historical critique of positions which reason continually undertakes proves only in what sense and in what direction the previously dogmatically accepted contexts of understanding have become problematic, i.e., questionable.[75]

The phenomenological "reduction to historical reason" is a reduction to open reason; and open reason is historical reason which changes in its structures of understanding. The form of self-confirmation taken for granted here and now by this reason is that of reflection and regression, and even such phenomenological matter-of-courseness can, indeed must, in turn become a theme for reduction.[76]

Phenomenology is, finally, also not "a set of axioms for possible metaphysics," i.e., a free-floating performance of unrestrained rationality. For it does not project a system of possible standpoints within which determinate matter-of-course convictions hold true; rather, it is historical, and this means that it goes into the historically *actually* temporalized positions (which are always "metaphysically founded positions") in order to disclose the constitutional connections only after the fact; it does not invent metaphysical positions, and it does not project sets of axioms.

So the situation for a phenomenology of reason is as follows: it starts with metaphysical attitudes which it accepts and discloses as belonging to particular contexts of understanding; it points out the humanity that reveals itself there and the consequences of a determinate lived-along (*dargelebt*) system of apprehension and attitude with all its affective, emotional, rational, with absolutely all mythical, onto-theological, and theoretical variants. However, it does not decide between the positions which serve as model, but merely carries out the correlation-analysis on them. Phenomenological reason, as the reason which wants to know further, deeper, and more, is distinguished from living, and hence also from life-worldly, reason. The latter lives only in "convictions." If phenomenological reason does not want to supplement such a naively habitual reason—on a different, higher level—with a new segment of unexhausted naiveté by retreating to a philosophical belief, then it must remain critically "with the object."[77] Either it can give an accounting of how the always dogmatic understanding of reality comes about—in which case it is, with its critical reflection, in principle, "objectifying"—or it does not succeed in finding a point of view from which what was taken for granted until then can be clarified, in which case it does not meet its own demand for rigorous scientific knowledge. That is the deeper sense of all phenomenological reduction. In critical reflection, reason is beyond the naiveté of "positional" consciousness—or it does not exist at all! As reflective reason, it preserves what naive reason mediates, and it makes it conscious by grounding it. To this extent, the reflective attitude reaches further than naiveté.[78] It is wrong to complain about the adoption of the critical and reflective attitude if it is a fact that one no longer lives successively in determinate earlier naive attitudes. A call back to the "lost original attitudes" does not bring back the naiveté of convictions. The intentional object is not the same in quiet simplicity as in conscious deliberation; and the naive attitude is not brought back by any performances of reflection. Reason has simply, case by case, entered a different stage of its development. Philosophy attests to this when it remains oriented by the phenomena as they appear. This "knowledge" and "cognition" is the issue, not a constantly belated "affirmation" of precritical positions.

Chapter Five

The Critical Suspension of the Horizons of Conviction

Critical phenomenology, as distinguished from descriptive phenomenology and any possible revelatory or laudatory phenomenology, is therefore the attempt to treat grounding questions scientifically, i.e., methodically and critically. Because of its investigatory and screening character it will bear a trait which can be briefly characterized as follows: it does not know and proclaim what position the individual must take, but goes back to the situationally given which is mediated within determinate horizons of conviction. Critical phenomenology begins with what is contextually pregiven, in such a way that it remains interested solely in the conditions for the possibility of such given appearances. It does not detach itself from historical developments; rather, it finds its peculiar field of work within the historical horizons. It devotes itself to historical knowledge, and it will logically have to become knowledge of horizons.[1]

The sciences of the natural-scientific as well as the human-scientific domains are certainly eminently critical in regard to their pregiven object: their entire task consists in research aimed directly at the given, in order to determine the properties and the mode of appearance of this object and the laws governing its connection with other objects. But this science, with its two major varieties, is not critical with regard to the ontic-ontologically matter-of-course positing of its research object, which results in an "original naiveté" stemming from the general understanding of life and the world which is reached from the "here and now" and carries along all the matter-of-course convictions typical of this very position. All science, like all normal conduct, starts from a context that is considered natural, which—as a context that is in fact metaphysically prejudged—it does not investigate, whose dogmatic presuppositions it often does not see, but which in any case it never makes as such the goal of its explanations. It does not seek to identify, e.g., the transcendental conditions which must be taken for granted as valid for the scientific attitude itself to be possible at all.[2] It can easily dispense with this, since it always keeps its investigations within a framework once established: within the framework of a "universal theorizing." It takes this theoretical framework for granted; it is the horizon of unquestioned validity.

The world within the scientific attitude looks different from the mythical, the prereflective, the unconscious worlds, from the world of belief and world view. That this attitude too is a position—just as much a position as the attitude of belief and world view—need not concern us, because science restricts its entire work to the objects that occur within the chosen attitude itself, and only to them. To the scientific attitude, questions which can be formulated nonscientifically are not questions at all—no objects of the realm under discussion here would correspond to them.

Decisive problems arise for philosophy at this point. On the one hand, since the Parmenidean-Platonic contrasting of *epistēmē* and *doxa*, it has repeatedly tried to become a really scientific discipline;[3] on the other hand, it does not, in its fundamental attitude, stand on a par with the individual scientific disciplines and strivings, since it does not, like them, investigate, from a pre-given position, a partial realm—for instance, a third partial realm of reality in addition to the natural and the human sciences, the real and the ideal sciences, the structural and the cultural sciences, the explanatory and the understanding sciences, and finally the sciences of being and of what-ought-to-be, etc.

But it is scientific—i.e., critical and comparative (not just descriptive, screening, classificatory)—when and only when its activity refers to the sole thing that can now still constantly be and remain a free object, even if it investigates no partial area of reality attainable from the universal scientific position: it can be critical only with respect to the conditions of possibility under which any such position is a position. Philosophy is thus necessarily "alien to the world."[4]

The claim to universality made by philosophy again and again in history can be justified only on this basis. The objects studied by the individual sciences are always different objects, at least intentionally, but they absolutely all belong as particular formations to one and the same prior world view declared to be natural by general consensus. What can happen here at all depends entirely upon the horizon which the scientific world view implicitly sets when it defines the problem and stipulates its methods. All objects which can possibly appear thus depend on the framework within which individual scientific research always stays.[5]

If philosophy, then, is not an individual science among others, it cannot find its field of work within the framework mentioned above, and so its specific field consists in investigating the conditions for what is given.[6] This means, in the present case, that it examines the position itself; it does not turn to a partial field of objects opened up from such a position. Only to this extent can it call itself universal, for the particular realms treated in the individual sciences always from a determinate "location" still belong to this same position which now becomes the object of philosophical research.

And if there were not just *one* such position which is considered to be the starting framework and recognized as matter-of-course, then philosophy's critical task consists precisely in inspecting all these positions together. As no individual science is purely descriptive, philosophy also cannot stop with the description of appearances which have become evident. It becomes science when, constantly more subtle and leading away from the obvious, it finds the grounding connections. Since the transcendental grounding conditions are, however, those of consciousness, philosophy will inevitably become at the same time a philosophy of consciousness and of reflection, because only in reflection can the "transcendental structure of consciousness" be disclosed and examined.[7] But since such a transcendental structure of thought is not one which can always be found just anywhere (i.e., utopianly) but only in the concrete thinking within each context, and since it seems to be topical as it appears in operation "here and now," this philosophy, which is not an individual science, deals with a phenomenon that can be grasped only from the "present situation." To penetrate through the phenomena to the underlying constitutive conditions, not merely accepting and describing them but asking foundational scientific questions about them, means to let what is taken for granted with its givenness become unnatural and questionable. This discipline, which tries to do such a thing in principle and lets it appear as a unique kind of phenomenon, is therefore called "critical phenomenology." In sum, this point must be kept firmly in mind.

If traditional philosophy has not yet made a genuine attempt in this direction, and if, as was mentioned, according to Husserl it therefore actually never did make a beginning as a science,[8] this is itself just a characteristic trait of consciousness which is in its turn evolving and developing and for which the direct attitude is at first more natural than any inward turn. Critical phenomenology is therefore, in any case, the discipline which, in such an "ever-renewed inward turn," studies and investigates what in the direct attitude happens naively and is only supposedly metaphysically neutral. Only in this respect does it dwell critically upon its objects; and only in this way does it have an object of its own that is strictly distinct from that of the individual sciences, although it is historically absolutely always variable.

Science, no doubt, aims at principles; and the whole complex of general knowledge arranged according to principles claims to be true. So everything depends on the principles upon which a scientific procedure is based.[9] To be sure, the principles governing a determinate behavior do not necessarily have to be known (with full consciousness) to the person who actually applies them. In the prescientific attitude, the principles to which experience is subject there too, as a rule actually go completely unnoticed and unknown; in the scientific attitude they are made known successively. In this case they can consciously be posited purely "by convention," or they can be accepted "hypothetically" (until proof of the opposite), or finally they can be derived really or supposedly "from the nature of the thing" and then be established "as principles."

One thing always becomes apparent: in the quest for certain particular truth contents by way of every kind of experience (prescientific as well as scientific), the methods depend on fundamental (consciously or unconsciously regulatory) attitudes. Obviously therefore only what can be manifested according to the approach observed in principle in each case will present itself as truth.[10] But the very mention of so-called prescientific experience, which has been superseded and overcome by scientific experience, now points directly to the consciousness for which one particular set of principles, or a different one, happens to hold good. Philosophy, if it understands itself rightly, and especially if it seeks to be a grounding discipline, can therefore never undertake the famous "turning to the object" for its own sake. It can "interrogate" this object, as it presents itself and as it is always already an object of research of an individual science, "concerning the conditions" under which it can be "this-there"—and only in this way does it have an object, only thereby does it become critical and transcendental-phenomenological. But in such an analysis, a determinate position represented in consciousness always emerges as the underlying basis.[11]

Principles guarantee and contain a synthesis; but if man's historically activated experiences are supposed to be based upon different principles, this expressly proves that consciousness has undergone a change, a modification with regard to the modes of synthesis functioning in each case. But the difference between prescientific and scientific knowledge and experience, a difference asserted constantly, suffices to ground the thesis of the multiplicity of forms of synthesis.[12]

It has rightly been pointed out that, philosophically, it is a question of the "principle that grounds the unity of experience as a whole."[13] This unity can be determined by means of empirical psychology; or it can be determined by logical analysis of its theses. But whether or not an *a posteriori* or an *a priori* grounding is undertaken, it always has repercussions on the "stringency" of the respectively occurring experience and on its scope. If, as was delineated, Husserl's thought, in its development, goes through at least five phases, then the norms are set by five different principles which guarantee the so-called concrete unity in a different way each time.

In the first phase, characterized by *On the Concept of Number* (1887) and the *Philosophy of Arithmetic* (1891), the psychological synthesis of counting is given as the ground of unity. The second phase, characterized by the *Logical Investigations* (1900/1), but also by the reports in the *Writings on Logic* (1897, 1903), involves logical mental processes and the meaning they contain, i.e., an aprioristic formal logic of the actually experiencing consciousness. With the third phase, that of *Ideas pertaining to a Pure Phenomenology and to a Phenomenological Philosophy* I (1913), it is the one and pure transcendental subjectity, pure consciousness with its completely general forms, that determines the synthesis as its ground of unity. With the fourth phase, represented mainly by the *Cartesian Meditations* (1929/1931, 1950), the transcendental ego (which we ourselves respectively are) as monad in the community of monads provides the common denominator for the synthesis by combining subjectity and intersubjectivity. Finally, in the fifth phase, i.e., the discourses on the *Crisis of European Sciences and Transcendental Phenomenology* (1935/1954), reason as clarified through and through and determining itself on its own (i.e., apodictically) will be the principle of unity, insofar as the attained historical stage of self-understanding expressly makes obsolete any "absolute" principle of unity, namely one considered valid once and for all.[14]

Husserl thus follows a course from the psychology of colligation, via the logic of forms of thought, to transcendental phenomenology, and, further, via the metaphysics of monads, finally to a historically oriented critique of reason. But (and this must expressly be kept in mind) it was always reflection that opened up avenues for grasping the principle of unity.[15] Even in the psychologistic *Philosophy of Arithmetic*, reflection on the psychic act of colligation is needed in order to grasp collective combination in its character of combination. In the *Logical Investigations*, the first reflection is what makes possible the fundamental distinction between the three concepts of consciousness analyzed by Husserl and leads to the characterization of consciousness itself.[16] *Ideas* I also leaves no doubt: "by the reflectional experiencing acts alone we know something of the stream of mental processes and of the necessary relatedness to the pure Ego."[17] For the significance of reflection at the height of the *Cartesian Medita-*

tions it is characteristically stated: "The task is not to open up transcendent being, but to understand it as an occurrence in transcendental subjectivity by disclosure of its constitution."[18] This, in turn, happens to be possible only through reflection. Finally, the *Crisis*, especially in the foundational section on Galileo and physicalistic objectivism,[19] speaks expressly of the fact that it is through the "garb of ideas" of mathematics and mathematical science that we take for true being what is a method;[20] but it is regressive reflection which then solves the problem of "hidden reason," by discovering and uncovering that whereby this reason, which has only now become apparent, "knows itself as reason."[21]

Quite contrary to every first expectation, "reflection" thus seems to be the principle that discovers the very ground of unity for valid principles. For the first expectation would really be that in phenomenological legitimations (*Ausweisungen*) one directly encounters phenomena. Only when it is remembered that Husserl's "principle of all principles"[22] demands that every originary presentative intuition should be considered a legitimizing source of authority for cognition, and that intuition gives content to every kind of evidence in consciousness, is it possible also to recognize the giving performances of "reflection" which in their execution mean not themselves, but the reflected connection, ascertaining something about it and bringing it to "intuition" through reflection.

Phenomenological positivism must be separated once and for all from Turgot-Hume-Comte-Mill-Mach positivism. For the Husserlian return to the things themselves is something totally different from a "positivist attempt to describe" applied to what is mediated by the senses. Certainly, positivism had intended to break off the high-flying idealistic speculations and the windy natural-philosophical inductions, in order to bring the things themselves to unprejudiced description neutrally, or at any rate free of metaphysics and independent of dogmas.

Phenomenological description, which does not ask what an *x* truly is but rather simply presents it in all aspects and strata so that what it really is all about becomes evident, is always just a preliminary stage of scientific work. Of course, again and again "conformity to the primal source [of validity], to that of pure intuition,"[23] is always supposed to be accomplished, but with respect to the objects of grounding science which are left for philosophy this adjustment is never direct, but always produced reflectively! This very knowledge that such an adjustment is resorted to in order to ground some state of affairs is already more than such a performance. Whoever does not take reflection into account fails completely to understand the phenomenological groundings. For here too phenomenology wants to be neither itself a position nor merely the reproduction of other positions (even with unsurpassable intuitive evi-

dence). It wants, above all, to show why on a certain level of consciousness something must seem evident. Even the entire distinction which can
be made between "judgmental and experiential evidence,"[24] i.e., which
exists between prepredicative and predicative experiences, is in turn
based on evidence provided by reflection! Only an uncritical phenomenology can be pure positivism. For positivism, which is itself again a
historical position, states unmistakably that the world, "apart from the
question of transcendence," is the way it appears to naive advertence.[25]
Husserl's positivism, if there is such a thing, would have to refer to the
following statement: "If 'positivism' is tantamount to an absolutely
unprejudiced grounding of all sciences on the 'positive,' that is to say, on
what can be seized upon originaliter, then *we* are the genuine positiv-
ists."[26] This means precisely that it is a matter of recognizing prejudices
as prejudices and, if not excluding them, at least restricting them to the
limits of their solely possible validity. This cannot be a direct giving
intuition, which in a determinate, straightforwardly apprehending attitude always has to do with things; only reflection which refers to
prejudgmental consciousness can accomplish this. All "standpoint-
philosophies"[27] have their "prejudice" precisely in their standpoint. That
this is the case is shown in evidence not by any experience devoted to
things, but always only by reflection; but of course reflection also submits
its own subject matter to "intuition."[28]

For reflection, when it turns inward, does not in such a turn relate to
the act itself which performs this turn, but to what is meant, to the
pregiven, hence prior, object of foregoing order. This object may,
however, be an object of a higher order; and so this phenomenon can then
in the new sense be, for instance, that "a connection exists between
subjective performances and objective structure": the inward-turned
reflection must, however, show completely originarily that this is so; it
can obtain it from nowhere else.[29]

Phenomenology's still unsurpassed significance does not consist simply
in its call for precise, careful, and unbiased description of what appears in
consciousness. This descriptively oriented phenomenology has always
found it hard to avoid setting such descriptions as "eidetic specifications"
and using them almost as substitutes for a definition. It should, however,
be clear at last that the pure description of an *x* must have absolutely
nothing to do with a determination of essence. For description captures
what is. The determination of essence leaves something out. The fact that
Husserl speaks of "ideating abstraction" makes this almost unmistakably
clear.[30] Every abstraction includes a selection process. It does not have
to take place in the manner of empiristic theories of abstraction; in fact,
in phenomenology that will not be the case. But it must remain a

controllable event. Thus a two-stage process is always involved: first, description of a phenomenon must be present; secondly, it must—indeed for certain descriptions of phenomena, on the basis of ideating abstractions—also be known that the existing description represents a selection process (involving the apprehension of essence). And what it intends must in turn be described precisely, so that it can be reexamined and brought clearly into grasp.

The criterion for sensory-empirical evidence is verifiability by, in principle, more than one observer; accordingly, the criterion for apriori-eidetic evidence would be a parallel verification of immediate nonsensory seeing (*noein*). Whereas in the first case such a verification is generally admitted to be possible, in the second we find the strongest doubts. Just as sensory experience can be continually clarified, similarly the nonsensory grasp of original (nonderivable) *qualia* should in principle also be verifiable. Husserl expressly argued against the objection that everything and anything can be presented as "evident" or as "intuition" from person to person or from philosophical school to philosophical school, i.e., basically against the objection that there is no clear criterion for nonsensory grasping. In the discussion of a "theory of knowledge on the grounds of psychophysiology and physics,"[31] he pointed out that a process genuinely parallel to so-called sensory experience actually exists. No doubt, even in the sphere of experience, the empiricists were doing a lot of mischief by their appeal to experience, and yet the verification of this experience could not be made dependent on the agreement of *all* thinking and feeling individuals in bearing witness to such experience, since this would result in an infinite process. And no doubt there is also a misuse of what is called evident, immediate, and intuitive insight into essence.[32] But the argument used in the case of experience must surely apply here too: the grasp of the connections under discussion upon assuming the appertinent (and stated) attitude should be possible and should be admitted because "all objections themselves make use of insights into essence" (considered matter-of-course and therefore not further grounded), thereby confirming their possibility.

The meaning of this indication, to which little attention is paid, can really be just to call serious attention to how much any evidence that is claimed to be eidetic is solidified by the fact that it is opposed. The opposition, in its turn, is based upon other "ultimate reasons," which, too, apparently are immediately certain. And eidetic research can be legitimated at all only by referring directly to its presence in all positional struggles. On the other hand, it follows from this that in the reciprocal opposition of such positions, that which forms the grounds of dispute must somehow be present and grasped, otherwise absolutely no possibility would be offered for discussion! Phenomenology would then itself become an unverifiable metaphysics, propounding a "doctrine" based on eidetic insight and the seeing of essences versus other doctrines; claiming for itself an eye for essences, while accusing the other, divergent standpoint of eidetic blindness; and finally, making the so-called phenomenological attitude into a personal affair of attitude and talent.[33]

That the formation of schools (increasingly in the case of Husserl himself, then in the circle around Scheler, and finally to an extreme through the formation of a circle around Heidegger) gave the impression that a secret, esoteric lore was involved must candidly be characterized as running strictly counter to the meaning of phenomenology. As long as reflection brings about the elimination of matter-of-course convictions,[34] and as long as reflection can rightly be credited with a universal methodical function,[35] as is actually the case in Husserl, phenomenology can never be transformed into a metaphysics of this or that dogmatically held "esoteric" position. The primordial demand of phenomenology remains that "the phenomenological method moves completely within acts of reflection"! It is expressly stated that "in principle infinite retrogressive inquiries" are to be made.[36] Only thus does phenomenology avoid the danger of becoming a "gnosis"[37] and draw back to pervasive critique. Of course, the critical self-clarification of consciousness, and hence the grasping of positions previously taken dogmatically-metaphysically as mere positions, will have to have as a presupposition precisely a transition from the static to the dynamic conception of reason. But it cannot be overlooked from the outset that rational activity does indeed reach this point.[38]

At first the *a priori* of subjectity discovered in phenomenological research perhaps seems to be always just one's own—that of one's own consciousness, which occasionally perhaps seems quite esoteric. Certainly, neither in Scheler's metaphysics of the person nor in Heidegger's metaphysics of being is any sort of tendency to critically investigate one's own position ever added. To this extent, it is basically false to classify Heidegger and Scheler within the circle of the strictly phenomenologically oriented efforts, since in the last analysis, their positions preclude the application of the principle of continual "grounding"; or, as their own writings show, it is at least open to misunderstanding to leave them in this context. With Husserl, it is different. The universally applied method of reflection does not stop even before the matter-of-course convictions taken for granted by any "positionally" bound consciousness. Philosophy as human self-reflection, as the "self-realization of reason"[39] called for in the *Crisis* does not reduce to the individual, but it goes back to him insofar as he lives in really "universal performances of reason," preserving experience and making it practical, whereby it in turn becomes universally investigatable and verifiable.

Phenomenology, so understood, remains a science as long as it sees through its own positional claims and continually abrogates them again. The transcendental subjectity which performs these abrogations is, moreover, "absolute" only to the extent that it really tries to free itself from all thetic positions and their naively demonstrated claim to ultimacy and continues to strive for a grounding.[40] There is here no mystical return to an ultimate authority which explains everything, but what is to be expected here is only "constitutional analysis" applied to the concrete case; and that means: which conditions are functional or which must be applied and recognized if precisely these appearances are phenomena?

If such a critical reflection does not begin, then of course what will be set absolutely is not this "regress" but rather one of the "positions" that was taken for granted in each case prior to the regress. To be sure, phrases introducing and confirming such a metaphysization can be cited; indeed, they can be cited all along the line, from Husserl to Heidegger. There is then talk of the "revelation of what a phenomenon is"—of "philosophy rising to ever higher summits"—of the "constantly progressing realization of the eternal idea of mankind"—of the "relatively perfect concrete 'adumbration' (Abschattung) of the idea of humanity"—of "science as title for absolute, timeless values"—of the "constant creation of world in us"—of "going to an original life," etc. These expressions could be compiled from Husserl. Similar statements from Scheler would have to be added: "Man is a direction of movement of the universe itself"— "Knowledge is a relationship of being"—all "knowledge is, in the last analysis, of the Godhead and for the Godhead"—"Man means something for determining the becoming of the Godhead" itself—the highest form of knowledge possible for men is "salvation-knowledge, is co-realization of God" by man. And finally, in Heidegger one reads: "Dasein is an existent that does not occur amid other existents"—the "existent whose analysis is the task at hand is respectively we ourselves"; the "being of this existent is respectively mine"—"in the being of this existent, this existent itself relates to its being," and the "required thinking is a more knowing and more thinking thinking than that of science" (which Heidegger rejects); it is opposed by the "speaking of the logos": the "logos brings the appearing, the forth-coming into presence, from itself to seeming, to opened self-showing."[41]

If phenomenology claims to be science and if it cannot stop with a pure effortless description of phenomena but also must not go over to the proclamation of metaphysical-speculative doctrines, it must from now on see its task as the critical mastery of the grounding connections which are secretly at work in each case. Only so does it remain with the things themselves, while the given "contextual connection," the lived situation, occasionally has them appear problematic and questionable, requiring further inquiry. Its goal can be only to introduce ever "new question-ableness," not to establish and consolidate metaphysical positions. Whether here an asserted "unconcealing," a "concentrated exclamatory speaking of the *logos*," is present or not must be examined, not simply asserted or proclaimed for a circle of awestruck esoterics.[42]

Undeniably, in contexts of assertions and teachings of every sort, especially in the metaphysical positions of Scheler and Heidegger, there is indeed a determinate transcendental structure of thinking. But to absolutize it is not phenomenology's task.[43] Any metaphysical position, from the positivist to the religio-Gnostic one, is out of the question for a critical, reflective philosophy that seeks grounding as a standpoint which is always just supposedly ultimate. Therefore, greater significance should be attached to the question of developing the adequate method in philosophy than generally occurs. If despite total elimination of positivist metaphysics, one still believes it necessary to admit a simple positivist method, that is simply too meager.[44] Description and analysis even of the "most positive" phenomena cannot possibly be the ultimate goal of a science.[45] Even in this sense, phenomenologically there should be no absolute positings. Methodical as well as dogmatic monism is a thesis and does not ground itself. For that reason, *openness* of possibilities must be demanded here. Every position relative to dogmas or methods contains absolute theses about reality and about scientific access to this reality. These theses cannot be grounded by themselves. Neither is it possible for positivism to ground its thesis—i.e., that only what is perceivable by the senses and verifiable by the senses is reality and is scientifically accessi-ble—by applying this very criterion of scientificity; nor does the method-ical positivism of mere phenomenon-description, despite all effort, have the capacity to derive any validities whatever from the portrayal of appearances: above all, it cannot in its turn make the "claim of the method" itself by plausible description.

As a matter of fact, phenomenological work is not exhausted in such descriptions.[46] Rather, it seeks from the outset the disclosure of *"if-then"* relations. That is, it asks which general forms of consciousness are present when certain objects are meant in a general way as such and such and stand in uncontested validity. Whether there really are universal, static, i.e., historically invariable, primitive concepts and elementary forms of connection, is already the question of the *Logical Investigations*. The *Lectures on the Phenomenology of Inner Time-Consciousness* (1905) seek to know which intentions are necessarily connected with which *intenta*. How *noesis* and *noema* correspond and result in a taken-for-granted constitutional connection is the object of investigation in the *Ideas* I (1913). How *cogitata* and *cogitationes* form a unity with the ego which stands in polarity to them and ascribes them to itself is the theme of *Cartesian Meditations* (1929). Why subjective performances of consciousness which have remained anonymous are to be posited and why life-worlds form the starting point for the work of phenomenological elucidation is described in the *Crisis* (1935 ff.). That is how Husserl's development is portrayed on a time scale.

Not the eidetic forms of ideal formations—whether they are of objective logic, objective ethics, or objective aesthetics (in Husserl himself, then in Scheler/Hartmann and in Geiger)—are the real goal of the work of clarification, but rather the "constitutive conditions," which are to be posited for them in their historical objective givenness. All descriptions and analyses remain at best a preparation for their discovery. Husserl's "eidetic," "transcendental," and "phenomenological" reduction is an external expression for the "method of regression": away from the thing, to the conditions which ground the thing in its "how." Although Husserl's Kant interpretations are subject to extraordinary changes and also do not have the same value, one thing must be remembered: without the Kantian idea that the laws and conditions of experience are the same as the laws and conditions of the objects of experience, transcendental regressive-reflective phenomenology cannot be understood. Certainly, phenomenology's concept of the phenomenon is so endlessly expanded compared with the Kantian one that it encompasses everything that is meaningfully constituted, and accordingly it must include, for instance, even what has the sense "God," the "Absolute," or "nothing."[47]

But only insofar as the laws of experience and the laws of the objects of experience are, in the very broadest sense, the same, does the principle "to the things" retain its meaning, namely as long as the regression from the constituted to the conditions of constitution is required. For the object of experience stands completely under the sign of the "forms of experience"; and so, in an at first unexpected inversion, subjectity is the sought thing itself.[48] Phenomenological discussion of transcendental clues has no other meaning than that of showing how apprehended sense points back to the apprehension of sense. And the implications of sense which emerge in the realm of experience suggest that one apprehended sense paves the way for a new one, which in turn points back to a corresponding apprehension.

The concrete subject with its experiential performances is, then, probably the starting basis,[49] but to discover the forms in which this (transcendentally determined) subject actually apprehends things remains the real goal of transcendental and constitutive phenomenology. Unlike fundamental ontology, no dictum such as "*Dasein* is that existent which in its being is concerned with that being itself" is set at the beginning, but rather the "clarification" of the basic composition of this subject is carried on constantly; the dictum is not accepted as a dictum, the position as a position! And the form in which the subject stands as phenomenon-constituting is "subjectity"—i.e., only insofar as it is possible to say that *we ourselves* are the transcendental subjectity.[50] The constant quest for a universal "ground" for this universal is (as in Kant) anchored in a general *a priori* "form" or "structure of consciousness," i.e., in subjectity. But the subject, the *Dasein*, the person, the individual consciousness in any case shows it! And this universal is presented first as the empirical unity of the subject, then as eidetic unity of the ego, and finally as transcendental unity of the absolutely constitutive subjectity.

The question concerning the being of this consciousness, i.e., of the unity to be posited here, cannot be answered again by a positing, but only by the continued recourse to the legitimations of reason.[51] Absolutely all the answers which the rational consciousness gives to such retrogressive inquiries abrogate (*aufheben*) the dogmatically and metaphysically posited positions and their contents by trying to ground them—and here grounding always means: to derive transcendentally. Phenomenology certainly does not have to regard that which is mediated in all seemingly natural world attitudes as the historical development of the Absolute. But it also seems doubtful that phenomenology itself, in all its steps of thought, is the appearance of truth, the development of the Absolute, the realization of the idea of humanity. That such a self-interpretation would remind us of the idealism of Fichte-Schelling-Hegel and its claim to absoluteness, has rightly been pointed out explicitly,[52] even if it would certainly be going too far to draw a parallel between Fichte-Schelling-Hegel, and Husserl-Scheler-Heidegger.

Phenomenology, as transcendental philosophy, is always right when it is eidetic and synthetic, insofar as it grasps all appearances *as* universals.[53] For a comprehending grasp, there is no such thing as the purely singular, individual, unique. Rather, the fact is that every *x* is understood as *x* only by the positing of universals which result from the "forms of synthesis" and can also be already found in the very structures of the language used. The *intentum*, the *noema*, the *cogitatum* constituted by consciousness is what it is as a unity of sense, or as an invariable it is the unity of a determinate sense. And when Husserl attaches all these unities of sense in their sense-function to forms of subjectity, from the outset he removes all Platonizing, all eternalizing character from them. They hold true "in-themselves" always only for the appertinent consciousness and system of consciousness—all other talk of an "in-itself" had indeed proven to be absurd. For nothing that appears withdraws from the possible ways of such appearance; and so it corresponds to them and is not "in- itself."[54] There should be no quarrel on this point.

Consciousness, which moves in world-designs considered natural, assigns to each object its place within the whole in terms of the binding framework: something is then considered to be this and not that from the vantage point of this whole; it is and remains an irreal unity of sense and meaning, valid in this and valid for that framework of consciousness, which is a horizon of interpretation. That absolute essence and the absolute grasping of essence are spoken of in this context does not abolish the "constitutedness of the given" in performances of subjectity.[55] Only for subjectity, and indeed in its current form, is the object what its noemic (irreal) sense shows.

When retrogression is to be made from the sensefully and meaningfully given to the constitutive authority, subjectity, this very subjectity can never itself come into view in a sense that transcends the context of apprehension and experience. Just as the object gets its sense from the whole framework of the project of apprehension considered to be natural, and becomes understandable in those terms (whereby this understanding holds true absolutely and unrestrictedly for the level of apprehension), likewise the sense and meaning of subjectity itself are demonstrable only from a determinate "basis of apprehension."[56] The correlation-connection between grasping and what is grasped holds good here too. This means, however, that subjectity—where it is posited and experienced—corresponds completely with the possibilities of legitimation of the preposited consciousness and never can occur and be known "in-itself" in a ("bad") sense that points beyond it. *Subjectity-philosophy is not onto-theological metaphysics.*

Since Heidegger, but especially since the secondary descriptions by Brecht, Landgrebe, and Szilasi, it has been stressed repeatedly that Husserl's phenomenology committed a serious omission by not asking about the "being of consciousness" or about the "being of transcendental subjectity."[57] What is meant by this reproach, which has become a dogma, is that the being-in-itself of this consciousness had not been brought out—as if in transcendental-phenomenological reflection there were any such "in-itself" of this kind! Where the correlation between conscious being and conscious content is universal, the suspension of the question of the being of consciousness will contain no failure to ask, but rather the avoidance of an absurdity.

Scheler's and Heidegger's metaphysical positions give answers to such a question; but in so doing, they abolish the basic correlation-connection between understanding and what is understood, so that suddenly they fall out of the correlation and discover something eternal, something valid in itself beyond such a correlation, something as being in its being, which suddenly (one knows not how or why) no longer remains bound to the context of understanding and its powers. That this should be possible is incompatible at least with the phenomenological starting position. Consequently from this point on, Scheler and Heidegger should no longer be called phenomenologists. If, however—henceforth contrary to the sense of the phenomenological method—it is nevertheless done, and if in the Schelerian-Heideggerian dicta a claim to universal validity, and no longer to a framework-validity, is alive, then such a position must be examined critically, lest a new belief in revelation be endorsed.

Even a reflection upon transcendental subjectity, whatever this may be, can make discoveries only within its given functional context, but not "in general" and "ultimately," or "in itself." Talk of transcendental subjectivity, or rather of transcendental subjectity, is misunderstood if in the sense of the so-called absolute idealism of Fichte-Schelling-Hegel it is provided with some index that is considered eternal, designating an "in-itself." Only what it allows to become visible in the correlation-connection of a given *noesis* and a given *noema* can be claimed by it— nothing in itself, and not once and for all beyond the correlation connection.[58]

Leading universal structures make it possible for x to be grasped as x in a concrete context; leading universal forms are, however, also what determine the apprehension of consciousness, of subjectity (an "objective genitive" is involved). Some determination-system with respect to objects, or some determination-system with respect to the grasping of the being of consciousness must in turn be posited as absolute, going beyond the preposited correlation analysis in such a way that it is thereby abolished and abrogated.

For the phenomenological consciousness, no natural conception, presented as evident, and no correlation-system is definitive, solely possible, and absolute—for the simple reason that questions of this kind cannot be formulated meaningfully within the stated approach. It is latent Kantianism that prevents one from taking phenomena for the "in-itself." It is latent Kantianism that protects phenomenology from allowing a determinate metaphysical position to stand as natural.[59] Finally, it is latent Kantianism that avoids the transformation of consciousness and subjectity into world.[60]

When the starting point is a correlationship between subjectity and possible objects, the two indeed go together but do not coincide. History, then, always varies the "systems of invariants" only as an unbroken whole, i.e., subjectity and objects. From here no road leads to "subjectity-in-itself" and to its genuine being. Only where a determinate subjectity, functioning in a determinate way, is singled out and posited as absolute must it coincide with facticity, because it is then cut off from anything beyond. This is the dilemma of a fundamental ontology.[61]

Thus it is clear from the methodical approach that phenomenological research need not be supplemented by an additional metaphysical *epoché*:[62] the fundamental emergence from the correlativism between subjective performance and objective appearance, together with the fundamental assumption of the historicity of rational consciousness, *is* metaphysical *epoché*.

All the intentional, noematic, cogitative structures of determinate sense are thus originally not idealized to the absolute, i.e., declared to exist in-themselves, but just interrogated for their sense and for the validity of being in which they stand. Husserl's suspension of the thesis of natural being served this purpose.[63] Likewise, the subjectity which occurs in each case as a component in the functional context, the "here and now," i.e., the transcendental consciousness at work in each case, cannot be posited as absolute. Paradoxically, it must even be said that every attempted absolutization here means basically a "naturalization." For subjectity (as "conditioning" for the "conditioned"), equated with a determinate condition and coinciding with it, could no longer be distinguished from what is conditioned by it: the condition would be dissolved completely in the conditioned and would be lost in it.

Only when phenomenological analysis holds firmly to the "historicity of reason" does it, on the one hand, avoid the absolutization of a determinate phase and, on the other, succeed in relativizing the problem of the "in-itself."[64] Inversely, in fundamental-ontological contemplation there is some discussion of the historicity of *Dasein*, but the determinate form of *Dasein* itself (which in its being is concerned with this being itself) is posited totally as absolute. The absolute is present by the way in which being becomes brighter in *Dasein*—here there is no "historicity." The ways of being (the existential structures) are forms of understanding posited absolutely, not variably possible and historically changeable forms of such an understanding.

Historicized, the self-understanding and the self-reflection of consciousness withdraw progressively from any positional metaphysics which sets up and promulgates doctrines of a contentual nature. If the epistemological problem has been promoted by the coming into view of the constitutional connection between sense-bestowing understanding and the apprehended sense, this does not mean at the same time that a new metaphysics has developed. In Husserl, there can be no question of any metaphysics after the legitimation of the intentions of the phase of the *Crisis*.[65] Inversely, where the epistemological problem is moved completely into the background, as in Scheler and Heidegger (and especially in the ontological school), only thetic metaphysics, disclosing itself in ultimate revelations, is left.

Metaphysics always deals with positings of reality which either have validity quasi-naturally or are undertaken explicitly. So again and again there are theses of being with regard to both the world, i.e., the correlate of the subjective performances of the understanding, and the subject, i.e., the correlate of the objective givens. But the two factors, consciousness and world, are not given absolutely in any of the interrelated constitutional and grounding relations.

Starting from consciousness, which always stands in connection only with the world disclosed by it at this very moment, no access of any kind to a world can ever be acquired that would transcend the present ("possible") constitutive connection. And inversely from the vantage point of the transcendental clues,[66] such as are contained in every concretely apprehended world as precisely this world, no return is open other than that to the "correlatively" appropriate consciousness. Every reflection that reaches back further once again is subject to the same schematization. In other words, phenomenological investigation remains caught within the description, analysis, and correlation of the phenomena of consciousness and the consciousness of phenomena, and has its field of work there. It attends to all constitution systems, takes them seriously, establishes for each of them valid essential connections between the subjective and the objective moments; but it never knows and never proves what subjectity in-itself and what world in-itself are.[67]

Phenomenological research is the quest for the presuppositions under which something comes to appearance *as* something; and it is also the discipline which sets out once more from the presuppositions, so primarily sought and eventually even found, toward a reality lying further back yet still pregiven, whereby it can in a certain sense anticipate it *a priori*.

The system of presuppositions in question remains strictly coordinated with what is conditioned and made possible by it. But it can be sought only by setting out from a world of appearances constantly encountered in a determinate sense, by starting with phenomena which have their specific logical, epistemological, and ontological place. All encountered appearances represent first of all the "natural world," and impose themselves in a "natural conception of the world." That what is supposedly so natural is not natural "in-itself" but is a constituted structure of experiencing, apprehending, and living in a certain mood, i.e., precisely of "historical" consciousness, is made clear by phenomenological analysis once it has found the principles which define the structure of univocalness in precisely this way. Sense-verifying syntheses are always involved when mental processes, apprehensions, and experiences are present.[68] That they are evident for the given context does not in the least prove that they still have the slightest sense outside the so depicted circle of understanding. Even to ask at all about their being there proves to be impossible, because the question remains meaningless in the absence of all corresponding transcendental clues. No road leads to a "metaphysical position in-itself."[69]

But that which stands within a determinate context of understanding cannot explain and verify this context as such in its occurrence. Phenomenological research verifies itself and proves to be really "phenomenological" only insofar as it occupies itself with the "given" appearances, using the ideal clues present in them to clarify the appertinent system of presuppositions (i.e., of historical subjectity) and elucidating the one by the other. These analyses of phenomena never lead beyond the correlation connections. Thus phenomenology is devoted to the object and it develops forms of consciousness. It encounters only this consciousness, which always is a complex of principles that must be presupposed within the given context; and it has to do only with this world which, as matter-of-course world, has matter-of-course forms of access and disclosure. So it remains in principle topically oriented.[70]

It can determine *that* this world and this consciousness, *that* this context of appearance and this subjectity belong together, and it can then ground one on the other; but it cannot ground *the fact that* this is so, and it cannot give any scientifically relevant answer to any explanation with respect to how this came about, insofar as it does not itself in turn become a "position," proclaim a "metaphysics," remain "dogma," all of which is not possible without charismatic claims. It is interested in nothing except what is scientifically relevant. Accordingly, the genuinely phenomenological attitude from the outset practices *epochē* toward all dogmatic-metaphysical positions and subjects them to an investigation of their immanent connection, since the absolute is not a given.

If the mythical-religious-metaphysical ideas of model and scheme are possibilities for ascertaining reality, then it is not permissible to distinguish between them, because each of them has a grounding character always only within its own finite circle, beyond which it does not extend. Consequently, on closer examination, they are all exhausted even as asserted positions, and under critical observation they retain only a "hypothetical" character related to their intentional objects and valid for them. Consequently, even Husserl's thesis of the world-realization of transcendental life is anything but metaphysical. It is the "self-experiencing of this consciousness" which is possible from a determinate stage of consciousness that says: *if* world is somehow given, then it is always matched by a corresponding consciousness which has reached a more or less obtrusive degree of clarity.[71] And this consciousness knows of its "constitutive" sense and of its "historical function," for it is a "consciousness enriched by historical experience." Nowhere is world, subjectity, being-in-itself thereby experienced; rather, the "sense of what is present" is taken up and analyzed. Finally, this also means that phenomenology remains phenomenology and does not become ontology, for even the sense of being, as it is meaningful in the systematic context, opens itself only in this very meaning from the vantage point of the phenomena and delivers "no universal metaphysics of being." To have shown this would not be the least achievement of critical phenomenology, which needs dogmatisms in order to raise itself above them, which lets the horizons of conviction become visible without binding itself to them, which uses the topical ground instead of absolutizing it, and which sees groundings where natural consciousness remains naive.[72]

Chapter Six

Topical Consciousness and the Utopian Regression To Ultimate Experience of the Life-World

Husserl's late work, *The Crisis of European Sciences and Transcendental Phenomenology* (1935/1954), is, on the whole, a piece of radical critique of dogmatism. Of course, Husserl inquired into grounding conditions in all his works; his purpose for investigating the given was to discover why and how and whether it is given in thus and such a way and can be given in precisely this way. The question is how to proceed when an explanation is required. Whoever starts with axioms and deduces from them what is made possible by them proceeds "thetically"—or rather "hypothetically," since he assumes what must be presupposed before the inferential mechanism can start to function. Whoever on the contrary starts with the given, seeks the still unknown (matter-of-course) presuppositions of "topical conditions," which are thus logically required. Husserl, the logician, chooses this second procedure. He thereby takes up the Kantian motif in such a way as in principle to ask everywhere concerning the conditions for possibility.[1] For this reason, as we have seen, no Husserlian phenomenon-description is concerned with description in-itself; rather, its aim is to uncover appertinent constitutive conditions.[2] Now, according to the investigations carried on above, some constitutions are "purely psychological," some are "logical," "transcendental-philosophical" or "metaphysical," and some also happen to be "topical-doxic-historical." Accordingly, the different constitutive conditions are described according to the regional difference of the object, in such a way that the grounding connections are clarified by description. Phenomenology is, here again, not phenomenon-description; it remains, rather, universal constitutional research that uses phenomenon description as its basis; it is transcendental philosophy.[3]

Now the expression "universal constitutional research" must be clarified. Through eidetic reduction, early phenomenology had prepared access from the "fact" to the "essence."[4] Phenomenological reduction[5] not only suspends the "natural thesis of being"; it points the way to recognition of the correlation connection between *intentio* and *intentum*, between *noesis* and *noema*, between *cogitatio* and *cogitatum*—whereby a premature metaphysics of reality in general and of things-in-themselves became impossible. Transcendental reduction[6] had started correlatively with the world and discovered the transcendentally reduced phenomenon "intentional world" and then in turn the "appertinent conscious life," which would never emerge from the given context and become metaphysically absolute. One could now say that two further moments which must be added to the doctrine of the reductions can be found in the *Crisis*. On retrogressing to ever new grounding circumstances, it becomes clear to Husserl that the regress can never end and that it is unlimited. What does this mean?

In view of the modified Cartesian intention, the goal of phenomenological research is to obtain an absolutely solid starting basis.[7] But the phenomena which present themselves to a first natural or eidetic description or to a second (contrived) one cannot provide this starting basis. As constituted phenomena they point back to the "forms of their formation," their origin, and their generation. Reflection, which now starts on this way back to the constitutive sense-formations, discovers the "subjective presuppositions of the objective." At the same time, it thereby first discovers the empirical subject, then metaphysical consciousness in general, then the ego as substratum of habitualities, and finally constitutive subjectity as intersubjectivity. For every object, of whatever kind, designates a "regular structure of the transcendental ego."[8] Everything must be included within this pervasive phenomenalization, and so in the last analysis even "science" itself is a phenomenon which, with all its claims to objectivity, is entirely "subject-relative."[9] Although all talk of the "in-itself" of a determinate world, of objective, logical theories, of science as the "totality of predicative theory"[10] may be taken for granted, the fact remains that here too sense-formations of an originary kind are present. This means that even the philosopher who approaches the world and the objects in the world in a scientific attitude can see that this attitude too is not "self-evident" and therefore must submit to reduction. But this means purely and simply that the scientific attitude, for instance in the form of the natural-scientific position, is just one attitude among others. It can as little be absolutized as can any other component out of the correlation connections of *cogitatio* and *cogitatum*. And if the scientific attitude stands completely on the basis of a life-worldly, prescientific having of the world, then it must be grounded from there too. Thus an indication is given not to break off the constitutive regressive inquiry prematurely.[11] The scientifically structured world is a theoretized world. As such it displays substructions which are not intrinsically "self-evident," but have become historically quasi-natural to scienticized thinking. Even the "scientific world" is not an image of the "world-in-itself"—science does not take the place of the old metaphysics as if *it* now mediates the true world. Science shapes the life-world insofar as it makes it "predictable." That is the point of view that guides it. But this point of view leads back to a consciousness to which it means something. The phenomenological method must be applied consistently against any attempt to absolutize this pre-reflective life-world, which now must be disclosed.

It falls short of its own intentions when it indeed characterizes the scientific theorizations and the scienticized world as "objective" merely for a determinate state of consciousness, but then is inclined to set the underlying life-world as absolute. Talk of the life-world then again betrays a "position," "positional metaphysics," and "transcendental dogmatism."[12] When the 13th International Congress for Philosophy, in Mexico, chose as one of its conference themes the Husserlian concept of "life-world," this implied that it is not necessary to investigate the sense of the Husserlian "method."[13] But the contributions of Luis Villora, José Gaos, Ludwig Landgrebe, Enzo Paci, and John Wild were to direct attention back to the Husserlian problem in a completely different sense. Life-world is not the metaphysical "ground of origin," discovered at last, from which phenomenology could become dogmatism. There is no life-world in-itself any more than there is a scientific world in-itself. Here too the regress to underlying syntheses must be undertaken. In reflection a critical ego discovers the life-world constitutions, and it thereby finds "itself." And the summarizing term "the life-world" already proves that an authority vouching for a determinate synthesis is at work here. In brief, on the first question—whether the phenomenological regress came to an end anywhere, for instance when the scientific world view was traced back to originary life-world conditions—it must be said: it cannot come to an end, for the thought of a state of consciousness, posited for itself, that would not be related to its appertinent world is just as utopian as that other idea that now at last there exists a world that is in-itself exactly the way it appears, yet without appearing for a determinate consciousness.[14] Even the life-world prior to the scientifically interpreted world, when and how we now bring it into grasp, is a world grasped critically and reflectively by consciousness. When it is what it is, it is the "correlate of an appertinent state of consciousness" of its own specific type; and insofar as a consciousness experiences itself reflectively as consciousness, the life-world is always what is opposite this consciousness. Even in the experience of the "life-world" a consciousness experiences itself; and this means that here, like everywhere else, neither consciousness nor the life-world can be posited "in-itself."

No content, as the foregoing considerations have shown, and in addition no life-worldly index, i.e., no phenomenon at all, is a phenomenon without correlatively assigned consciousness. And so finally the life-world is not a world in-itself, from whose perspective everything opens up. Whoever believes that he can begin the journey to genuine being here has once again not applied the phenomenological method as a method.[15] Hence there is no reason, no consciousness, without something that appears in it, but also no scientific, life-worldly, or archaic appearance without a corresponding consciousness and without a correlative reason.

"Life-world metaphysics" can be indispensable and makes good sense as a provisional metaphysics.[16] To dismantle this life-world metaphysics again by including it in phenomenological reductions has once more become the task of the reiterative phenomenological constitutional analysis. At no point can the analysis break through the connection between the state of understanding and what is understood; hence, not here either. Formulated in the language of traditional idealism, this means that I can grasp no being without the self; "from the perspective of the ego, all being must be defined as non-ego and to that extent as relative to the ego. But the opposite must equally be recognized; no ego is without reference to the non-ego. The idea of an ego posited by itself, i.e., an absolute ego, is inconceivable and unreal."[17] In the language of phenomenology, this means, accordingly, that no consciousness and no reason, on the one hand, but also no world of knowledge, faith, or life, on the other, is absolute or can be posited as absolute. In all correlation connections a "topical consciousness," a topical reason prevails. The points of view, the *topoi* which determine the state of correlation, must be disclosed by phenomenological analytics, which then discovers that it cannot come to an end, because it must itself refer the life-worldly syntheses, i.e., the syntheses which lead to a life-world, back to the worlds which are lived singly in every case, and these worlds are still not the "life-world in-itself."

The second question was that of the unlimitedness of reflective regress. It has become clear that no world, not even a life-world, is without appertinent constitutive transcendental consciousness. Since, conversely, no consciousness, no reason remains without an attached world, a topical reduction must make it evident that even the consciousness which must be posited for this must not be called absolute, but represents basically just a determinate doxic consciousness. A reduction that could perhaps be called "topical-doxic" would show that here a "historical" moment comes into view—consciousness and reason emerge only in confrontation with something about which an at first doxic apprehension is present and emerging. It represents a relapse into the absolutizing thinking of the objective scientific mental attitude when it is said that here—for instance, in the life-world—one now has the whole, undistorted reality at hand or in hand,[18] that the elaboration of a "natural concept of the world" has successfully been developed here and now. Yet one thing is quite evident: for the world-concept of the objective-theoretical sciences, the world-concept of the life-world philosophy is "more natural" only because it is immediately grounded in the given context, and only against this background does it seem matter-of-course.[19] Phenomenology is destroyed by internal inconsistency if it allows these merely life-worldly matter-of-course convictions (which appear more original and more natural to the scientific consciousness) to stand as definitive starting bases in general, and does not try to ground them too. It would be systematically the same whether Heidegger in *Being and Time* uses *Dasein* as the ultimate disclosing authority or Husserl metaphysicizes a "life-worldly consciousness." But in the end, Husserl does not do this at all, as is asserted by his interpreters who are oriented by Heidegger and interpret him retroactively from the Heideggerian vantage point. He speaks expressly of a world-consciousness in "constant movement," of the "change" of affections and motives.[20] And this topical-doxic consciousness is discovered to be "topical-doxic" only through a rational reduction that is universal. Hence it is "reduction to reason in the changing of its theses," positions, and concepts. The phenomenology of reason thus had to refer to reason in its constant movement of self-clarification.[21] It is certainly not fashionable to speak of such a new, "consistent rationalism," but that does not prevent this rationalism from remaining indispensable.

The phenomenology of reason can now appeal to the fact that a really new moment is present here. Transcendental reduction generally had reduced to the "ego," to the "community of monads," to "transcendental subjectity" as intersubjectivity; now, when the title "reason" is used (as in the *Crisis*), no rhetorical variation of style is involved, but something new is actually meant. Transcendental reduction makes it clear that the state of consciousness of subjectivity, on the one hand, and the sense-context of objectity (*Objektität*), on the other, belong together correlatively and generally. Rational reduction, however, discloses that reason is in motion, i.e., that it is historical: "Reason is the specific characteristic of man, as a being living in personal activities and habitualities. This life, as personal life, is a constant becoming through a constant intentionality of development. What becomes, in this life, is the person himself. His being is forever becoming."[22]

The historicity of reason, then, first allows objective history to emerge. Correlatively with the subjective performances, it is what has become objective—the course of history corresponds to the constitution of consciousness. But even the stage now disclosed in the regress (as the apparently lowest matter-of-course apprehension of the world and of life) is not the natural world as such. It remains the "more natural" one only as previously given and accustomed. "Natural" is itself just a formal concept for what is taken for granted in any determinate state of consciousness. Husserl was completely right when in *Ideas* I he characterized a natural attitude in the following words: "I am conscious of a world endlessly spread out in space, endlessly becoming and endlessly become in time. . . . By my seeing, touching, hearing, and so forth, and in the different modes of sensuous perception, corporeal physical things with some spatial distribution or other are *simply there for me*, on hand in the literal or figurative sense. . . . Animate beings too—human beings, let us say—are immediately there for me."[23] In the Husserl-Heidegger controversy, all those who wanted to enthrone the prescientific metaphysics against the scientific one attacked this passage, using it to accuse Husserl of theoretical prejudice, of blindness to the universal reality of being and of a lack of understanding for the facticity of *Dasein*.[24] The reproaches are explained if one does not take into account that thinking must be topical and cannot draw its examples from utopia.

Metaphysical dogmatists of the ontology of being have, from their position, had to regard the position of scientific matter-of-course assumptions as completely unnatural. They have not, however, taken into account that every position has its matter-of-course assumptions and its quasi-natural attitude. And there is none that does *not* possess a determinate starting point, a state of givenness with its appertinent assumptions; that is, each is topical. Only to believe that it is not so is utopian. The ontology of *Dasein* starts with "invariant" forms of existence, existential structures. Husserl in *Ideas* I has shown with the greatest clarity what was considered natural in *one* time, namely what was recognized as matter-of-course according to the scientific world-design; now in the *Crisis* he has likewise depicted the naturalness, viz., quasi-naturalness of the life-world approach. "Naturalness" is—as this shows—a historical concept through and through. To have seen this raises Husserl's analyses far above anything which the metaphysics of being then always immediately resolidified; and this metaphysics of being, when it comes across Husserl's life-world, would like to undertake the definition and metaphysical dogmatization even of the life-world.

Thus in the treatment of the "methodological problem of the transcendental science of the life-world a priori,"[25] it was believed necessary to equate Husserl's ultimate constituting ego with Heidegger's "ever mineness." But this is to overlook that the Heideggerian *Dasein* permits no history precisely for the form of his *Dasein* as sense-disclosing authority, whereas in Husserl the decisive thing is that reason remains in a constant movement of self-development—i.e., it probably also changes its transcendental form—and it shows this only when it changes the forms of its transcendental structure and as long as it does this, namely when critical reflection rises above mere living along in matter-of-course assumptions. It does this, accordingly, when it is always being determined anew in reflection, which abolishes prior assumptions. In Heidegger's *Being and Time* the existential structure is absolutely fixed, and only "what" proceeds from it in historical temporalization permits a certain range of variation. The form of existence, however, remains once and for all the one which the "hermeneutics and analytics of *Dasein*" has disclosed; there is now absolutely no more historicity; that is, historicity remains, in Heidegger, strictly a foreground phenomenon.[26]

For Husserl, however, in the fundamental correlation connection between phenomenon and phenomenon-disclosure, the transcendental structure of reason is always affected whenever something new emerges in the concept of the world. That is, Husserl's further work, from the *Ideas* I to the *Crisis*, proves implicitly the corroboration of his thesis of phenomenology *as a methodology* which must not be understood as metaphysics. To this extent, one can thus speak here of a really universal method of regression. No world, but also no subject, no empirical ego, no *Dasein*, no consciousness whatsoever, no life-world consciousness will be left standing as absolute unity of determinate contentual fixation; rather, it is first referred simply to its function in the context together with what is disclosed thereby. Reflection is absolute only formally, since it knows and recognizes no boundaries at which it would have to give up its activity: reflection is, however, not absolute materially, for it does not posit or deduce the worlds, but only recognizes already pregiven worlds as *there* and performs work of constitutional analysis on them.[27]

In this connection, Husserl spoke early of a universal *epoché*. The second volume of the *First Philosophy* (1923/4) is called *Theory of Phenomenological Reduction* and expressly adds to phenomenological and transcendental reduction an apodictic reduction.[28] The universal *epoché* is characterized by the fact that it always encounters and must encounter a specifically determined consciousness, which is always held within specific horizons, but which in each case is new and can assume new forms. Husserl declares: "This universal *epochē* becomes possible through the essential peculiarity of my life, that in every present phase it has a—though empty—form-consciousness, a horizon-consciousness, and that in it in a universal way everything is implied that ever was, is, and will be objective for me and is implied as intentional correlate of my whole, i.e., my co-implicit, life."[29] Universal reduction to my consciousness, my reason, and my life thus means inclusion of all apprehensions of being and time, which then become possible on the basis of a determinate state of consciousness of precisely *this* transcendental life. So I then acquire, according to Husserl, pure universal life in the continuum of reflective regressions, and the worldly universe is changed into universal intentional objectivity as such, just as it belongs to life itself as an inseparable correlate.[30] Then there arises the possibility of a "phenomenology of phenomenological reduction,"[31] because no phenomenological reflection stands still with the given, not even with that phenomenological position of simply performing a few determinate reductions. It seeks everywhere the grounding synthesis for the correlates of states of consciousness and reason. This explains why even for the connections which constantly emerge anew in reductive regresses new names which appear ever more originary are used: "primordial structures," "primal institution," "originary development of the universal in the essence of a transcendental subjectivity," "innate a priori," "logos of all conceivable being," "ultimately functioning and achieving subjectivity," "primal ego,"[32] "absolutely unique, ultimately functioning ego," etc.[33]

Since all this involves correlation conditions, and since every authority—however absolute it is called and however ultimately functioning (i.e., primal ego, the absolutely pure subjectity)—always lets itself be known only in and with its connections of grasping from which and in which it understands itself, what we have here is still not a "metaphysical idealism" that would seek to "derive" the system of the world from a definitive ultimate authority.[34] On the contrary, it is as follows: a world opens up in each case somehow always conceived with subjective structures, with structures of being and value, with horizons of grasping and understanding; and the question is which ego-structure, which kind of ordering of subjectity belongs to a total conception opened up in that precise way. Here nothing is derived from an absolute, but rather the method of bringing together is applied universally: what does the reason which can allow this and only this topical given to arise look like? That is the question of the "method of critical reflection."

In his *Formal and Transcendental Logic*, Husserl had pointed out that even in all universal claims, transcendental subjectity does not create positions, but rather investigates them. For if one says that every existent is constituted in subjectity, this means that it receives its sense and its characteristic of being assigned to it from there; but it does not mean that this subjectity made this existent real or generated it.[35]

Such subjectity must, of course, always first be "discovered." For "no one has to first discover his empirical natural self, himself as a human being. Every adult awake person finds himself present as a human being with a human self and human psychical life. He exercises natural self-experience in natural reflection."[36] And further, the transcendental subjectity "had to be discovered first of all; each one must discover it for himself and must first of all discover his own. And he discovers it only by a method which frees him from the motivational compulsion of natural life."[37] What is natural or what seems to be natural thus undergoes changes.

A so-called "natural" psychological reflection, then, still remains worldly experience, and it follows from this that phenomenological as well as transcendental reductions have only the one sense of making visible in each case the entire transcendental structure on which such a worldly experience is built. Thus it is premundane: "only when nothing more 'exists' for me in the strictest sense as existing reality can I grasp myself as transcendental subject, as the irreality which presupposes all reality."[38]

The world, every world, is what it is when I (as subject) grasp it as transcendentally articulated. This insight must in turn be reobtained again and again from the given context and does not mean that a pure transcendental ego, an absolute subjectity, could be split off from concrete consciousness and "set free." Naturally (and probably quasi-matter-of-coursely) consciousness always constitutes some horizons of grasping or other. That is, concrete consciousness always lives in an articulated world which it takes to mean *the* world.[39] Here everything is articulated topically, doxically, metaphysically. But as a reflective "be-ing," consciousness which has become concrete goes further and further and overreaches itself and the contentually grasped existent in the course of distinctions. That is how sense-connections and correlation-connections are "understood." On the other hand, the understanding just achieved in turn has itself a matter-of-course ground and refers to the applicable preconditions that make possible the understanding of sense and can be reflectively uncovered with an ever new start. Here what would have to apply already to metaphysical idealism also holds true for phenomeno-logical idealism: "Sense is not something instituted, which a subject existing for itself assigns to an existent imagined as chaos, nor is sense read off from the existent as something objectively present. There is sense only for an ego that reflects itself in its relation to the existent. Sense is the underivable basic determination which no longer can be outdone, under which the ego must always think itself in its relation to the existent—and without this relation the ego is only a completely empty, null and void x."[40]

Historically, transcendental subjectity (the very ego which becomes thematic with respect to the existent) is also discovered in "acts of reflection."[41] For it holds true apodictically that reflection remains bound to the transcendental inner relation between subjectity and the existent, which it comprehends but does not produce. Thus Husserl says: "I now distinguish between this transcendental reduction or phenomenological reduction and the apodictic reduction associated with it. Apodictic reduction designates a task that is made possible only by phenomenological reduction. Before I exercise apodictic critique, I must have a field of critique, here a realm of experience."[42] The experiences which the concrete ego has are, however, always topical, doxic, complex. That they take place on the ground of theoretical scientific substructions, i.e., starting from this determinate topical situation, a, is an experience that has come about through phenomenological reflection on the horizon—that they occur on the ground of life-worldly matter-of-course assumptions, i.e., from a possible situation b, is also disclosed by such a transcendental-phenomenological reflection. The realm of experience is, as a realm of experience, ever "different," i.e., structured as historically variable and transcendental; and that structural and constitutional connections are present here is itself a completely new experience—precisely speaking, an experience through transcendental-phenomenologically apodictic reflection. For according to consistent transcendental phenomenology, I have this realm of self-experience, of transcendental experience, only due to the method of phenomenological reflection.[43]

Husserl expressly admits that even questions of a "possible transformation of the method of phenomenological reduction soon intrude."[44] Thus in this context there actually has been talk of the universal reduction to reason, and for good cause: the structures of reason are reflected in the relationship of consciousness to that which it grasps—there is nowhere else for them to be grasped. And "reflection" always achieves the grasping of that relation. To that extent, reflective consciousness is apodictic. It experiences itself only when such relations are present, but it always experiences itself then; overreaching these relations and leaving them behind (that is, if something is really experienced as ground), reflective consciousness operates under the prevailing points of view of its critical reflection, and with them it sets boundaries for and delimits itself by "proceeding" in one direction.

From this angle, a way now opens for historical reduction, i.e., for a return to historically developing consciousness. The *Crisis*, of course, constantly speaks of this.[45] Yet in the analysis of the life-world, the historicization seems to be brought to a stop again. To state it clearly: it must be examined whether Husserl has the point of departure from the life-world actually hold true as an absolutely ultimate point of departure. That would mean that relational structures are left standing as matter-of-coursely valid and are not understood in the phenomenological sense. That is how the Husserl interpretation which starts from fundamental-ontological positions sees the matter. It must therefore be discussed.

According to that interpretation, functioning transcendental subjectivity, which "exists" apophantically only in reflection on the pregiven relations between concrete consciousness and concrete horizon, is suspended and can make no appearance, precisely when the relation between conscious life and the content of consciousness is not transcended reflectively and hence understood as sense-connection.

For understanding is not just the simple possession of certain *qualia*, but also and especially the grounding possession.[46] The life-world problematic is linked with the question of a historical reduction as follows. A radical "epistemological issue" is involved—namely, the question whether the so-called world of the sciences, with its implicit claims to objectivity, is in its turn a "historical fact," and then as such to be dismantled. The regress behind the world determined by the sciences and presupposed by them, i.e., the regress to prescientific matter-of-course assumptions and life-world experiences, is itself something that requires validity in its investigations. It cannot simply go back to life-world experiences merely because the sciences "are in crisis" and no longer seem able to account for the sense of their actions;[47] moreover, the cogency of this procedure and an appertinent inner logic must still be presupposed. The life-world problematic thus involves mainly the problem of a prescientific knowledge. This prescientific knowledge is, however, not immediately given here and now, i.e., in our scienticized world-conception, in a naive prescientific attitude, but rather must first be uncovered most toilsomely.[48] In this uncovering, as must be said right away—perhaps going further than Husserl does—disclosing structures of consciousness are also involved; they are the reason why the life-world is not simply life-world, but is understood as the presupposition that precedes and conditions the sciences as their underlying or indispensable precondition. This is more than the life-world knows about itself.

It would be a mistake to react to the crisis of the sciences by seeking merely to return to life-worldly circumstances which are the primary support for the sciences, while failing to see that this return itself is anything but a life-world phenomenon. In reflection the life-world is understood as life-world, and through reflection the scientific world attitude which is quite naturally accepted as valid here and now is probably also connoted. That is more than science—and also more than the life-world—does for itself. By going back to how science emerged and built itself up from life-world experiences, reason temporalizes itself in a specifically new, previously unknown manner. The reflection that takes place here goes beyond conceptions which seem natural and are temporarily taken for granted. Thus in the *Crisis* the important thing is not that it is shown, especially in the Galileo paragraphs,[49] how science developed historically and what the motives for this were. Important, rather, is the critique-function of reflection—repeated there—which demonstrates the historicity of consciousness. For neither science nor the life-world discloses itself as its sense (*Sinn*). This occurs in reflection, and reflection is not always there in respect to the world of science and the life-world; rather, it appears at some time or other "as an event," now, at the critical moment, or, in effect, "historically." The decisive factor in the *Crisis* is, therefore, not the opening of a way to life-world metaphysics, apparently offered so unquestioningly, but rather the fact that even this metaphysics becomes understandable in critique as metaphysics, as positional dogmatism, and thus is simultaneously stripped of its claims to absoluteness.[50]

For even when it is said that here an originary life-world not altered by science seems graspable and when this life-world is then taken for granted as prescientifically matter-of-course, this matter-of-courseness of the life-world conception must in its turn remain provisional through and through. Quite analogously to the procedure of phenomenological regressive reflection elsewhere, here too a critical interrelation of the appertinent life-world consciousness and the life-world must be undertaken. Phenomenology has, even so, not discovered any supposedly primary experience—it (the current experience) must be traced back to the *cogitatio-cogitatum* relation. It could rightly be said that in building up their world, the sciences operate with the "hypothesis of the being-in-itself of nature processed by them, which is always determinate in each case."[51] But the tracing back of this (merely presumed) being-in-itself to a scientific hypothesis and the suspension of that hypothesis must not, in a naiveté that reaches further back, lead one to count on a being-in-itself of the life-world. The procedure of reflective regression does not stop even before the life-world, and it breaks down even the life-world into situative, contextual, and single-topic life-connections, which originated historically and can be led back together to "*the*" life-world only by an additional synthesis. Even the idea of the life-world is a hypothesis which is not immediately known and recognized as a hypothesis.

Landgrebe pointed out quite rightly that the sciences and philosophies of the early modern era did not view this hypothesis of nature's being-in-itself "as a hypothesis."[52] They sought to devalue everything prescientific as *doxa*, as mere opinion, and denounced it as prejudice. Husserl criticizes the apparent, the merely so-called "objectivism" of this position because such a so-called "objectivism" does not see how the framework of objective and universal thinking is and remains a subjectively posited framework. The main result of objectivism, before it is analyzed critically, is that the prior experiential reality of the life-world is now considered to be the realm of the merely "subjective-relative," concerning which there could be no true knowledge and no true science.[53] In short, the position of the scientific world-conception is naturally itself topical. But to trace the evidences considered scientific back to primary evidences, in which the life-world constantly remains pregiven, would thus be the task. About this, Husserl states: "This life-world is nothing else but the world of the mere *doxa*, traditionally treated with contempt; of course, in extrascientific life it has not a trace of such disparagement."[54]

All this—to take and recognize the life-world as pre-historic world, to posit it as world from direct experience of nature—is so plausible that hardly anything, it seems, can be said against it. On the other hand, the really lived topical and doxic positions of immediate and original world experience are so "subjective" that they would have to exclude everything "universal," and "any community."

Two decisive problems arise at this point: first an "ontological" one, and second an "epistemological" one. 1. The concrete subjective, doxic-topical conceptions diverge so much that Husserl directly asks the question whether there can be, besides "objective truth," a second, "subjective" one?[55] But at the same time, the universal aspect of the life-world conceptions is brought out again:[56] The "life-world" always existed for mankind even "prior to science," just as it then also continued its existential power during the scientific epoch. Thus the problem is already given. On the one hand, the life-world conceptions are topical-doxic, i.e., completely context-related. They are thus singular, individual, occasional. On the other hand, they are said to be the circle of old familiar certitudes accepted in human life as unconditionally valid prior to any needs for scientific grounding and proven in practice.[57] Under the first aspect, life-world experiences isolate; under the second, they form a common but not scientific fund of direct understanding! Actually the prescientific experiences are each in themselves completely different, and they take on the appearance of a new dimension only when they are all bunched together as a whole as simply "nonscientific" conceptions under the collective name of "life-world experiences." But certainly, that is possible only *after* the rise of scientific experience. This is just a historical synthesis—one which becomes possible after the rise of scientific endeavors in general. Formerly, before the development of science, there was absolutely no such thing as *the* life-world experience, but just thousands of experiences, each assigned to its specific conscious life, experiences which then coalesced *post eventum* into a so-called style of life-world experience, opposite to the scientific attitude which had arisen in time and against the background of the scientific world view. On closer examination, the metaphysics of the so-called life-world points further back to the immeasurable abundance of positions of individual topical-doxic conceptions actually ever lived, i.e., back to the thousand dogmatic systems of life, which always show first the purely individual-subjective constitution and never a group-subjective constitution, of these life-worlds. Perhaps the certitudes sought in the life-world through inductions of every kind may make possible an endlessly expanded prospect in the sciences.[58] But certainly the respective life-world position, i.e., the one actually adopted concretely, is not a universal one. It is entirely topical; and the regress to a life-world metaphysics is prohibited because there is no such metaphysics in the first place before it is discovered by reflection as a foil to the scientific conception of the world, i.e., before it becomes "objective" in correlation with this performance of reflection which has been handed down by a series of events. The universality of that position is first opened up by the present reflection, whereby it must be kept available as *foil* for understanding the emergence of the sciences. Phenomenological reflection can, here too, always merely subject the actually given situations between consciousness and world to a correlation analysis. It cannot analyze a universal life-world metaphysics if there is no universal bearer, i.e., if there is for it no concrete universal consciousness that could be assigned to an absolute metaphysics of science and its bearer.

But this means, in the last analysis, that "life-world" is a "structure of sense" which the person bound to the life-world himself does not know as such.[59] The concept has its sense only in connection with that discussion which asks how "the sciences" probably arose. The analysis of this genesis of the sciences and their "tracing-back to determinate life-worldly views," and finally their suspension does not clear the way out of a supposed crisis of the contemporary sciences, for the really naive life-worldly discrepancies are, in their singularity, even more divergent in each case than the ones which arise through the sciences. The regress to the so-called life-world presuppositions of the sciences, too, shows only how much it is *man* who dares to make absolutely all world designs. Reflection can disclose this. It then proves that, e.g., even the scientific world view reworked into technology is based on very determinate subjective presuppositions. It can thereby give an indication that here too everything depends on the transcendental pattern of apprehension of conscious-unconscious man. Phenomenological analysis lets it become transparent how much even theoretical reason is practical. This provides an opportunity. But analysis of the life-world can in no way anticipate for current consciousness how the man of self-reflection will and should relate to the problems of life-world and world-design once he is freed from scientific conceptions of the world.[60] Only correlations entered into between the apprehending subject and the apprehended world fall into the realm of its sense-clarifications, which are themselves not thetic, positional, metaphysical positings. For what actually happens during the dismantling of a dogmatic, i.e., a prescientific or a scienticized world-conception, cannot be anticipated by any life-world analysis. It must "count on a release of fully uncontrollable irrationalisms." Or else it can only point to the fact that here possibilities are set free which can be perceived, and that the subjects, in an irrational unbinding of their decision-making capacity, also cannot with their views flow into the natural-scientific interpretation of the world. Assuming that in the twentieth century there actually is a crisis of humanity which points back to an emptying of sense through scientifically conditioned technicization, then the phenomenological task is that of formulating the question of the origin of the technological world-conception—not, however, that of postulating an anti-scientific metaphysics.[61]

2. The epistemological problem consists in the following. The *doxa* and its right are supposed to be restored. This is done by a regress to the "naiveté of life," but precisely in a reflection that rises above it.[62] This has been interpreted in such a way that Husserl—late, but not too late—by his regress to the life-world, and the performances that make it possible, abandons the ground of the metaphysical thinking of the modern age and now at last also sees the task which Heidegger had previously taken in hand in *Being and Time, What is Metaphysics?* and *Kant and the Problem of Metaphysics*: to initiate the "return to the ground of metaphysics."[63] The attempt to bring Husserl back closer to Heidegger and, after he had long been accused of forgetting the problem and of lacking self-understanding, to let him receive a part of the glory for his share in bringing about the naively welcomed turn to metaphysics, is evident.

But the interpretation itself is not so evident. For the epistemological problem emerges here too. It must be expressly established, even if occasionally it is emphasized didactically, that only the "pre-Socratically cleared regress to the sources" and to the ground of metaphysics has made possible the distinction between *epistēmē* and *doxa*.[64]

The return to the ground of metaphysics is, in Heidegger for instance, the return to the self-clarifying being which attains self-grasping in *Dasein* and here finds a place for proclamation (*Verkündigung*).[65] In Husserl, the return to the ground of metaphysics consists entirely of research into correlations. In Heidegger, what being says must be accepted, and it brings itself to speech in all forms of understanding. The place of understanding is, first, *Dasein*; *Dasein* has command of forms, it is a determinate form of understanding; and so access to the sense of being is found here, and only here. For Husserl, accesses to what counts as being in determinate states of consciousness must be posited only in correlation with them. Nowhere does being as such disclose itself. It is always a matter of that sense of being which belongs to a determinate apprehension of being as "corresponding." Access to the sense of being is obtained by clarifying the apprehension relations. It is not that "being" brings itself to speech (a dogmatic assertion, which one can just as well recognize as reject), but that reflection clarifies in which consciousness which existent can be apprehended as "this- there" and what being means there in each case.[66]

When Husserl speaks of a dimension of ultimate evidences, this must be understood to mean only the dimension which sees the objectities (*Objektitäten*) of a prescientific world as products of the subject, as positings of transcendental performances which must be taken correlatively. Traditional philosophy, as universal philosophy, always had in mind the realm of constituted structures. It mainly let that too, as objectively posited, simply stand as such for its study. Thus it is not universal. It would be universal if it had given the "grounding" for these objectivities. The foundational connections which belong here cannot all simply be disregarded. If this part of the work is missing, then it is not comprehensive and complete. That is the task of phenomenology as transcendental philosophy, which becomes "rigorous science" only by tackling the foundational task as absolutely universal.[67]

As can be seen, two different concepts of science are at work here. The first is the one developed by the so-called exact natural sciences and it simply counts on a pregiven world of objective entities. The second becomes possible when the right to fundamental critique of grounds and correlations is admitted; and only if that is the case can transcendental reflection legitimately disclose the connections that exist between constitution and what is constituted. Contemporary science and traditional philosophy stand on the ground of a determinate metaphysical world-conception. Simply standing on this ground, they are not universal.

"Universality" would require that they know about the "subjective presuppositions" of physicalistic-objectivist thinking of the world. The philosophy which includes in its investigations the transcendental motives for the scientific world view is, at any rate, more universal. Of course, it can be called really universal science in the strict sense only if it does this always and everywhere. This "task" is obviously the ultimate one.[68] It can, then, not stop short of itself in elucidating positional circumstances. But that means the following: the concept of exact science is historically oriented by the concept of natural-scientific knowledge. The natural-scientific world, however, can be understood as subject-conditioned elaboration of certain motifs of the life-world. If the physicalistic, objectivistic world-design is subject-conditioned, then the kind of science that discovers this connection is more universal than the one which remains entangled in it without seeing through it.

But certainly cognition, knowledge, i.e., science, is itself still needed to grasp this connection.[69] It too wants to communicate truth; and it even gives it in the sense that the genesis of the so-called objective concept of truth seems understandable. Thus, a concept of knowledge which is not directed at "objects" as things of nature and segments of the world as such, but at the "constitution of objects," is at work here. But precisely these constitutional conditions should provide this knowledge.

The life-world knows absolutely nothing about the constitution which belongs to it and leads to it; and the scientific transformation of the life-world, which is the quasi-natural starting basis of twentieth century thinking, is likewise characterized by the fact that it declares its objects to exist in themselves and not to be constitutional correlates. For the life-world and for science, "objective" knowledge is "knowledge of an object." Of course, transcendental phenomenology can communicate no knowledge in this sense. For this knowledge is given away to the individual sciences within such a pregiven realm. But this does not mean that, out of an attitude of opposition, transcendental phenomenology would have to restore the subjective truths of the life-worldly topical-doxic consciousness after it has first unmasked the truths of science, which claim objectivity, as subjectively conditioned.

It is illogical to attack the scientific world view and its claims to objectivity by pointing out that this world view is itself subjectively conditioned through and through, only then to grant complete validity to life-world conceptions of a topical-doxic consciousness which are admittedly also completely subject-conditioned. This entire process, however, does not at all result from a life-worldly "living along" which is itself naive. Neither the "life-worldly *doxa*" nor the "natural-scientific *epistēmē*" sees through its foundations.[70] That the one as well as the other is subject-conditioned is revealed only by phenomenological reflection which discloses correlation connections, and indeed is oriented by precisely this intentional phenomenon. This reflection is, then, not a naively subjectivistic opinion, and it is certainly also not knowledge of objects; still, it remains objective by virtue of its critical relatedness to a pregiven existent, which it investigates for its constitutional conditions. Even the fundamental-ontological elaborations of existential structures, which do not at all deal with objects, are not void in such a sense, but objective.

The transcendentally constitutive "full concrete being and life"[71] is thus never given in itself, but comes to appearance in the grasping of a sense— and an existent has sense always only for an ego. So in regressive reflection knowledge always remains "objective"—namely, related to existents, to objects of a determinate framework of understanding, which framework must be clarified in its configuration. Only thus can there be objective knowledge of life-world frameworks, scientific horizons, and circles of understanding.

That phenomenological critique is to achieve this, that it can bring these connections to givenness as what they intrinsically mean, is the presupposition under which the transcendental method of reflection and regression itself stands.[72] This would surely be a dogmatically accepted method if it were simply practiced and did not somehow and sometime become questionable to itself with respect to its own (at first taken for granted) validity. Thus the epistemological problem inevitably becomes more acute. The phenomenology of transcendental reflection goes beyond life-world metaphysics and physicalistic objectivism only when it shows which presuppositions are implicitly valid in each case, without being known to the respective position itself. But it thereby *always* "goes *beyond*" them. It does not go back to any position which would be quasi-natural, but it goes one step further in the self-clarification of reason, which on this occasion proves to be less and less naive on at least one point.

The "historicity of reason" results only from this context. For reflection ascertains which sense belongs constitutively to which conception of sense. To see this is not once again natural and matter-of-course and does not represent a finding already deposited somewhere, which could be reacquired by regresses to determinate historical ("still unquestioned") appearances (such as the "pre-Socratics" or the "etymological forestructure"). It is always natural and matter-of-course to remain within the given framework of apprehension and to manifest one's understanding according to it. But that this connection forever existing between ego and appertinent world-horizon is so quite dogmatically is more than this context itself informs us about. Here critical reason which repeatedly goes beyond the circumstances must come into play.[73] It discloses the sense-objectifying connection between this ego and that world-horizon and makes it understandable.

Such a reflection, then, which goes beyond what is casually understood as naturally matter-of-course, is the historical moment *par excellence*. On the one hand, it commands the knowledge which is obtained in every position as positional content, and on the other hand, it makes it understandable by tracing it back to the constitutive relations. To this extent, reflection remains bound to what in the present understanding is an object, i.e., it remains attached as starting basis to this knowledge which it is only supposed to ground: this knowledge of reflection is objective precisely in such an "object-relatedness," or it is nothing. An unrelated knowledge, a having that has nothing from anywhere, is a concept simply devoid of sense; it is utopian.

A knowledge does not lose the character of objectivity by the fact that it is perhaps no longer related to "world-objects" and rises above the ground of the natural thesis of being.[74] That the object-world is not a world-in-itself and that it is subject-conditioned does not abolish the objectivity of this cognition or these ascertainments whose object happens to be the phenomenological object, i.e., that phenomenon about whose being-in-itself absolutely nothing can be said. The objectivity of these objects which are to be called phenomena rests not on any metaphysically definitive mark of distinction, but on the "universality" in which they hold good. To elucidate "validity pre-suppositions" is the task of phenomenology—and it discovers thereby that validities are historically "variable." Thus it must say farewell to every demand for ascertainment of an ontically absolute "in-itself." With the correlation connections between ego and non-ego,[75] it always has in hand something that appears only historically yet is epistemologically grounded beyond question and absolutely valid within its context, but never metaphysically ultimate. This rational-critical correlation analysis, too, can now become a phenomenological object for itself. But it can be its own theme only on the occasion of an actually present sense-connection between ego and non-ego. It thus clarifies itself by a "material" which it *does not produce*. In that lies its object-relatedness, its objectivity.

To study the life-world for its "conditions of formation" is something different than to practice "life-world naiveté." To see the effect of the life-worldly apprehensions alongside an otherwise mostly scienticized interpretation of the world is something quite different from an unmindful living-along in life-world and science. But something must always be given, the one or the other—the life-world, the world of science, or something else[76]—so that on this occasion of givenness, the attempt can be made at all to disclose constitutional conditions.

Nor does the phenomenologist make the objects; he discovers them—he recognizes them as constituted this way or that. In so doing he is, of course, always already beyond the naiveté of determinate topical attitudes to the world and life. To that extent this framework of understanding, as framework and as reflective thinking that discovers horizon, is always "pre-mundane." This does not mean, however, that it could be anything at all without these world-contents; it is something with reference to them—namely, critical reflective thinking, which transcends the givens it needs as basis; and these givens are historical.[77]

The idea must be given up that transcendental subjectity is the "absolute ground for the generation of reality." It is the ground of objective knowledge which ascertains constitutional conditions and hence sense-connections—of knowledge which is related to these objects and makes statements about why they are the way they are.

The rediscovered naturalness and "self-evidence" of the so-called life-world has for phenomenological contemplation only the sense that here, in this eminent opportunity, implicitly the eternal demand to dismantle naturalness and matter-of-courseness—and particularly to ground the circumstances of understanding which exist here too—again becomes transparent. It will not be possible to go back with assurance to the matter-of-course assumptions of life-world conditions; rather, critical reason will here find one more "opportunity" to prove the regressive method. In short, transcendental phenomenology, even in the context of the life-world problematic, also discovers just metaphysics as a lived, as a "secret metaphysics," but it does not identify with any of these metaphysical positions.[78] If it did so, it would be giving itself up as a method. As a method it remains "clarification in the constant movement of self-elucidation." This means that its position—namely, knowledge presupposed to be universal and not just topical-doxic—can henceforth be maintained only if with respect to the topical-doxic positions something is discovered to be valid for all of them together. This something is, namely, that they actually are all "correlates of apprehending consciousness," correlates of structured reason. This is the assumption, the preliminary hypothesis. This is phenomenology's position. But, expressed in other terms, this means that its position is to be constantly repeated methodical-critical reflection. And precisely this emphasis on transcendental methodology prohibits any metaphysics of being, life-world, and science. It is when it gives up the connection with the topical-doxic positions that philosophy in general becomes utopian.[79]

To be sure, it also does not coincide with these positions. Naturally, understanding always exists already prephilosophically. But to bring understanding and what is understood into "constitutive relation-connections," to examine what is taken for granted for the grounds of its coming about is a task resulting from an original will to know which always transcends the matter-of-course once again. Philosophy devotes itself to precisely this totally unnatural and non-matter-of-course work on the phenomena. And that in the continual process of clarifying the sense-connections it also clarifies and brings to light the possibilities of reason itself is the historical aspect of all critical reflections.[80]

Critical reflection exists when, opposite the given, viewpoints which are not already simply present in the given are applied. To that extent, "critique of phenomena" is always more than "description of phenomena"; and phenomenology in its constant movement of self-elucidation clarifies itself by reapplying points of view which can have a grounding effect in a given situation. That reason now sees the phenomena as phenomena, that it apprehends worlds as constituted, transcendentally dependent worlds, may be the "self-evidence" through which phenomenology in its turn appears as transcendental ontology. It cannot be anticipated that even this starting situation of critical-reflective consciousness will become the object of renewed regression. But if it does, then the "movement to constant self-clarification of reason" is continued precisely thereby.[81] Phenomenologically, every metaphysical position—including this one— can without restriction be considered the starting basis for constitutional analyses; and none remains as given "in-itself." And so there is no possible metaphysics of reason or consciousness other than the "provisional" one— which lasts only until it is shown to be topical-doxic when the universal methodological postulate is applied. The return to the life-world *doxa* and to the appertinent "*topos* of understanding" is "*methodical*" *and not* "*metaphysical*" *reduction*. There result from it self-clarifications of reason, which are of a determinate kind but are themselves again objective— because bound to their determinate object. This knowledge, which keeps strictly within the framework of "*if-then*" connections, belongs to philosophy as a rigorous science, as it determines the grounding connections.

Chapter Seven

Phenomenological Method and Rigorous Science

In the essay *Philosophy as Rigorous Science* (1911), Husserl said of traditional academic philosophy that as science it had not yet begun; indeed, the reason for its inability to do so was basically that it had not become aware of the totally subjective beginning of all philosophical scientific positions. What tradition failed to do, phenomenology is supposed to accomplish. It is supposed to become science in the perfect sense—science which meets the highest theoretical requirements and in an ethical religious sense makes a life governed by pure norms of reason possible.[1]

The fact that it is possible to disclose an underlying life-world stratum behind the scientific world view, which now seems natural and matter-of-course, raises once again the problem of scientific knowledge, of knowledge in general.

Knowledge—in the realm of the scientific world-view—is the disclosure of world conditions which, contrary to all subjective appearance, exist "in-themselves" and have validity "for-themselves." But this knowledge in the sense of objective scientificity goes back, as was delineated above, to a "subjective world-design" which has gained acceptance historically and only for that reason has gone so completely unquestioned that now it seems to be "matter-of-course."[2] Galileo's "mathematization of nature" reinterpreted nature, which is topically-doxically pregiven.[3] With Husserl we can say, citing a key passage: "Prescientifically, in everyday sense experience, the world is given in a subjectively relative way. Each of us has his own appearances; and for each of us they count as [*gelten als*] that which actually is. In dealing with one another, we have long since become aware of this discrepancy between our various ontic validities.

But we do not think that, because of this, there are many worlds. Necessarily we believe in *the* world, whose things only appear to us differently but are the same. [Now] have we nothing more than the empty, necessary idea of things which exist objectively in themselves? Is there not in the appearances themselves a content we must ascribe to true nature? Surely this includes everything which pure geometry, and in general the mathematics of the pure form of space-time, teaches us, with the self-evidence of absolute, universal validity, about the pure shapes it can construct *idealiter*. . . ."[4] The question is whether the natural-scientifically contrived world, whether the mathematized world is the true world.

The Galilean "self-evidences" of a particular conception of nature can *de facto* be unmasked as historical (historically developed) matter-of-course assumptions—i.e., as something which is precisely not "in-itself," but corresponds to a determinate interpretation-design of subjectity. From the vantage point of the scientific world view, the life-world appearances are absolutely all pure *doxa*: merely subjective opinions about a determinate subjectively relevant *topos* of what exists. Indeed, for the scientist, the life-world is not the world in itself. That is also why, to science's objective look, the life-world seems to be completely insignificant. To the very extent that it has no connection with the supposed world-in-itself, the life-world is ignored or dissolved in the scientific attitude.

The "scienticized world view," which, according to Husserl, stands completely under the sign of Galileo, relates only to the general aspect of an object graspable in size and number, which object then in turn, as a concrete object, simply represents a particular case of the appertinent law. Its essence lies in the laws of its fixed constitution, which is the mathematized one.

With such a concept of knowledge, there can hardly be a science of the life-world encompassing the very province of what remains prescientific. This dilemma necessarily leads to a discussion of the "concept of knowledge" in general and, at the same time, a discussion of the subjectivity of the scientific world-design.

If a philosophical or a phenomenological consideration guarantees a science of the appearances in the sense that it discloses the foundational connections existing between given appearances, on the one hand, and the appertinent states of consciousness that condition these appearances transcendentally, on the other, and if the life-world is a phenomenon, then it must—as was shown above—also investigate the connections between the life-world and life-worldly consciousness. For nowhere is it written that a scientific clarification of these relations must take place only on the basis of Galileo's world view, i.e., a world view with natural-scientific overtones but one which originated historically. Nowhere is it said, also, that the actual positing-in-itself of a particular world view—for instance, the natural-scientific one—makes impossible an adequate scientific experience of its presuppositions and of the presuppositions of worlds other than the natural-scientific one, especially not if this positing-in-itself of the natural-scientifically interpreted world is not performed conjointly.[5]

In its fundamental reflective regression to the conditions of possibility, phenomenology obviously no longer presupposes that the natural-scientific world view is "self-evident," but at the same time it does not want to become "unscientific." In short, it does not go along with the absolutization of any particular world-design, not even the positivistic, physicalistic, or conventionalistic one, but rather, in reflection, it lets each one emerge from the conditions of its possibility. That is why "constitutional analysis" exists; that is the purpose of correlation research in the broadest sense. Implicitly, however, this means two things: science is not possible only on the basis of the natural thesis of being—and science still refers to objects, i.e., it is objectively conditioned, even when the objects are not those of the natural-scientifically "experienceable" world.[6]

Although life-world experience may seem secondary and irrelevant from the natural-scientific vantage point since it practically excludes an exact scientific treatment, it will not be called irrelevant if, and only if, the one world-design present here may assert its own right alongside natural science's different world-design of theorizations and substructions. This, in turn, will be completely the case only if the subject-relation also of the Galilean, i.e., of the so-called scientific, world-conception in general (which, strictly speaking, is just a "natural-scientific *doxa*") can be described. For only this invalidates its claim to absoluteness, which asserts that natural-scientific experience guarantees the mediation of such a thing as world-in-itself.

If this too is a historically temporalized and only subject-relative interpretation-design, i.e., one understanding of the world among other possible ways of understanding it, only then does a right exist to draw the life-world back into the light and let it play its role in its topical-doxic statements. So it is not just a question of how philosophy is a science, but also of the extent to which "science is already a philosophy."[7]

Rightly understood, this cannot be a matter of playing off the so-called life-world against Galileo's world and of wanting to find, in the life-world, the Absolute which the natural-scientific world no longer provides once it has been unmasked as conditioned by the subject. That would merely push the problem back by one historical stage. The historically earlier is not, just because it is earlier, one single bit closer to the Absolute. The "mystique of the earlier," the more original, the first, merely conceals the universal constitutional relation. The life-world conceptions which happen to precede the natural-scientifically interpreted world as a different design of subjective performances must not therefore be called more absolute simply because they are earlier or because they provide the starting basis for the formation of the natural-scientific world view.

That life-world experience, in contrast with experience conditioned by natural science, has this or that character is precisely not known to life-world experience itself. Not earlier/later, not original/derived, is the name of the opposition, but rather naive understanding on one hand and grounded understanding on the other is the way the phenomenologically formulated antithesis reads.

All positional understanding—i.e., all understanding that starts from a particular positing and accordingly must be declared to be topical-doxic—is and remains naive.[8] The "matter-of-courseness" of this naive uncritical understanding has nothing to do with earlier or later! The person caught up in the life-world takes his world view for granted as much as does the person living along quite naturally and "matter-of-coursely" in the scienticized world. The one and the other finds his apodictic ways of understanding completely "natural," or rather, "quasi-natural," however much they may differ from one another and however much one position—historically—may be conditioned by and depend upon the other.

Understanding may be called "not naive" only when it does not move within these matter-of-course assumptions, but takes itself as theme. Thus phenomenological reflection transcends both the life-world conception and the natural-scientific world-conception.

Enzo Paci, in a study of "life-world science," which thus apparently is quasi-naively considered possible, says the following: "The life-world must not remain as what it is in anonymous normal life, in everyday practice: it must become scientific."[9] And Paci presents this as Husserl's opinion. But such a statement is dubious. For why must the life-world become scientific? The life-world as life-world achieves in prescientific consciousness precisely what is expected of it: it is the "unquestioned" correlate of an understanding taken completely for granted. Why should it become the object of scientific elucidation after the fact? And furthermore, can it be so at all adequately?

Obviously, it does not at all have to do so by virtue of the life-world claims themselves. Only after the fact, for a "reflective" thinking that seeks to "ground" and to "understand," must the life-world be included in the circle of constitutional analyses. The meaning of knowledge and of science is obviously not exhausted, as this shows, with knowledge and with science as they are given in the life-world and in the natural-scientific realm or in a world substructed by natural science. Of course, knowledge about the origination of the prescientific and the scientific conceptions of the world and of life is also possible.[10] The opposition between the life-world and the natural-scientific conception of the world can thus be reduced to the following: what is an object, in the natural-scientific conception of the world, is for it the "in-itself" of things; and accordingly, to the natural sciences "objectivity" means that they are on the trail of and mediate the "in-itself" of things. On the contrary, what is apprehended in the life-world is *never* oriented "objectively and generally" toward the natural-scientific "in-itself," but rather it remains topically most proximate; and the plain ascertainment of what is most proximate is pure *doxa*.

Husserl, on the contrary, explains: "What is actually first is the 'merely subjective-relative' intuition of prescientific world-life."[11] But it is easy to see that this—his knowledge of subjective constitution—is not itself again merely subjective knowledge (or cryptic lore): as knowledge it is "objective," namely, related to what lies before it, about which something happens to be known."[12] Husserl and the interpreters of the life-world make their task more difficult by not clarifying the epistemological concept of knowledge and science. Knowledge does not become non-objective because it does not refer to the object in the natural-scientific sense. Conversely, it is logically forbidden to speak of a "subjective concept of truth" and of merely subjective knowledge, when actually what we have is "knowledge of something subjectively considered true." Knowledge of the subjective, knowledge also of the subjectively grounded, does not in the least subjectivize this knowledge, which is and remains a knowledge of a second kind: namely, ascertainment of what can be known in respect to the subject and the subjective grasping of the phenomenon.[13] This is the "object," and the knowledge that refers to it remains "objective." Husserl (and with him Enzo Paci and Ludwig Landgrebe) wants to establish a new concept of scientificity unencumbered by any trace of the natural-scientific substructions. So if the "rigorous science"[14] they call for is expressly not objective but is supposed to be subjective, then what this can and may at all mean must be examined.

The life-world conceptions are certainly not natural-scientific conceptions; accordingly, they have nothing to do with any scientific world-design accepted today. In correlation research, however, phenomenological constitutional analysis discloses that they too contain a world-design, although not that of the natural-scientific world conception, which came later. But that the data of the life-world are not and cannot be interpreted natural-scientifically is first discovered by *reflection*, which, however, does not thereby aim to state just any opinion whatever.

It is thus misleading to want to contrast "subjective sciences" (i.e., sciences of the life-world) with the "objective sciences" (i.e., those of the natural-scientific world view). Nor is that necessary at all. The phenomenological concept of phenomenon simply does not coincide with the Kantian concept of phenomenon. It does not have the content of being a phenomenon in the sense of the empirical natural-scientific world. But then it is not just knowledge of the phenomenon in the Kantian sense that is objective and universal, but perhaps also knowledge of the phenomenon in the broadest sense of a determinate other unity of sense and meaning that can be called objective and universal.[15] The phenomenological object is obviously a phenomenon in such a sense!

The objectivity of a knowledge and a science does not depend on whether that phenomenon which becomes the object of observation is a subject or an object in the worldly sense. Knowledge is objective and is a science whenever general meanings for a particular pregiven can be ascertained.[16] The fact that life-worldly consciousness and the life-world are interrelated, as well as the fact that the truths recognized there are relative, does not in the slightest relativize the ascertainment of such a relation.[17] And if the "physicalistic objectivism" inaugurated by Galileo means that on the basis of particular theoretical premises only the mathematical world represents the world-in-itself, then here too a "relational" connection exists between the presupposed apprehensions, on the one hand, and what results from them, on the other. Though natural-scientific truths constituted in a certain way have validity relative to Galileo's world-design, still the ascertainment of this relationality of the connection is not relativized again but holds true objectively—namely, in respect to the very connection present in reflection.

The scientific analysis of connections of apprehension, i.e., the analysis consisting of the phenomenological reductive approach and frequently mentioned together with Heidegger's "connections of understanding," always deals with subjective states of consciousness of the most primitive or the most sublimated kind, on the one hand, and with what is understood to take place in these subjective states, on the other. This constitutional connection is always unambiguous as to the phenomenology of the object, and the step-by-step description of this very connection is objective. The truth with regard to subjective performances does not now become a subjective truth simply because its theme is subjectity in its relation to the subjectively opened objective horizon.[18]

What makes the life-world phenomenologically important is not that essential orders of founding[19] with regard to the natural-scientific point of view can be discovered, as if one had gotten in hand the more underlying "in-itself" of all apprehensions; rather, the only thing that makes the life-world significant is that its analysis lets the historicity of all apprehension-designs of reason come clearly to light. This analysis too is not "matter-of-course," but demands on its part a particular state of consciousness, which in a particular sense is topical and disinterested.

When Husserl, in describing the classical scientific attitude, speaks of the "disinterested observer,"[20] this has the following meaning. Any understanding is locked within certain ways of being able to understand. Husserl analyzes, for instance, that of the "kinesthetic feeling of the body,"[21] Heidegger that of "*Dasein*, which in its being is concerned about this being itself."[22] These ways of understanding, as different and as stratified as they may be, must always already be present if they are to be "understood" as modes of a particular subjective design. However, this happens in reflection—which does not thereby kill the original understanding, but provides a fundamental proof for the "historical vitality of reason" in this very moment of reflection. For the attitude of reflection is the attitude of the disinterested observer insofar as in it the naive casual understanding interested purely in the pregiven is transcended! Whoever discovers the "matter-of-course" assumptions of a particular understanding, e.g., the sleepwalker-like unquestionedness of its performance, no longer stands within that understanding in naive performance. It is, then, not a matter of the pure repetition of the performance, but of understanding the "matter-of-course" assumptions in question—for this happens out of a new state of consciousness.

So even the "disinterested" phenomenological observer is "interested."[23] He is simply not interested in what was meaningful to naive understanding, but rather in grounding this interested relation! His interest is an interest raised to a higher "valence." It is directed at objectively ascertaining what emerges as life-world, as the world of knowledge, and as the world of *Dasein* in completely subjective and subjectively interested performances of understanding.

The "disinterested" observer still relates to an entity which he wants to clarify. But in order to disclose that entity, he cannot merely follow it imitatively. The phenomenological consciousness of this disinterested observer finds itself by historically critiquing positions pregiven in each case, and only by such critique. Critique and reflection show a self-limitation of subjectity which comes to light topically and, in the regresses to the present connections of understanding, does not simply keep going along with and prolonging them, but understands them objectively as subjective-objective context of understanding (i.e., as this givenness of a new order or higher sphere). Thus more always happens in reflection than

could be given in the original understanding. That the life-world is understood as preliminary stage for natural-scientifically possible substructions reaches further than what the life-world knows about itself.
Natural-scientific objectivistic research does not itself say that the natural-
scientific thesis of physicalistic objectivism and of the "in-itself" of the
mathematized world is subject-conditioned and subject-related, and hence
fully historical. Such a statement becomes possible only for reflective
consciousness which advances historically beyond this position. [24]

If the cognitive ego with its desire for knowledge, the subject, the human
being, *Dasein*, subjectity, always stopped with the above-mentioned performances taken for granted at the moment and were utterly engrossed in
their performance, that would produce "no historicization of reason."
Reason is really historical only once the connections of understanding are
understood, for example, as subjective-objective, i.e., once they are
"leaped over" in their topical ascertainment. But that is the case only in
the subsequent reflection. Reflection proves that reason is historical, and
to what extent—for with every critical reflection, it passes beyond the
naively practiced attitudes of understanding and abolishes them in their
temporarily taken-for-granted or postulated unquestionableness. That too
is one meaning of "universal reduction." [25]

Transcendental subjectivity, historical reason, is, then, the name not
for a metaphysical authority (*Instanz*) that stands in the background, that
is realized or clears itself successively. It is rather this concrete ego, this
subject, this human understanding itself, insofar as in the encounter with
the existent it always determines itself anew and distinguishes itself from
other things, or comes back to them reflectively. [26] And the entity that is
present before it is in each case the entire subjective-objective correlation-connection, which had previously gone unquestioned. By this correlation-connection (in the way it is interpreted and understood) reason
distinguishes itself historically from what it is not. For phenomenological
reflection, the life-world is as much a subjective "world-design" as is
physicalistic objectivism's world of knowledge. The ego reflecting upon
this topic has fixed and determined itself in a determinate manner, but
nonetheless absolutely objectively[27]—namely, with respect to the pre-
established givens meant in each case, which are either the life-world or
the natural-scientifically interpreted world, over which it elevates itself
with this reflection. Reason does not arise just anyhow and anywhere, but
with respect to something.

Critical reflection shows why consciousness has reached beyond the
situation of understanding in which everything is still mastered "matter-
of-coursely." To this extent, the attitude of the disinterested observer has
been called the attitude of the person who has "overcome and left behind

the fetishization of the world."[28] And it is right to say: "Phenomenological reduction should free us from fetishized interest, in order to make us accessible to a historical-teleological interest," as long as some unknown *telos* or other is not again made into a fetish![29] For the phenomenalizing of the world means, indeed, that the things, matters, and objects which have become phenomena always have their sense within an assigned context, but also that they retain that sense only there. Whoever stands in the midst of this context and does not step beyond it—for him of course the comprehensible phenomena at hand, on hand, and understandable within such a context, always mean "world-in-itself." Only the person who goes beyond the state of understanding can discover what is accessible on the particular grounds for conviction as relationally referred to and can therefore refer it to its appropriate framework of understanding. By the same token, however, every absolutization has been made impossible once and for all.

The phenomenological concept of knowledge and science which is manifestly involved in all the present inquiries claims that to objective reflection, subjective-objective connections remain generally accessible as those which they are "phansically." It is true that the theoretical disinterestedness which Husserl wants to anchor in principle by means of his phenomenological reductions is the precondition for the development of a non-dogmatized, non-metaphysicalized, non-fetishized interest.[30] But since the entire work of reflection consists in coming back to something given, phenomenological reflection—though it may step back as far as it will—can also never itself become a "tabooed position" or recommend a metaphysical position concretely for acceptance. It would even thereafter be able to make pregiven metaphysical dogmatisms the occasion for reflective regressive inquiry with regard to constitutional and validational connections.

Neither a "consciousness" in general, nor a "personal being," nor *Dasein*, which in its being is concerned about this being itself, are, then, for the phenomenological attitude "ultimates" in the absolute sense.[31] These Husserlian-Heideggerian criteria of understanding are always transcended in reflection, including in the current one, and by that very fact they are stripped of their absolute character, for they hold good for the respectively co-posited structure of understanding, and only for it. And *Dasein*, the personal being, the Cartesian *cogito*, is always already transcended when ways of understanding, of being, and of spirit, which provide the *universal* structures beyond the particularity of an actually existent *Dasein*, a concrete person, or a determinate habitualized ego, are ascertained in it.

Critical reflection, which apprehends something *as* something and as different from something else, is always proof of a "new state of consciousness."[32] Once again it becomes clear: it is not the earlier state of consciousness that is the more comprehensive one, but the one which seeks to give transcendentally valid grounds for the naive apprehensional attitudes. Naturally, science is an achievement of the human spirit, which presupposes its intuitive point of departure with historic specificity.[33] But the intuitions of science and of the life-world themselves must be interrogated as to what they have "in common." One is only too easily tempted to speak of a science of the life-world, in which the concept "life-world" has a meaning only as a counter-concept to the scientific world of physicalistic objectivism, and possibly is not intrinsically unitary at all and is a given only after the fact, for reflection.

If phenomenological constitutional analysis, as has been stressed again and again, tries to lead back to the relation existing between certain performances of the human mind which open up transcendentally, on the one hand, and what is made possible by these performances, on the other, then it accepts the *telos* governing them. But it would be wrong to conclude therefore that phenomenology is the science of the "secret *telos* of things," which must be disclosed in every single part of the world. It is a matter of the immanent *telos* of a particular state of consciousness, such as is contained in the correlation connection between the act of understanding and what is understood, not of a universal *telos* pervasively encompassing absolutely all states of consciousness and the worlds correlatively connected with them. That would be graspable only "speculatively";[34] and phenomenology, as long as it determines itself by the given, refrains from this very speculation.

When speaking of a "science of the life-world," as has become customary today in the aftermath of Husserl's *Crisis*, it must be asked what the particular scientificity of this discipline can consist in, since from the outset it admittedly is concerned only with what is apprehended topically and doxically.[35] The point of departure surely is that a prescientific experience lies at the basis of scientific experience; and this prescientific experience is also often called "pure experience."[36] But the astonishing thing about this is that—although it is supposed to be a matter of the doxic-topical as such (i.e., in each case of the singular and concrete), surprisingly, doxic-topical opinions are, in turn, interesting only from the viewpoint that they have "universal" forms. That, too, is absolutely not "self-evident," but should be raised to matter-of-courseness by the "arts of interpretation."

The Platonic form of world-doubling is known. Here, in the Husserlian life-world/world-of-science discussion, a world-reduplication with a complete change of ground seems to be involved. In Plato, the world of Ideas is first and original, while the world of things is an imitation, and also temporally later. In Husserl, the relation between life-world and world of science is apparently the opposite: the life-world with its typical structures apparently comes first, and based upon it, natural science first develops a system valid "in-itself," which actually is validated by that very fact.[37]

In this context a sharp distinction must be made between "methodological" and "metaphysical" treatment of the life-world problematic. The metaphysical point of view aims to make the science of the life-world into a universal science dealing with the one world of experience common to all.[38] Husserl himself seems to promote talk of the fundamental science of experience. For he expressly states: "Is not the life-world as such what we know best, what is always taken for granted in all human life, always familiar to us in its typology through experience? Are not all its horizons of the unknown simply horizons of what is just incompletely known, i.e., known in advance in respect of its most general typology?"[39] That these "matter-of-course" convictions are sufficient for life-world consciousness is certain. But that phenomenological analysis from the outset begins with the common features of the life-world must also become a problem.

For the "lived" topical and doxic positions too are not unitary and hardly ever display common features, except precisely this one: in none of them is the start made from the natural-scientific world-concept. Does this common feature justify speaking of a life-world only negatively?

Is the "substruction" of mathematized natural science—that the world erected by it involves the world-in-itself—now repeated by the fact that one universal typology of intuition and experience essentially peculiar to "man" as such is subsumed and ascribed to the thousands of different topical-doxic attitudes? Is the same line of inquiry as resulted from disclosure of the presuppositions in the Galilean world-design being repeated here, but just one step further back? Galileo's "physicalistic objectivism" could be unmasked as a "subjective hypothesis" which, however, lost its character of hypothesis with the passage of time and became the metaphysical dogma of the self-existing, mathematically determinable nature. Must the "life-world problematic" now be examined so that the installation of the life-world as final authority—desired analogously by the philosophers of being—turns out to be metaphysics?[40]

The metaphysics that underlies physicalistic objectivism has been shown by constitutional analysis to be a subjective attempt (corresponding exactly to a determinate state of consciousness). Thus talk of the life-world, and the life-world itself, must probably also be reduced to the appertinent state of consciousness. Man's so-called one, universal, and permanent state of consciousness, which is always reconfirmed in pure experience, such as he is supposed to possess completely unchanged—in the kinesthetic experience, for instance—this taken-for-grantedness, which has come to a stop in the life-world's naive orientation, must certainly again be made the theme of phenomenology.[41]

The "*a priori* of the life-world" should thus be brought out in contrast with the "objective-logical *a priori*" of the natural sciences.[42] This means no less than that the topical-doxic historically relative life-world, in all its relativities and thousands of particularizations, has a "general" structure of its own.[43] The analyses furnished as proof of this should for the present be regarded as successful. Yet whether such a universal structure, so acquired, would not have to be sought actually right *within* the topically-doxically isolating modes of behavior still remains an unsolved problem.

If the topical-doxic apprehensions, too, are determined by a regular structure, they appear to be constructed in full parallel with the natural-scientific conceptions modeled upon them, for which, in their particularity, they make determinate other regular structures binding. Husserl states expressly that as life-world the world has, even prior to science, the "same" structures that the objective sciences in their substruction of a world existing "in-itself" presuppose as *a priori* structures.[44] The world-reduplication becomes complete when one reads that the life-world is a spatio-temporal world, that it contains the bodies so familiar to us also as bodies, etc. Indeed, it is even added that the "categorical features of the life-world have the same names," but are not concerned, so to speak, with the theoretical idealizations and the hypothetical substructions of the geometrician and physicist.[45]

Although physicalist-objectivist reality is a subjectively contrived reality, it evidently does not lack a certain *fundamentum in re*—its *fundamentum in re* is the structure already universal in the life-world. In short, the universal is now being sought and found within the life-world in a formal-universal element which remains invariable amid all changes of the concrete life-worldly relativities.[46]

Certainly, the life-world as life-world has no knowledge of this common structure which is supposed to belong to it in general. The retrogression to life-worldly consciousness *as* life-worldly can thus not be the one that makes it possible to overcome the contradictions between lived life-world and contrived world of science. Since all "lived life" has its experiences topically and doxically, and since these experiences are constantly different, finally since the topical-doxic object of experience is *not* itself the object of topical-doxic experience, the retrogression to the life-world as metaphysics of the life-world can certainly not accomplish what the neometaphysical brand of transcendental phenomenology expects of investigations into the life-world: namely, the finite and unsurmountable overcoming of the lived contradictions.

Only methodological reflection can overcome these contradictions. For only it discovers the common structure of life-world experience, which in its "content" is absolutely antagonistic.[47] The fact that particular experiences occur on the basis of the same structural mode of lived experience does not in the least prevent an antagonism *in re* which can be seen from the contents. If, for instance, kinesthetic experiences of "I move," "I do," etc. display a general regular structure, this does not in the least abolish the fact that my bodily experience and the analogous experience of another's body come about in activity directed toward one another which may well be classified as hostile, antagonistic, or particularly articulated.

One too readily overlooks the topical-doxic, actually lived contents, reassuring oneself with the statement that as different as these contents may be, they are, at least in a general way, formed according to the same "formal," general structure. A return to life-worldly metaphysics would also bring back all these "contentual" antagonisms formed on the basis of the same constitutional conditions! This can certainly not be the goal of life-world investigations and of the demands erroneously attached to them! Only when the life-world science is carried on without thoroughly problematic metaphysical goals but purely for methodical reasons can a meaning compatible with the other tendencies of phenomenology be obtained.[48]

The regress to the life-world circumstances and structures satisfies certain requirements of knowledge: the natural sciences, with their claims to objectivity, are understood when they can be interpreted as developments of life-worldly types of experiences which have come about "historically." They are understood *then*; and the life-world conditions are also then understood in this, their "basis-function." But as soon as this life-world is in turn absolutized and presented as absolutely the only ground of experience that can in practice serve as starting point, the regress to the life-world no longer satisfies justified elucidating demands of knowledge.[49]

That this cannot be the case is immediately evident when one reflects that precisely the life-world is grasped not as life-world, i.e., as itself "grounded" subjectively and prescientifically. "Life-world," in this sense, is just the abbreviation for certain contents. The common form of these contents is precisely not "given" in the antagonistic life-worldly experiences, and so it is not a phenomenon. Here too the experiential ground of reflection lies beyond both the life-world and natural science, since it makes statements about both in their connection and in their relationship of dependency, statements which are absolutely beyond the reach of life-worldly and of natural-scientific apprehension. Any absolutization after the fact is something different than the life-worldly or natural-scientific apprehension, which is always lived naively and considered absolute. Phenomenological reflection recognizes both as subjectively grounded and grasps them as relatively referred to and relying upon a determinate state of consciousness. By recognizing this, which neither the life-world nor the natural-scientific conception was capable of doing, it makes obsolete every supposed journey back to the "mothers of being," to the absolute "sources of pure experience" which can be found somewhere or other—for the simple reason that pure experience does not experience itself as pure experience. It would betray an extraordinarily "unhistorical" thinking if historical reason, after having discovered by critical reflection that the world substructed by natural science and the life-worldly naive world are subjective correlates of certain appertinent modes of experience, were to terminate its continuous historical activity by an act of self-surrender, setting all hopes on the most recently discovered, fashionable life-world structures. Reason is historical reason only when it proves it by a continual process. And this process would be abolished if the initial life-world structures were posited absolutely, whereby such continuous proofs would be prohibited, decisionistically prevented by a *tour de force*.[50]

It is, on the contrary, a fact that reflection is always the reflection of a concrete person. And this concrete person with his reflection must constantly rely on pregivens about which he reflects and about which perhaps *only* he, in this particular situation, can reflect. By reflecting upon current reality he determines himself to what he is. He carries out his possibilities in dealings with what is pregiven.[51] The (Husserlian) man of the twentieth century reflects legitimately on what is "assigned" and "pregiven" to him. What is "closest to his heart" is the structure of the physicalist-objectivist natural science and its derivation from the prior life-worldly understanding. In this reflection, however, life-world and scientific designs, as the subject matter of reflection, never emerge from their relatedness to reflective consciousness. They are what they are here within the framework of possibilities which depend on that concrete reflective consciousness. This means that none of the correlates to which reflection refers can have absolute validity and be posited in themselves. They have obtained their particular meaning in reflection and with reflection; they retain it there, and only there.

Before phenomenological reflection upon the so-called "common structures" of the life-world apprehensions, the life-world was purely and simply different with respect to its real contents. It was infinitely split up topically and doxically. That it represents a structural whole of a particular kind becomes clear when historical reason lifts itself in critical reflection above the controversial standpoints naively held at each earlier stage. In this sense, the "methodical retrogression to the life-world" is also always a rising above it. For now it is interpreted, now it is no longer lived as a position. This, as well as the following remarks, is based on Husserl.[52]

The life-worldly consciousness, too, is a transcendental consciousness and, as phenomenological, it does not tolerate the slightest attempt to make it absolute. If the life-world were absolutized, the reflective attempt at grounding would fail, and what would be left is an absolutely posited world with determinate world-contents and world structures together with accesses to understanding.

The seductive idea of absolutizing the life-world goes back to the following reasons. Whereas the "substructions," the "idealizations," and the "logicizations" which must be assigned to every scienticized world view cannot be experienced directly, it is apparently possible to grasp the life-world in self-experience as it itself—indeed, unintermittently.[53] The life-world has the direct evidences which are missing in the scientific perspective. If, further, it is true that the life-world is directly present in perception, that the evidently given is given as itself experienced in immediate presence or as itself recollected in memory, then this life-world experience has a reference to time experienced and lived-through, in which all this happens, whereas mathematical substructions and idealizations lack such a temporally shaded experienceability.[54]

Finally, if it further holds true that the science of the life-world has the grounding task of bringing to validation the privileged status of "temporal experienceability," on which all objective-logical construction is grounded,[55] then the eminently temporal experience of critical reflection also asserts the claim to this same privileged status. For it is indispensable to all reflection that the moments to which it refers be experienced. Only when they are experienced can reflection make them its object. Thus if in the twentieth century the relation between the apprehension of life and the scientific point of view is the object of discussion, then reflection must be able to repeat both the life-world apprehensions and the arguments of science, in order to be able to refer to them in reflection. For both the life-world moments and the scientific ones exist nowhere in a Platonic, heavenly, glorified place, but only in the reflecting consciousness here and now. Here they have their place; and only here, from this relation to them, does reflection acquire its objectivity.[56]

If life is experienceable, one may always say that it is experienced directly through "seeing" and "intuition." However, it is not just that seeing or intuition grasps forms in life, but that the seeing itself has a particular "form," of which it is assumed even in the life-world that it is a universal form. Whether this form is typical and lasting would have to be determined by a phenomenological analysis of the lived topical and doxic attitudes. Though one may also speak of the temporal life-world's "intuitive mode of revealing itself,"[57] this does not exclude the possibility that there are totally different modes of intuition. Intuition and perception are themselves considered to be "typical" forms, whose typicality is obviously given for reflection and only for reflection.

Phenomenology, which claimed to offer rigorous science and showed that it is unscientific to leave certain moments of reality uninvestigated, then actually devoted itself to these moments. It did not allow itself to be harnessed to the pregiven world-framework; rather, it initiated the regress to the origin of this world framework, thereby making visible the subjective conditions under which certain objective statements can have validity. Further, it pointed out the subjective elements in physicalist objectivism and historicized this approach, too.[58] Finally, it highlighted analytically the connections that exist between the prescientific, immediately experienceable life-world and Galileo's scientifically interpreted world. This linkage was possible because the universal structures of the life-world supposedly anticipate the general structures of the world which is scientifically posited as in-itself. By this entire procedure the scientific world-conception has been stripped of its claim to absoluteness in Galileo's sense and the grounding right of life-worldly experiences has been regained.

Since all the above-mentioned experiences were not made "naively" but were acquired by reflective reason, which makes its appearance historically, the metaphysical regress to *one* of those moments—which cannot become transparent to themselves in their mode of functioning—is prohibited as an absolute solution precisely by virtue of the results obtained. Methodical regress thus continues to be required: it is a *conditio sine qua non* of all reflection. Without the reference to experiences it hangs in the air. But reference to experiences and the recognition of these experiences as the absolute ground are two different things.[59]

Even the absolutization of the life-world and of the experiences determined by the life-world cannot prevent reason, which temporalizes itself historically, from inquiring into these new "matter-of-course" convictions which are simply taken for granted by *opinio communis*—i.e., it must ask why it is assumed that these pure life-world experiences, or any others, can be posited absolutely. Under what conditions is such a procedure meaningful, and what presuppositions must be present for such an interpretation to take place? This is what it wants to know.[60]

The reflective approach to knowledge always reaches beyond what is given in any other kind of knowledge. Reflection asks about the grounding of all cognitive claims made anyhow or anywhere.[61] In order to be able to reflect on them, it must have gone through all these positions. However, it repeats them, not for the sake of repetition, but in order to establish correlation connections between a determinate understanding and knowledge, on the one hand, and what is communicated thereby, on the other. The same thing also holds true when the life-world science is supposed to be the ultimate starting ground. Only for a very determinate consciousness, and not for just any consciousness, can the life-world science provide the ultimate, and ultimately binding, evidences. So how this consciousness, which can satisfy those claims and hence corresponds to that view, must look if it is to clarify this is from now on the urgent task of phenomenological reduction. In short, phenomenological reduction is not at all finished because an "outline" of the various stages has been listed. Phenomenological reduction means *continual* tracing-back to self-enclosed grounding horizons. Only from this vantage point can the "new life-world dogmatism" then also be given its modest right—the right to be one positional metaphysics among many other possible ones, one which, in any case, has been and is now being advocated decisionistically.

An ever open system of knowledge acquired by reflection starts here.[62] What is "prepredicatively hidden" becomes an object of investigation, and in turn the phenomenological method proves to be a method of legitimation and not a construction of final solutions or speculation on ultimate positings. Even when the so-called life-world science is supposed to be grounded in the "world of common life"[63] or in the world of "straightforward intersubjective experience,"[64] precisely this is a position at first merely assumed to be matter-of-course. But a particular conception of the life-world is envisaged thereby: a "life-world of common features." It would easily be possible to disclose a life-world of completely incompatible oppositions which is not a construct, but is lived just as originarily, naively, and unreflectedly as the life-world of the so-called formal common features, discerned only after the fact.

For it makes a difference whether what interests me about the actual life-world are the "structures," which are common, or the lived "contents," which stand in the sharpest opposition to one another! The life-world is *not* characterized just by the fact that the structures, for instance, of hatred or anger, or physical sensations and qualities of motion, are typically inherent in its structure. It is characterized at least as much by the circumstance that my anger is directed against his anger, my sensation against his sensation, and thus is something completely different in content. What needs to be said on this subject can be summed up as follows.

Even the "direction of interest" at the formal or structural moment—

which allows interest in the actual concrete content of antagonisms to recede in favor of the sameness of the modes of apprehension—is itself a direction of interest within a determinate, concrete ("existential") state of consciousness. It is in no way matter-of-course, but rather is also historically grounded. Only the person who disregards the material content of all topical-doxic experiences, i.e., the really concrete-historical contents of life-worlds, which are subjectively dispersed in an infinite variety of forms, will catch sight of the formal structure of such a thing as "life-world in-itself."[65] For such a consciousness, and only for it, *"the"* life-world science will become the ultimate ground of absolute evidences in the sense described above, i.e., the metaphysical starting ground. Whoever, on the contrary, remains aware of the subjective conditions for all positings, even those meant most absolutely and most objectively, will, even here, have to inquire concerning the conditions of possibility. He will then apply phenomenology's "methodical conception of knowledge"—namely, that knowledge is given only where groundings have been provided, although they may also again and again be recognized historically as valid only within a determinate horizon of understanding.[66] In critical reflection this horizon has its appropriate place.

Husserl's attempt to describe the life-worldly problematic can be characterized as follows: contrary to all derivations *from above*, now a disclosure *from below* should be carried out.[67] The true *a priori* of knowledge, then, lies not in just any transcendental, metaphysical positings-in-themselves, i.e., neither in Platonic Ideas, nor in Augustinian creative thoughts of God, nor in Leibnizian "possibilities of a divine intellect," but rather in the evidences of the prescientifically apprehended life-world. The *Crisis* seems in some passages to want to claim by the given positive analyses that the objective *a priori* of the Galilean sciences is already grounded in general structures of immediate ("life-world") experience. Although the life-world remains concretely doxic through and through, it always intrinsically contains the universal which authenticates science. The immediate experience of spatiotemporality is differentiated from the categorial structure of space and time as conceptualized form of intuition.

The required life-world "science" can disclose what the person engaging in life-world opinions does not see and what the person standing on the ground of the objective natural sciences in principle excludes as not worth knowing. Thus the theory of a universal "prelogical *a priori*" is developed here.[68] Husserl called it a pure "theory of essence of the life-world."[69] Even if it is now stated that the newly found structures must not be separated from life itself, which flows along in time, from which they were obtained and in which alone they have their reality, one problem must not be overlooked. Certainly, the re-Platonization of the typical structurings, i.e., their transposition to a region of so-called eternal essences, must be excluded from the outset. But if this also actually succeeds, nevertheless in principle the question as to whether the "in-itself" of reality may not now have been found in the "life-worldly structures" after all still remains open. If that were the case, then phenomenology as the science of the life-world would end in a metaphysics of the "typical forms" of "straightforward intersubjective experience," of "common life,"[70] of intuitive "schematizations," etc. But the fact remains, on the contrary, that in the encounter with such a "permanent and typical factor,"[71] which seems to be taken for granted as the universal ground of experience, phenomenology can only raise the question of the genesis of this assumed certainty; it cannot, however, settle for the retreat to, or profession of, any matter-of-course convictions.

Whether, when the basic life-worldly structures of the later scienticized view are sought, it is a question of "immutable" forms—this is and remains a problem. It is not just a matter of disclosing the universal forms of the life-world; the genuinely phenomenological goal can only be to ask whether the apparently evident immutability actually contains a genuine immutability and under what conditions it stands. And even if there are formal universal structures of the life-world, it always remains an open question whether there are, in addition, formal-universal structures of the "self-development of the life-world."[72]

And phenomenology, in applying its correlation method, can never stop just anywhere. In the last analysis, this means that even the structures and universal forms belonging to life-worldly consciousness are not "in-themselves" and provide no "world-in-itself"; they permit an "absolute" knowledge only within the concretely given context. However, to posit this context in metaphysical absoluteness, and hence to make it definitive, is, in principle, not possible for the phenomenological method. The task of phenomenology is to transform what is simply given "ontically" within a particular horizon of experience into something "ontologically" experienced. Phenomenology determines why this or that ontic element, with all its horizonal indications, is constituted. Thus it becomes implicitly an ontology of temporal reason, namely of reason that "temporalizes" itself. Reason and consciousness do not exist just anywhere; rather, they exist only within the horizon-experiences of a grasping that is always structured transcendentally in a particular way.[73] Since this grasping varies, the grasped worlds and world-connections, including all theoretical, emotional, volitional, and existential correlates of understanding, also vary with it.[74] Tracing down the changes in this grasping means to get to, or at least to try to get to, the forms of change in the transcendental structure of rational consciousness.

In conclusion, the life-world reduction means that it is certainly possible to go from the substructions of science back to the immediate typical experiences of common life. If thereby the liberation from a "determinate fetishization"[75] is accomplished, still no other solution has yet been found. A "grounding-science reduction" must also be carried out, and its content would be a return to the "basic form of scientificity" in general, i.e., the form of critical-grounding knowledge beyond all metaphysicizations.[76] What matters is not the "content" of any world of science, persons, *Dasein*, or life, which has become ontically-ontologically manifest, but only the form of uninterrupted and incessant reexamination. Only then is even the thought of a fetishization, of a metaphysics "from below," starting from the life-world, shown to be impossible in principle, and phenomenology is performed as "rigorous science."[77]

Chapter Eight

What is Appearance in its Appearance?

Phenomenology is thus what it is by virtue of its method of legitimation; and this legitimation too takes place through reflection. This method claims to attain and guarantee a special degree of scientific reliability. Moreover, it is supposed to be applicable to the treatment of questions about subjectity and objectity which traditionally were excluded from philosophical discussion—to transcendental meta-questions.[1] If phenomenology claims to be a "universal," "absolutely grounded," self-justifying science, this claim must now be no less grounded with respect to method.[2] This means that the asserted and demanded universal self-legitimation will also have to occur with respect to itself—it must make itself eminently conspicuous in elaborating this method, and it makes possible the discussion of the grounding science![3] This means that a discussion and description of the phenomenological method can, in any case, offer no report on the course of Husserlian, Heideggerian, or Schelerian phenomenological research into method up to now. For that very reason the motif of "transcendental self-grounding" must again and again, rightly, be placed in the center of methodological discussion, although this certainly was not an obvious *leitmotif* of phenomenological research since its beginnings. For to carry on phenomenology at first meant to push ahead into the sense-horizons which opened up from the things and to disclose the grounding connections, which possibly are contained in the pregiven data precisely as "anonymous" prior performances of reason. Moreover, this is the approach for all phenomenological analysis and hermeneutics. If ultimately the double meaning of "appearance," *phainomenon* and *phansis*[4] (which phenomenology, as its name suggests, had in mind), must be emphasized and made the starting point of more far-reaching interpretations, this is another indication of the extent to which the results of phenomenological explication inherently press to "ultimate" motivations. Where Husserl's work, which has already become historical, ends, current research must begin.

Naturally, the phenomena with which phenomenology generally must deal are phenomena of consciousness and only of consciousness. This consciousness, as intentional consciousness, constitutes its objects, but it does not create them. Phenomenology's method will, then, be intentional analysis which uncovers objectivities as unities of sense. It always resorts to direct evidences; the question is only whether this intentional analysis does not need to be complemented by a higher-level procedure when, for instance, the egoicalness of the ego, which is the opposite of mundane objectivity (*Gegenständlichkeit*), comes into view.[5] Moreover, it must be remembered that intentionality at first probably designated simply the peculiarity of consciousness that it always is consciousness *of* something— and hence it was a purely psychological concept—and also that the field of the psyche, like everything that must be called "objective" in the broadest sense, is also part of the domain of what is meaningfully constituted and legitimated. It must therefore be asked how "intentionality," a technical term in psychology, ever became a basic phenomenological term.[6] The arguments on this subject are as numerous as they are well-known. They can be summarized as follows.

The fact that perception requires something perceived; that judgment requires something judged (and adjudged); hence, in sum, that "something" stands in relation to psychic processes as processes of consciousness, "something" which is given in all these processes without coinciding with them—this fact is clearly known and relevant in the area of psychological research. Here we already have "transcendence within immanence."[7] The question still remains as to how such a fact is supposed to have more far-reaching systematic effects. At best one can probably say at the outset only that it involves a correlation connection which is just one fact among many other possible facts. The state of the question can apparently be radicalized only once the really observable single connection has been shown to be a "universal constitutional connection." This would mean that everything we deal with when something appears in consciousness is a phenomenon. Such a radicalization of the approach naturally entails the renunciation of all customary ideas of things-in-themselves and appearances in which, as mere appearances, precisely the essential does not appear.[8] So if the phenomenological method wants to be a universal method, it will have to be responsible even for the treatment of so-called metaphysical questions. Metaphysics will, however, no longer be a science of realms and things that lie behind the appearances; instead, if the constitutional problematic is really grasped, it will pay attention to the performances which must start prior to the "having of any object"—i.e., to the performances in which an intentional correlate of cogitative accomplishments (*vermeinende Vollzüge*) enters into view and interprets itself, so that it is possible at all to speak of "something." Even the so-called metaphysical object legitimating itself as this or that remains a phenomenon. This view, of course, runs counter to tradition. Husserl therefore gives detailed information about the tradition and the proclamation of an epoch-making beginning.[9]

Implicitly contained in the general view of the nature of consciousness as an intentional consciousness is the possibility of attaining a single, quite determinate metaphysics—a metaphysics which has to do with the "presuppositions" under which that which is and comes to appearance as being can be given. That this does not result simply in a reference to Kantian philosophy must, of course, be shown again and again as intentional analysis and constitutional research are carried out. [10] But from the beginning, the decisive difference becomes clear: if by phenomenon is understood whatever presents itself at all in a determinate sense to consciousness, then even the Kantian thing-in-itself can show itself only as a phenomenon (in phenomenological terms, namely, as legitimating itself in a determinate sense as "this-there"), or it simply is not accessible—and that means, in terms of consciousness-theory, that it "is" not. Phenomenology, in its formation and further development, no doubt takes a universal transcendental turn, but this does not mean a turning to Kant in the sense of refurbishing Kantian idealism and critique. Transcendental philosophy and Kantian philosophy are certainly not synonymous.[11] And reference to a "crypto-Kantianism" leads nowhere.

Phenomenology, having made the concept of intentionality an underlying basic concept of its discussions, goes beyond the mere classification and description of "psychic phenomena" (in Brentano's sense): the essential difference between the execution of an act and what the act means can generally be shown whenever one inquires into the mode of being of any scientifically relevant objects. For example, the phenomenological "foundation of a pure logic" and its radical separation from empirical psychology contributed to this proof—for the concepts of logic, the states-of-affairs, relations, judgments, conclusions, and proofs command their own inner objective relationship to one another.[12] Subjective processes must, indeed, always be initiated so that objective structures may appear in consciousness here and now. For Husserl first develops the procedure of intentional analysis "when analyzing what happens when a judgment or a colligation is made, and the manner in which the difference between an evident and a false judgment is revealed in this subjective act of judgment and in which talk of the truth and falsehood of the judgment refers to processes which can be shown in these differences" (Landgrebe). So phenomenology deals with the sense which must be disclosed successively. Logical, aesthetic, ethical sense is just as much a particular case of intended sense in general as is "ontological sense."[13] Phenomenology is universal sense-research at the very moment when every existent or what is considered to be an existent, when every given or what is considered to be given, when every mental object or what is considered to be a mental object, is grasped and interpreted as sense-determined in this consideration.[14] Everything that is pregiven, that becomes transparent in consciousness, that in any way makes itself noticeable as relevant, is, as something determined in that way, a bearer of sense. But a new sense is also obtained from the so-called fundamental ontological questions themselves.[15] If an existent, regardless of its kind, can always be, for the apprehending consciousness, just the existent of a particular sense, then the road to grasping being goes via the explication of the sense of the existent; and even "fundamental ontology" is a "philosophy of sense" (*Sinn*) insofar as it is concerned with the *sense of being*. Phenomenology thus grounds ontology; ontology does not precede phenomenology. Such an explication occurs in so-called "experiencing presence" (*erfahrendes Dabeisein*), which term we can use to designate the originary self-bestowing, the warranting evidence. The concept of being is here obtained from how an existent makes itself evident in its sense.[16] Since such explication, however, takes place in subjective processes (for the merely objective cannot see through itself), sense attains givenness at all only in them. Thus the subjective processes must be characterized as sense-bestowing and hence as constitutive: there is no intentionality of consciousness without a sense-bestowing function! But the conveying of ever determinate existential validity characterizes sense-formation as a whole, for nothing that becomes graspable as "something" lacks a determinate character of being.[17]

At this point, of course, the question arises as to what the term "subjective" has to mean. For certainly objects, things, the world of things, for example, are not dependent on being experienced individually ("subjectively"). What is present here and now as a psychic process, and as such can in turn become the object of oblique reflection, certainly does not *produce* things in reality. Rather, the thing, any thing, stands—as what it is and means—more or less evidently before the individual's receptive look, in which it is merely grasped consciously.[18] But that this thing is independent of our apprehending individual gaze, and that it remains what it is, belongs to the very sense that constitutes it; this is the "sense of the object," of the "mundane object." The question of the nature of the external world in itself is quite a different question, a metaphysical question.

The individual subject, in his experiencing life, appropriates the determinations of being and sense which hold true of an object.[19] To do so, he uses his own original experience, as well as the communications of others or the traditional views. To this extent reproductions of past sense-constitutions always take place. In other words, what is present in consciousness is, in the apprehension of the pregiven, always pre-explicated in a determinate way; thus it implicitly contains within itself the sense-bestowing performances of others—"sense-implications" which refer to other performances and other intentions which can in turn be investigated anew.[20] Facts, objects, and states are and remain what they are independently of whether their sense is grasped by me or not. But if their sense is grasped at all, precisely its independence of the subjective, experiencing, individual thinking is, in each case, one of its essential determinations: such an intersubjective encounterability—which is possible in principle—belongs to the sense of "objectivity."[21] Natural phenomena and objective (objectified) psychical processes are thus explicated according to their sense "by me" alone, but in principle they are grasped in coinciding explications and only thereby identified. The sense of that phenomenon which we call the "objective" or "objectively existing" object consists in the fact that what it means is reached in its sense only when it is grasped and accepted as something objective accessible to everyone. What "objective being" is, is thus reduced exclusively to this sense. The phenomenon that is right before our eyes in this way is all that consciousness can attain. No thing-in-itself and no "supra-existent," "transcendent" realm lies behind it. When something is grasped *as* something, it stands in view in a certain sense, and its apprehension is exhausted in this.[22] There is no other metaphysics than the analytics of presuppositions.

Actually something understood as "objective" contains a reference to other persons, who in principle must be able to grasp the "objectively" meant object as to its sense in the same way as I. Precisely this implication now also leads further. Intentional analysis shows that when—for instance, in subjective performances—I experience something as objective, I must, with this experience (something is "objective," i.e., has "general" validity), continue to rely on the possible subjective performances and experiences of others, who are ideally co-posited or co-intended. From here new horizons of constituted sense-formations constantly open up. Any question about the determinate kind of existent, about its "what" and "how," can be answered only in a determinate sense. And the same is true if, for instance, one places the question of being itself at the beginning. Even the question of being and the question of the kinds and particularities of being already become as questions "questions of sense." Consequently, science, including the grounding science, deals only with structures of sense.[23] But if sense always refers back correlatively to the performances in which it becomes graspable, then the analysis of these subjective operations is not irrelevant. Intentional analysis draws its justification from here. Moreover, it must not be forgotten that the correlative appertinence of performance and sense also requires constitutional research, because sense and meaning are conveyed in the intentional performances of consciousness. In these sense-bestowings is constituted what is considered at all as a "this-there." That is where the groundings take place. Yet facticity is the field not of phenomenology and logic, but of metaphysics.[24]

Wherever the question of an object's mode of being is encountered—whether in delimiting the logical from the psychological, or in separating value from ideal—the very question as such always demands a relation back to some sense. Even being can be spoken of only in a determinate sense. Thus the regress to sense-research is complete. And it follows from this that one cannot simply start dogmatically with being; rather, constitutional problems in the area of sense are ultimate—for the sense of being is likewise just a case of constituted sense in general.[25] Ontology is really something secondary compared with the evidences of phenomenology.[26] This statement makes no prejudgment at all about the special sense in which such being of any ontology is understood. To be present, past, or future, to be beautiful, good, right, real, ideal, irreal, etc., designates in each case a particular sense through which something is an existent for consciousness in this its determinability. Where sense is present (and it is present in the so-called fictional, hallucinated, phantasied, no less than in what is perceived, felt, experienced), structures are meant which can be investigated. Here the field of a "universal analytics and hermeneutics" opens up. For the sense-formations which first make an x into a being for us are everywhere accessible to further explication and have an inner relation to possible new experience—not just in the realm of representations. If one allows "the things themselves" to speak, experience must not be conceived uniformly, i.e., determinate contexts of experience lead to a determinate sense of being.[27] To know something new can actually lead to a new type of cognition. Thus being, in the sense of traditional logic, depends on correlatively attached and appertinent contexts of experience—the predicative judgments, inference, etc. Therefore even here the possibility and importance of prepredicative experiences becomes apparent, and the so-called "life-world experiences" constitute a case of experiences, and only *one* case.

The phenomenological "principle of self-legitimation" forbids that *one* context of possible experience, as for instance merely the predicative, or only the prepredicative, be posited as absolute. Accordingly, even from this it can be shown, among other things, that being-on-hand, as it is present in the predicative judgments as being in the sense of logic, cannot exhaust the entire sense of being, as long as an immediate living-through of the operations (and not merely a grasping of what is meant in these operations, i.e., of the sense) is considered possible.[28] For just as different kinds of connections of subjective experience correspond to every different mode of being, similarly one can start from the functioning experiences, on which then (because of their qualitative difference) in each case something different, i.e., possibly also a differently intended way of being, depends, together with a different entity existing in a different manner. Once again, "to constitute something different" can be read as "different constituting."[29] For "every phenomenology, consistently elaborated, must come to all possible objectivities as objectivities of possible knowledge."[30]

Intentionality, as a basic concept of phenomenology thereby achieves it not only that the correlative connection between the ways of experiencing and the appertinent determinate sense is grasped, but also that the constitutional problematic becomes generally visible. This starting point acquires philosophical significance. In the psychological realm, empirical consciousness stands opposite pregiven things, which are taken into grasp by inclusion of corresponding ways of experience. However, where matters, things, objects themselves are understood as sense-formations, the intentionality of the determinate consciousness is disclosed as a functioning performance through which this or that sense is mediated. The *intentio recta* grasps givens; the *intentio obliqua* makes this presumed simple grasping of objects understandable as the constitution of objects.[31] Transcendental lines of inquiry are brought into view by this reflection. For intentionality acts constitutively even when it is a mediated immediacy. If that is so, then the existent, which is indeed always an existent in a determinate sense, contains within itself the reference to the constitutive performances that lead to it. In short, the existent, in its determinate particularity, serves necessarily as clue in the quest for the correlatively appertinent constitutive performances.[32] This means that decisively advanced philosophical research in search of grounding connections and foundations can no longer start or stop "anywhere" with pregivens, but must trace "everything" that is presumed to be simply "given" back to the subjective, intentional, constitutive, transcendental functions through which what is, is for consciousness.[33] The existent itself, which remains something sense-determined wherever it is present as a phenomenon, is placed inside given constitutive sense-connections and queried concerning the grounding, giving performances. Yet it is a phenomenological conviction that it is not just the actual experience occurring here and now that is important; rather, the essential connection and the essential relation must be clarified with respect to constitutions. Of course, the question arises as to whether this marks a boundary of the phenomenology carried on by Husserl which does not necessarily mark the limits of phenomenological research in general.[34] For just as, say, the ego becomes a phenomenon and then— since the essential relations are supposed to be sought out—statements are made with regard to an *eidos*, "ego," is then not precisely *that* lost about the ego which makes up its uniqueness, its thisness, and is universalized in the *eidos* "ego" or, in brief, is "objectified"? As in fundamental ontology there is the distinction between "existential *Dasein*" and "existential structure," here perhaps the opposition between ego-reflection and immediate self-consciousness must be noted. There is no doubt that reflection, in experiencing co-presence (*Dabeisein*), objectifies any *x* whatsoever. The question is only whether the egoicalness of the ego can be experienced only by way of reflection, or whether there is here a peculiar way of living-through which the ego does not objectify and make into an existing meaningful whole, but which on the other hand is not nothing. Husserl, no doubt, posits the standpoint of reflection absolutely.[35] Current phenomenological research, which goes beyond Husserl and takes into account the problematic statements of existential ontology, must devote itself to a discussion of these questions. In so doing, it must, among other things, reach back to the results of general epistemology and formal linguistics.[36] For they refer to reason; and "reason itself, including theoretical reason in particular, is a form-concept."[37] That is the location of the universal.

But it must be established first of all that universal sense-research is understood primarily in such a way that the sense-connections considered in principle to be intersubjective are disclosed, whereby the actual subjective giving performances remain accidental and serve only as an example for certain essential performances. If the things themselves in their sense point to particular forms of access, then this determinateness implies that the actual individual access in each case is merely a case of accessability that is in principle possible. Intentional analysis is thus not analysis of merely actual but of any possible connections; and it accordingly relates not to unique but rather to essential circumstances. Here again it must be left open how it relates to the ego and to functioning egoicalness. Can egoicalness be grasped in its essence at all, or does this contain an inadmissible anticipation, i.e., "objectivation"? In any case,

Husserl repeatedly initiates sense-investigation (*Besinnung*)—"sense-investigation as activity and the phenomenology of sense-investigation about the goal of a universal science."[38] But sense-investigation always seems to remain "reflection."

Any psychological reflection that adverts to psychical facts takes the "object" of its advertence ("the psychical") to be something given, constituted, present—that is, it persists in the space of the constituted and does not bother with the constitutional connection which is inherent to the essence of intentionality. On the contrary, the phenomenological expansion of consciousness goes only so far as to claim that it indeed contains everything that can be thought meaningful, necessarily in this its sense "that it can occur only for consciousness."[39]

For psychology cannot be the "fundamental science." Psychological reflection takes the world, the subject, and the subject-object connection as an existing, indeed present linkage, whereby the existing subject can somehow relate to the likewise existing object and establish a particular describable relation. Existents and contexts of being are indeed experienced in psychology—but they do not become clear *as* constitutive connections of intentional consciousness. That products of sense-formation are present when the ego has to do with existents interpreted in this way or that does not become clear, because it is not the individual ego-subject here and now, with his actual psychical experiences, who produces "objects" or does anything at all to the existent. Psychology does, of course, have to do with this concrete empirical ego. But there is in this regard a double "latency" of the ego—the originary latency of the subject which has not yet developed to self-consciousness, and the latency of the human ego, which is subject of the act.[40] Experiencing, grasping, comprehending, understanding, knowing are characterized in normal language usage as acceptance of the self-existent, as acceptance of something that is. Psychological reflection brings to visibility only actual, empirical, conscious advertences of a subject to such a, so to speak, self-existent entity (to which nothing happens through these advertences). The subject already understood in this way or that has precisely this or that relation to an object standing opposite it, which is not ontically "generated" or "created" in this relation. The phenomenological method, however, wants to exhibit the transcendental constitution of objects as they are present and can be encountered as phenomena in ontic consciousness. For this purpose, reiteration of the disclosure of the latent is necessary.[41] It has nothing to do with the ontic "generation" and "creation" of things or of the "world." The problem of constitution is and remains a transcendental-philosophical, an "epistemological" problem.[42] It belongs to the sense of transcendentality to be the logical presupposition for something real. If phenomena as phenomena of consciousness always depend on the performances through which they become present in consciousness, then these performances, too, function in a particular sense and are not empty performances. When an existent is known at all (i.e., when it is a phenomenon in consciousness), then determinate performances of consciousness functioning in a determinate sense must have been done, must have happened; so they remain implicitly (correlatively) attached to the sense of this phenomenon. Hence the first task which the phenomenological method has to fulfill is shown to be the universal disclosure of this implicative combination.[43] But "life as a performing goes first; it becomes thematic in critique."[44] Sense is the sedimentation of sense-constitutive transcendental performances. It serves, on the other hand, as a clue for seeking out these performances of life, which at first remain hidden. The sense-implications refer directly to the constitutional problematic. It becomes the theme in every form of critique. Intentional implication is thus a key point for discussing the problem of constitution. It makes intentional analysis possible at all. Here then the statement holds true: "That such constitutive performances have always already happened, so that some existent or other can be pregiven to us simply as such and such—that is nothing that would simply be disclosed. Rather, the performances are implied in its sense in such a way that it refers to them; these references can be disclosed as such which necessarily belong to the stock of being of the existent" (Landgrebe). But "strictest science would require that in the beginning nothing be presupposed of the world, not even the being of a world at all. . . . What is left? Naturally, the subjective itself."[45]

The references lead matter-of-coursely to horizons always opening up anew. For the implicative co-positings need not have become explicit from the first. Very often they are first disclosed by clues in the inner sense of the given, and the disclosure is guided empirically by the "principle of significancy." And the disclosure continues until the legitimation of "pure transcendental subjectivity."[46] The continuous course of scientific research and the formation of ever more complex life-experiences finds a grounding here. Nothing else is present here but the expansion of the horizon of the known. Yet such experience naturally always takes place on the ground of mundane processes of experience accentuated by the context. It is a trait of mundaneness that something is implicitly posited as experienceable in principle (i.e., not just accessible to *me*). Such experienceability requires that intersubjective encounterability be part of the sense of the meant object. Something is objective when it carries this accent of sense. That is to say, the relation to others (in principle to everyone) is a trait of objectivity, because the notion "objective" means what is accessible not just to *me* in my individual subjective acts. Here the whole problematic of solipsism follows.[47] The thing indeed depends on sense-bestowing performances, but not as if those performances were the empirical acts of real subjects here and now. It belongs to the sense of anything objective that it can in principle enter into possible experiential processes of others, and can enter them as the same. It follows from this that even in examining the theoretical sciences dealing with objective givens, implicitly the other is associatively co-posited in each case, because the phenomenon of "objectivity" makes no sense without others as potential apprehenders.[48] Here we have before us just one example of determinate phenomenological explication of sense.[49] These associative, not secondary, but sense-constitutive references represent a distinct possible area of analytical research. And if these associative co-positings are not directly sought, they nevertheless do exist. For example, for something to be considered an "objective existent" for us, there must be some such thing as the unity of sense "of others." Objective experience is possible in a world which is intentionally constituted as communal (and not merely individual-subjective). At the same time, "world" means the horizon within which something can be encountered as "intersubjectively encounterable," i.e., as objectively experienceable and as objectively existing; and the "*intentionalia*," then, designate the particular modes of being of the intentional, i.e., of experiencing life.[50]

Mundaneness, then, means intersubjective encounterability. For "world" is that within which we find ourselves present as individual empirical subjects, as existents among existents, so that "world" as a whole forms the horizon for possible further psychological and material experiences of every kind.[51] What exists always refers to other existents, and psychic phenomena stand no less in associative connection with other psychic phenomena than objective phenomena do with other objects. What can here become the object of possible experience has a typical structure which is immediately known (though also perhaps not expressly), since it is the structure of mundaneness; and that means that everything that occurs here must in principle be intersubjectively experienceable.[52] The type of givenness seems to be that of presence-on-hand. It follows from this that something present-on-hand arouses determinate expectations with regard to a different possible present-on-hand by which this expectation can be fulfilled or disappointed. The associative (empty or filled) references all occur, however, within the scope of what is in principle experienceable, i.e., of so-called "objectivity." But certainly the structure of mundaneness, objectivity, intersubjective encounterability, and the life-world is not something pregiven, in the same sense as "objects" which emerge within the intersubjectively constituted "world" are pregivens. Yet it probably is a matter of meaningfully addressable phenomena, though phenomena of a different order.[53]

The subjective psychic-mental acts of single individuals all occur within the realm of possible experience, i.e., primarily within the mundane realm of objective experienceability. The sense of mundaneness, of objectivity, of intersubjective encounterability, which lies at the basis of experienceability and which never becomes thematic in the *intentio recta*, now as sense itself in turn refers to new subjective performances of consciousness which must be examined if indeed nothing that imposes itself on consciousness as a phenomenon is supposed to be left standing unquestioned as an existent. So reflection is given its due.[54] The sense of mundaneness, objectivity, etc., also requires a phenomenological grounding. For if for the natural attitude a world is always already there and is grasped as the outer horizon of possible experience, then here too sense-formations, to which precisely this moment of sense belongs, must be posited. The field of constitution is opened up by reflection, for phenomenology "is supposed to be the science that justifies itself absolutely and at the same time the universal science."[55]

In the realm of the objectively experienceable, i.e., in the *world*, of course experiences of every possible kind can be had. First of all, it is an important phenomenon that experiences can be shared with others, that our world never is completely "our" world, but a world of culture. Culture encompasses "formations of praxis which as such are apprehended cognitively by an understanding after the fact of the relevant acts of feeling and will. And what is understood after the fact can become the object of the experiential grasp, of predicative determination, and even of the scientific problematic."[56] Living together grounds exchange of information, communication. Learning, education, and culture are possible where the so-called world-structure is present. For that is precisely where the possession of experience is won, expanded, built up, since it is never single and alone, but is based in the broadest sense on transmittability. Growing into cultural and educational horizons depends on this. But the world of the experienceable is always already interpreted in a certain sense as the world on hand, and it is in principle intersubjectively encounterable. This holds true of the world from the natural-scientific aspect as well as from the historical point of view.[57] Surrounding world, historical situation, tradition, language-space, etc., imply sense-formative performances which are learned from others and appropriated. Everywhere, if genuine explanation is striven for, a "fallback into transcendental philosophy" will follow.[58] Psychological, anthropological, and especially cultural-anthropological research here has its field of work. But, no matter how many "worlds" may come into view, the structure of the "world" is thereby not yet discovered and understood as a presupposition which lies there at the basis, a presupposition which merely states that when something is present as a component of nature or of history, it is one existent among other existents and so is of a determinate structure, for instance that of presence-on-hand.[59]

Whenever intentional sense-bestowing performances of consciousness are to be posited, they are either originary (constitutive) or imitative (interpretative) performances. In every case they must have happened if something is to come into view. The center of such constitutive performances, which possibly point further associatively, is the ego, i.e., we ourselves, or, in principle, subjectity. If the ego or ourself is thus spoken of here, that must not be understood as if the so-called "outside world," in its structure, depended henceforth on "psychic interiority," i.e., as if the "soul," the "psychic subject," "man" as this particular person, were the origin of "world-formations" and thus at the same time the cause for the (Protagoran) relativities.[60] If absolutely everything that is encompassed by such names is a phenomenon of consciousness, it represents only in principle a constitutive correlate of sense-formative performances in general. Where "inner, psychic processes" are brought into opposition with the "outside world," these processes are themselves already grasped as objectified, mundanized, constituted. To understand these supposedly originary processes of a psychic interiority as opposite to an outside means that mundanizing acts of understanding have already been performed.[61] Where "interior," "interiority," or "interior being" are discussed, we are still on the ground of world-constitution. For only within a world constituted as objective is it possible to speak meaningfully of interior and exterior, of localization and objective place in time. These sense-formations are the very ones which must be brought into view. We ourselves remain centers of these sense-formations, but not as psychic subjects fixed here and now, for the characterization as psychic, worldly subjects represents once again the performance of an already prior sense-constitution. Again, psychology, which has as its object precisely these objectified subjects (as should paradoxically be said), does not reach the ground-laying problematic of constitution. Genuine understanding always refers further back to the prior foundational connections, the transcendental connections of apprehension.[62]

In this context, phenomenological reduction means simply that the empirical-psychological subject is being disregarded. Not that it stands at the beginning; rather, it is itself constituted in self-apprehension and apprehension of the other as "this-there" with a determinate sense. That is how it expresses and enunciates itself. But where everything that is simply given as *there* may be disregarded, and where the grounding connections are to be pursued down to the last one, one must proceed in all radicalness. It is not an existent (neither in the sense of a Cartesian *res* nor in the sense of a psychological ego) that can stand at the beginning, where even such being is traced back to sense. Accordingly, the point of departure can absolutely not be an entity of any kind, but only the performance of the evident sense-formation.[63] In these performances emerges what stands as pregiven, as natural, as psychic, as worldly, etc., indeed as what is accepted in the evidence of the linguistic expression. Accordingly, from any given sense one must ask back to the sense-constitutive presuppositions, and this "reiteratively" and "regressively" without end, for transcendental phenomenology is ultimately the development of the "logos of all conceivable being."[64] Therefore, the center of these functioning performances can itself be no metaphysical "entity," no real or ideal existent. As authority which first lets objectivities arise according to their sense, i.e., be understood, it represents the opposite of something itself objective. It is not objective, but rather it posits objectivities. It is accordingly also not itself psychical, empirical, worldly, i.e., it is not psychical spirituality or subjectivity, but the authority that constitutes *all these* and, furthermore, *all possible* sense-factors. Basically, it is the abbreviation for the sequence of legitimating *cogitationes*, to which the reflections also belong.[65] Accordingly, it represents the counter-concept and the prior concept to all mundane objectivities and subjectivities, and reveals itself only in its functioning as transcendental subjectivity—to subsequent reflection. Even the so-called metaphysical questions, if they have sense and seek meaningful answers, require functioning subjectity, which can be nothing else but the very same flux of sense-legitimating *cogitationes*. Evidence, wherever and however it enunciates itself, cannot be outplayed, and it gives itself in transcendental modes and forms of experiencing, apprehending, having, and giving.[66]

Even the question concerning being, the individual existent, and the "metaphysical hinterworld," the soul, the self, and the ego comes to a decision here and nowhere else. Sense-connections absolutely all refer to the constitution of sense in general—so that sense-formations can be spoken of only when they become manifest in the *cogitationes*. They cannot depend on pregivens, since all pregivens are pregiven, by the *cogitationes*, as constituted. Reiterative regress is the last word, and history really brings something new! But what is the reason why free, formative, functioning subjectity gets started at all? In view of these problems, fundamental ontology starts with the fact that such a subjectity does not function purely and simply by constituting unities of sense, but is concerned with being-in-the-world in general, which must already have been experienced as threatened and put in question. Husserl explains that reflection is originally such in the will; the subject, by determining himself as the philosophical subject, has indeed made a decision of will directed at his entire future cognitive life.[67]

The Heideggerian concrete answer—which requires the anchoring of philosophy in "existence from care," which is distinguished by the understanding of being—seems thoroughly problematic. The application of the phenomenological method certainly need not stop with referring once and for all merely to a quite determinate subjectity, namely one characterized by the care-structure as a free, functioning, decisionistic activity. Genuine grounding certainly requires penetration into the "depths of subjectivity" (as Husserl says). And precisely this insight occurs historically in each case, i.e., starting with the situative context. If Husserl's late phenomenology accordingly betrays his increasing preoccupation with egological problems, it can certainly not be denied that only indications are present.[68] However, to disclose the ground for the functioning of transcendental subjectity is also a philosophical task. For Husserl, it consists in free self-investigation.[69] A portrayal of the phenomenological method that is carried to this point should serve, out of the inner motives of the universal grounding problematic, to make visible the necessity of continued phenomenological analyses. The desire for radical, reflective clarity[70] must itself be analyzed again. That reflection must be directed toward a "phansiology," "arche-ology," and "egology"—i.e., that the ground is found in *phansis* as coming-into-appearance, or in *archē* as performance— must naturally not just be said, but legitimated.[71] The self-explication of transcendental subjectity, which ends in the constitution of relations of being, can start only from a being as recognized ultimate point, namely as performance. Thus phenomenology will not become ontology in the sense of fundamental ontology. Even if the inquiry is carried beyond the purely formative activity of transcendental subjectity to the concern (*Betroffenheit*) in which the subject always finds himself, it is an anticipation (*Vorgriff*) to interpret this concern generally in the sense of care (*Sorge*). Where "being" does not stand at the beginning, one must perhaps start with "what-ought-to-be" and with the problem of relevance. Husserl, however, leaves this question open, because it could only be settled from case to case and not generally.[72] The result is this: transcendental subjectity does not represent an entity of some kind or other, neither in the sense of a psychological subject nor of a logical consciousness in general. We ourselves are it when we "disclose" that we are centers of constitutive sense-formations, and precisely therein and therewith the constituted subject of self-apprehension and of the apprehension of others. The phenomenological principle of self-legitimation makes it possible to take what is constituted as sense completely seriously. This becomes important when one traces the individual constitutive performances which are always situatively found, contextually fixed, historically conditioned, and topically characterized. Among them are not just those in which others are apprehended as "persons," as "subjects" in the world, but also those in which Others appear (appresentatively, as Husserl says) themselves as "centers of intentional sense-formation."[73] They are as such precisely not things among things; rather, through phenomenological empathy they too are experienced as themselves functioning egoicalness. It belongs to their sense, in which they are accessible to us, that they too experience themselves as centers of constitutive performances, whereby of course this— their being as center—cannot itself be given to me originarily (for that would mean that *I* would be an *alter ego*). Here problems with further implications arise. The decisive point to see in this is that there are certainly not just experiences which grasp sense natural-scientifically. Such questions must in any case be investigated when *phansis* and *phainomenon* are treated.[74] On the basis of the most varied performances, one sees others in immediate prepredicative fashion, experienceable as functioning centers of constitution, which in turn in their performances grasp us as centers of intentional sense-formation; and accordingly the starting point that must be set phenomenologically at the beginning is transcendentally functioning subjectivity in the form of monadic intersubjectivity. The "monad" becomes the point of departure because one must go back to one's own founding performances; we call it "intersubjective" because in its performances of intentional constitutions, the monad always appears as a member of a historically fixed "community of monads" which can as such, for example, first make the phenomenon of objectivity explainable.[75] The originary self-legitimation finds a boundary where the *alter ego* is constituted in a certain way ("analogically") in consciousness; but, as what it really is, namely the center of constitutive performances, it is not experienced and it is not experienceable. The *alter ego* as center of constitution appears in the apprehending experiences as a constituted structure and thus precisely not itself as constitutive. It is an understood other person. Since in the appresenting experiences leading up to this point what is experienced is certainly not nothing, it would have to be clarified whether the question concerning the sense of being is not given a new decisive turn. In short, under certain circumstances must not being be spoken of precisely where there is nothing graspable as a unity of sense? And must not this being then simply be called "understanding" in its performance? To all appearances, this is probably Husserl's opinion.[76]

The reduction of the inquiry to transcendental subjectity contains no standpoint-bound metaphysical presuppositions. All that is said is that the ultimate ground of constitutive "formations of world and object" in the free understanding activity of this subjectity (simply the flow of *cogitationes*) must lie in the praxis of theory, whereby the entire self-understanding—with all existential, historical, situative, and life-world components—remains the product of constitutive, grounding performances. The "ground" of these formations cannot, however, itself be again something pregiven (and hence also constituted); it must be postulated, and can probably be found only—in a way yet to be clarified—in what-ought-to-be. The disclosure of the implications of sense leads only this far. Thus intentional analysis does not reach the absolute ground; since reflection always strides back, it again and again discloses only grounds.[77]

Based on the disclosures of the performances of sense-formation which have always already happened, the result is a history of consciousness in its performance. For functions must always be operative, or be posited as operative, so that the individual, empirical understanding of self and being is filled at all here and now. Yet the disclosure of these connections is not what is really relevant historically. That particular functioning performances occur with their appertinent correlates, and indeed occur eventfully without attachment to pregivens—that must be "historical" *par excellence*. But what is precisely not oriented by the pregiven, but rather posits and grounds itself, is reason in its free performing, is also reflection in its unanticipatable occurrence. For reason, only what should be, can be. What the concept "thinking," for instance, connotes, thinking always already is.[78] When the possibilities of free subjectity—or also existence in its existing—are spoken of, the concept of possibility must certainly not be understood in the sense of the *possibile logicum*. Where the point of departure is self-grounding reason, what is possible can only be the real, i.e., what is brought functionally into appearance—whose action is understanding.

Transcendental subjectity, which, let it be said in conclusion, we ourselves functionally are, does not represent a "pregivenness of a higher kind," but can be characterized only as the constitutive freedom of the origin.[79] Genuine origin, however, must probably be reason with its evidences, on which everything depends. It results in the grounding of pregivens; it produces the attempt at self-understanding; it brings about what admittedly "is." Thus it represents the absolute ground of free possibilities. These possibilities, however, must not, like Leibniz's *possibilitates*, themselves again be considered as constituted pregivens (mental pregivens located in the *intellectus divinus*), for which or against which a decision is made. There is not the least Platonism here! Rather, where integral rationalism[80] is the last word, only what enters into appearance, which is transcendentally conditioned, can be called "possible"! Possibility is then not a word for the hovering state between two alternatives posited as finished; possibility designates, rather, the opening for the occurrence of an appearance. Thus phenomenology, which allegedly had no relationship of any kind to the problem of the historical, acquires direct access to the essence of history. The historical event *par excellence* is the occurrence of appearances, i.e., the making possible of sense, as it is manifested in the emergence of reason. The transcendental relation of constitution is cleared up by the very fact that we always understand ourselves in a certain way and can ask about ourselves as well as about our mode of understanding. We are not simply *there*; we must not be posited simply as "pregivens," but rather as "potentially" self-conscious centers of sense-formation. We let all this be spoken aloud in linguistic explication. Starting from the topically given, reiterative regression discloses what the condition of possibility is. Since absolutely all phenomena are sense-formations, phenomenology will have to become universal investigation of sense. It can achieve what it is supposed to only if it remains a critical, reflective science of foundations. Thus it moves in the realm of the theoretical, and it is concerned only with the "things themselves" and with their foundations. And reiterative-regressive reflection, by rising above what is taken for granted in concrete understanding, proves the historicity of reason, which it itself again raises completely to consciousness. Thereby it clarifies what man can be, without asking the question of man's essence. Reiterative regressive reflection makes it clear that a phenomenology carried out in this way is more than the experiential science of man, developed in the naive attitude.

Chapter Nine

Conclusion: Foundational Knowledge and Philosophy of Consciousness

The question of the essence and the existence of man is just one among other possible questions. It has especially characterized philosophical discussion perhaps only in the twentieth century, but it is not the fundamental question purely and simply.[1] Actually, the procedure is time-conditioned. Philosophical anthropology as a foundational science is something modern, even more modern than philosophy as fundamental ontology. Even if it is true that in every philosophically posed question man himself is also implicitly or explicitly put in question,[2] this does not prevent the first rank from being conceded to the *actually* exercised historical self-interpretation of man (which does not have to begin with man).

There is no "absolute priority" of one question over the other, unless one were to accept a particular metaphysics as "position" from the outset! If in the real historical accomplishment of being, man turns to things as his things and does not ascribe the least significance to the question of the essence of man, that is indeed of extraordinary, essential, unmasking significance for the determination and characterization of such a mankind, but it in no way justifies ascribing absolute priority to this question about his own being and *Dasein*, apparently not asked by man himself, compared with the problems he obviously treats as important.

Certainly man is what he is only *with* his questions and his attempts at answering them. To reproach him for the "questions he does not ask" and the solutions he does *not* undertake is really possible only if what man really is and what he really ought to do is clear in advance. But what he really is, is shown precisely in the projects and performances which are important "to him." Man simply does not strive continuously and hectically to be just a man as such, but, on the contrary, by a historical decision taking this or that to be important, he becomes the man that it is really possible for him to be. Thus the question concerning "man as such" cannot be the "main" question. *Wherever* man begins to ask—not just when he asks about man's being—he abolishes what was previously taken for granted. Philosophical reflection shatters the pregiven world-order, which is always lived along in a naively metaphysical, dogmatic context, by finding something questionable in some place or other.

Certainly, man appears to be the problematic, the problem-discovering being *par excellence*. There is no absolute priority for any one of these problems. But all together, in whatever manner they may be posed and approached, they say something about man. And the question of man's essence, expressly formulated, is for him "no more distinctive than the omission of this question." Man as the being who is ardently interested in clearing up objective questions may be characterized as forgetful of being, while man as the being interested in the meaning of his existence may appear to be characterized as oblivious to objectivity.[3] The priority of the one question over the other should apparently be based on the fact that "the essence of being" can be cleared up only in terms of "the essence of *Dasein*," whereby finally a light would then also fall on the being of things and objects. This convincing argument relies on taking being as the most general concept, which, with a certain unadmitted taken-for-grantedness, somehow lies at the basis of all thing-conceptions and cannot be circumvented. Further, it is assumed that the one who asks questions has thereby himself, in a determinate sense, a character of being. Moreover, if an understanding of being is a determination of the being of a particular existent, then this understanding of being is (as Heidegger says) ontically distinguished by the fact that a particular existent is "in its being concerned with this being itself"; but at the same time, it undergoes an ontological revaluation upward, since it also concomitantly makes possible the understanding of all being of a non-*Dasein*-like kind.

All this will ground the ontic, the ontological, and the ontico-ontological priority of that particular existent which Heidegger calls "existence" (*Existenz*).[4]

If the task of Husserlian phenomenology in all its varieties is, supposedly, to make "the things themselves" speak, still the things that especially need to be given voice to are the very ones which initially are hidden. And most hidden of all are the things taken for granted in any human reality, namely man's understanding of his world, his self, and his understanding.[5] But the pinnacle of what remains hidden again and again is the sense of being, which each person somehow counts on and about which no one really can say anything valid. The question of being, therefore, acquires priority for these two reasons: first, in any other question a character of being is always included and connoted, even if this occurs only implicitly; second, the question of being is the genuinely philosophical question because here what-is-hidden *par excellence* lets itself be made the problem. That is approximately the point of departure.

Naturally, it is possible, in contrast with this clear and discernible development of the problem, to argue in such a way that one declares that even problems of being (questions of being of every kind) are "questions of sense" which require "meaningful answers"—which as such in turn can come to light only as "legitimations in the understanding, in consciousness." What is even more taken for granted and left unquestioned in posing or in forgetting the question of being is the positing of understanding, of the ability to grasp meaning, to make meaning possible, i.e., consciousness in its broadest sense. That *Dasein* is privileged both ontically and ontologically—this assertion already counts on the fact of understanding in the manner of an understanding of being. Fundamental ontology thus assumes and takes understanding for granted in order to be able to make some determinate, privileged existent the starting point of its investigations.

Only on the basis of prior performances of understanding can questions of sense be asked at all. This is true not just for questions of being, but for questions in general. If understanding of being is the "being-determination" of *Dasein*, then understanding will constitute the being of this existent. This understanding would then encompass everything that was validated.

It is immaterial whether one holds to the use of the term "understanding" or rediscovers in it academic philosophy's "consciousness." What matters is this: fundamental ontology must, in order to remain "ontology," become a philosophy of understanding and consciousness, and ultimately the philosophy of the transcendental determinations and forms of this consciousness. Insofar and as long as it is this, even in Heidegger, it has to do with a "*veritas transcendentalis.*"[6] The turn from transcendental to transcendent philosophy begins where it is said that it is "being-in-itself" that makes itself clear and where understanding becomes just a *causa occasionalis* for the "clearing of being." At this moment, being, in its openness, is no longer a corresponding (variable) correlate for certain determinate and peculiar legitimations in the understanding; rather, this being is posited absolutely, and the clearings are relative.

There can be no doubt that this type of transformed transcendental philosophy, i.e., this metaphysics of being, ultimately must be unphenomenological. Beyond the given clearings, what clears itself here is dogmatized as the metaphysical existent-in-itself. The result is that we have here a starting point for a reiterative and—even here—regressive sense-analysis still able to clarify these connections phenomenologically.

Such a clarification is, from the ground of the "metaphysics of being," declared inappropriate, because phenomenological sense-analysis is not spared the reproach of fundamental-ontological hermeneutics that it is oriented by a "derivative mode of understanding being" and that it does not go beyond an objectifying mode of thinking, thus missing from the very outset the genuine position of a metaphysics of being. This is certainly wrong: for something can be called "derivative" only when it is not an equally-ranked correlate of a correlation connection. Precisely this correlate, however, stands at the beginning of all phenomenological constitutions, which are not creations.

Any talk of "objectifying thinking" must, then, be submitted to scrutiny. In principle it must from the outset be asked whether there can ever be such a thing as a non-objectifying thinking in a philosophy which seeks to communicate, or whether the polemics against objectifying thinking must not be attributed to a lack of clarity in the concept of object.[7] So much, at any rate, is certain, that even clearings of being should "convey sense" and that this being becomes graspable. But if it does become so, then by the same token it remains "sense which has become a phenomenon." No "turning" whatsoever can change this.

Certainly, "object" does not have to mean something "present-at-hand." For Husserl's phenomenological reductions had begun precisely with the point that at first no use was to be made of the "universal thesis of being," and yet on the one hand an "absolute consciousness" as the "residuum after the annihilation of the world," and on the other, the whole "natural world as a correlate of consciousness" was left over.[8] It was a matter of clarifying, purely in their sense, precisely these objects, which now could no longer be characterized as present-at-hand. Whether it is right that the concept of object is oriented by objects of the natural world (which, however, is basically always already scientifically transformed) may be left completely out of consideration, since after reduction questions of being can be treated only as questions of sense (*Sinn*). And even in determining the "sense of being," in bringing out the "modes of being," etc., precisely sense is to be the issue.

In *Being and Time*, *Dasein*, which in its being is concerned with this being itself, is never the "concrete" individual *Dasein*, but always the form of *Dasein*.[9] No individual description of phenomena applies to existence in its concrete existing—each relates to what would have to be called "form of existence." The existentials are ways of being of *Dasein*, not of this or that existent (*Daseienden*) in its existing, which is really particular in each case. In short, they are forms. They can be identified as such. They contain and designate a fixed sense, and by the same token they are themselves the object of a legitimating performance that affects precisely them. They are phenomena of the appertinent access-forms of understanding. Yet it is quite immaterial whether the route of reflection is rejected for the acquisition of these existentials and a direct awareness of their own is claimed. Existence in its existing is always one thing, while "existence in knowledge of the forms of its existence" is another (different) thing. The existentials, of course, are objects of the apprehending consciousness, just as are the categories in the realm of things present-at-hand. Everything that becomes the subject of a proposition is at the same time the object of understanding, the object of consciousness. Nothing (in Husserl) is an exception to this, neither discussion of God nor discussion of nothingness.[10]

The only objection that could be made is that of course all statements entail objectifications; however, what is meant in the statements is absolutely not something objective, but pure possibility. This objection cannot be valid, because in the question of the being of something, the answer still has all paths open. It can be answered to the effect that what is meant by the "sense" is something possible, involves something really present-at-hand, means being-projected. For precisely this is what the question inquired about, and if it is answered, the answer must deal with the object of the question, i.e., correspond exclusively to its sense.

Heidegger also treats the object which is at issue in inquiry under various aspects: when it is an inquiry about being, there is "something which is asked about" (*etwas Gefragtes*); and there is the sense of being as "that which is to be found out by asking" (*das Erfragte*), and finally the being of the only existent which can give information in response to questions, namely the being of *Dasein*, "that which is interrogated" (*das Befragte*).[11] Under these three aspects—that which is asked about, that which is to be found out by asking, and that which is interrogated—something different always stands in the intentionally directed view, but it always remains in this view as a unity of the same "sense," i.e., as an object, as a phenomenon on a particular level of sense-clarification.

Object-directed thinking and the self-certainty of the *ego cogito* are generally traced back to Descartes.[12] Yet it must be pointed out that Descartes, to consolidate certainty, must begin a return to metaphysics and to God—to the Creator God, who alone guarantees the existence of the ego, which this ego cannot guarantee for itself because of its doubting considerations, not even after overcoming the methodical point of departure from doubt.[13] Cartesian thinking is object-directed only in the above sketched sense that no subject that is to hold good as an ego can be thought *without* consciousness of an object. The subject does not stand opposite objects, each finished and independent in its kind; rather, the subject *is* world-consciousness, dream-consciousness, fiction-conscious ness—and always with the thing. That is the absolutely indubitable point of departure. Even if Descartes' God were deceptive, "he may deceive as much as he can, but never will he cause me to be nothing, as long as I believe myself to be something."[14] Only as long as consciousness has something as content is it consciousness.

In Descartes there can be no "autonomy of the ego," of the subject; thus the independence of the subject opposite the objects is not found in Descartes either. Not from its own reason does the ego in Descartes obtain certainty, but because God preserves the ego, which the ego can only accept but not ground. And the "subject" is not, for instance, "alien to the object."

The idea of the "autonomy of reason" must be traced back to Kant. But this idea is modestly clad in the form of a demand. Autonomy is not a fact, just as little as freedom is a fact, but rather a demand of reason which cannot sensibly be avoided. Accordingly, it always involves something that "must be done." And it is not possible to speak of a crisis of reason, since it is reason itself that not only brings up this discussion, but also grounds it—and thereby abolishes it again. Who else but reason, who else but consciousness, then, corrects the view that man is connected with the world only as *animal rationale*? The strata of the lived body and the drives, the emotions and volitions, can say nothing about themselves and their right; only reason and reflective consciousness can do so. Even the crisis of a mankind is determined by reflective consciousness.[15]

Even where man has, with exaggerated individualism, understood himself as a singular ego-subject, where he must rely on himself in his isolated individuality and tries to derive all communal structures of culture and history, of society and state, from the individual subjects and an agreement between them, this very same man—with his self-correcting reason and with the continuously controlling consciousness—replaces this interpretation with a new one. Talk of the "crisis of consciousness" and of the "crisis of reason" is indeed popular, but what on earth could bring the crisis situation as such to consciousness, if not this rational consciousness itself. This crisis—which is, moreover, the very same crisis which only reason and consciousness can discover and make understandable—is already overcome by the fact that the contentually dogmatized interpretation is removed from matter-of-courseness and made questionable.

In the history of philosophy and of ideas, most portrayals of the development up to the present make their task so difficult by not holding

firmly to the "historicity" of thinking, which they themselves proclaim. [16]
Again and again there is still talk of "crisis situations" and of revolutionary
changes which necessarily draw in their aftermath historically reverber-
ating devaluations and reestimations of reason, viz., of consciousness, as
if these historical appearances are one thing, and the world-knowledge
posited as absolute (but shared by the respective author) another. What
we have here, however, are still adaptations of those views which asserted
a universal, divine, absolute, and spiritual knowledge of the *intellectus
divinus* or World Spirit. In a real historicization of rational consciousness,
however, it is *this* consciousness itself that allows all such crisis situations
and revolutionary changes to take shape as it detects them. There are no
crises unless we thought them and brought them to consciousness! A
general "malaise in culture" is a phenomenon of consciousness, otherwise
nothing; and it can be "unmasked" as what it is only by consciousness.

The history of philosophy is a telling of fairy tales when it portrays the
context as if first abstract rational knowledge existed and then a certainty
of the human claim to dominate nature were built upon that knowledge.
In reality, it is certainly true that in a determinate attitude of consciousness the intentional objects graspable in it are completely mastered and
that domination resides in that mastery. Technical consciousness, for
example, is domination; it does not first need to raise itself up to
domination by an upsurge. But it is always subjectity in whose performances that which then appears as given is brought to legitimation.

All metaphysicizing schools of the present, especially the "metaphysics
of being" of the late Heidegger school, assert that the so-called basic
tendency of previous modern philosophy is a "philosophy of subjectivity"
which must be dissolved and overcome by speculation. [17] Not the
ego-subject, but rather an operational organon must be the starting point
for every understanding of the world. [18] But there can be no doubt that
the "concrete" experiences of "life" and the actual decisions of existence
for these metaphysical tendencies, activated singly in each case, remain
completely inconsequential, since they are interested only in the forms of
life and the elaboration of the ways of being—i.e., in objectified
disclosures of something that cannot be immediately conscious to itself.

But what should be called "philosophy of subjectity" (not of subjectivity) consists in this very process. [19]

When at a particular historical hour man no longer considers himself an
abstract rational being, but a concrete sensory-corporeal, emotional-
volitive unity, it is still not the sensory-corporeal moments, nor the
emotions and volitions, that bring about this revised image; rather, it is a
matter of the sensory-corporeal factors "grasped" and "understood" in
their scope, and it is the "comprehended" emotions and volitions that

play a role here—that can play a role because regressive steps of consciousness have made it possible. Only a rational consciousness can assign its role in the human economy to what is in itself *not* rational and conscious, and then understand the whole man as this and that on the basis of these functions. Sensoriness, corporeality, emotion, and volition do not achieve this.

So it must be asked what the battle cry "overcoming the philosophy of subjectity" can mean. Either it is supposed to mean a Pelasgian twilight existence; then even such an "understood" twilight existence is still more than the naive and original performance of this twilight. Or else the overcoming of subjectivity means the overcoming of the claim of reason and consciousness to dominate life.

The first case is clearly absurd. The so-called overcoming of a state of consciousness of any particular degree can never bring about the restoration of a pre-conscious state by means of consciousness. Naiveté of the old kind cannot be reestablished with consciousness and on the basis of consciousness.

The second case contains an error. Conscious reason is the only ability which can, without ceasing to be rational consciousness, recognize in its performances the non-rational and the unconscious in mediated immediacy and insert them within their own rights. This is just what the pre-rational and the pre-conscious cannot do. For that reason, the watchword really cannot be the overcoming of the philosophy of subjectity, but on the contrary only the strengthening and promotion of such a philosophy of subjectity.

Karl Marx's dictum, "Man is man's world," stands alongside Dilthey's adage: "We learn what man is from history." Both statements demonstrate an explicit idea of immanence. When man organizes his life-world and economy according to the needs of his animal-social structure through work, as in Marx, and when he develops his life into historical-cultural contexts of sense through inventions and adaptations to the naturally given surrounding worlds, as in Dilthey, he stands, as this socioeconomic or historical-biological unity, behind the secondarily developed contexts of life and milieu, whose presumed specific laws point to him as the bearer and producer of these quasi-natural facts.

The bearers of life, behind which one should go no further back, are concrete enough. Whether life is, as in Marx, what is known from the outside—namely through alienation—or whether, as in Dilthey, it is what is known only from within as it opens up in historical understanding, may remain less important. In either case, it is a matter of understanding. And this understanding is communicable, it is universal, and it counts on a meaning that is determinable in each case. The only question remaining is *who* is concretely the bearer of this understanding. In Marx it is the "classes"; in Dilthey, rather, the "spirits of nations" with their particular sociohistorical structures.

Husserl, in his *Ideas* I (1913) and in his *Cartesian Meditations* (1931, 1950), again raised the question of the origin of a more certain knowledge, and he found such a knowledge bound to the performances of intersubjectivity. In the *cogito* is determined what awareness, feeling, will, corporeality, and community mean as precisely this, and what role is attributable to these moments in the total economy of human life. To this extent it is right to say that there is here a "return to thinking as thinking," and the actual performance of subjectity would thus be rationalistic in the old sense.

The breakdown of Husserlian rationalism,[20] which was soon scorned in the age of irrationalisms, is now said to have been completed in the history of ideas by Scheler and Heidegger. This now poses the task of examining the vitalist and fundamental-ontological interpretations, too, for their degree of "cogency." They can be binding only if they have validity. But that they have validity seems to be determinable only in a *cogitatio* that belongs here. In any case, the polemics against the philosophy of consciousness must not be allowed to mix and confuse rational cogitation and non-rational opinion. And whether there is and can be anything non-objectively understandable happens to be the question. Thus the positions of Husserl, Scheler, and Heidegger with respect to man's essence and the understanding of man would have to be developed in succession. For this is where it can best be shown whether it is a matter of a poet's rhapsodic legend or of mediations with a valid claim.

Philosophy, before it abandons its task, must deal with experience in the broadest sense. This experience is always a historical possession. This means that all given available knowledge contains matter-of-course assumptions which have gone unexamined because they were adopted as person-constitutive. Knowledge in the twentieth century contains all the matter-of-course assumptions of a natural-scientifically determined world view. If the question now aims at taking in grasp the world as such, i.e., also beyond the natural scientific reshaping, then this demand falls under the rubric: "establishment of an original experience."[21] Yet one must remain conscious of the paradox: original experience is one thing, reestablishment of such an original experience is something completely different.

The "history" of reason has led to the natural-scientific theoretizations. If one wants to penetrate through them, then the given world is perhaps indeed free of *these* theoretizations, but no more than that. The world, so discovered, is certainly no longer originary, but it is geared toward the originary. To want to get the things themselves into view means in Husserlian language actually, first of all, to go back behind scientific theoretizations. Every experience is an awareness which later should have this goal: to draw closer to the origins. The analysis of the phenomena for the meaning deposited in them will—in that opinion—bring it about that an original experience becomes distinguishable from one believed to be so only here and now.

Experiences now sediment into expressions. These expressions can mean what is meant in an empty fashion, or a sense-fulfillment can take place in the use of the expressions. Thus it has been said: "To test or examine experience as to its originary character means thus above all to take the linguistic expressions as the starting point of an inquiry into the inner perceptions from which they derive their meaning and significance."[22] When phenomenology applies the process of reduction, its purpose is to go back from the sense to the sense-bestowing mental processes. Everything one can speak of meaningfully is a phenomenon—thus also everything that comes into appearance is a possible object of regressive inquiry. Phenomenological intentional analysis will, then, bring the "what" of what-is-meant and the "how" of the meaning into correlation. Evidence results only via a particular qualitativeness within an appertinent attitude, and never absolutely.

If the existent, if the "what" of this existent, is at all to be brought into grasp, then it is only in the manner that it becomes an object of consciousness. And since the adequate grasping of the respective "what" must rely on the appropriate appertinent mode of apprehension, phenomenology must come upon the validating performances and experiences of consciousness as the ultimate ground for the possibility of absolutely all findings, i.e., the "how."

In the realm of every philosophical anthropology one can speak meaningfully of any being only insofar as it shows itself in consciousness.[23] The constitutional problematic is here too, just a "secret," "hidden" problematic of sense. If one wants to speak of the given, ever different sense of objects as clues in the quest for the correlatively appertinent modes of mediation, one can likewise do this with respect to man. Whatever can be spoken of meaningfully emerges in the *ego cogito*. The *cogitationes* represent the field of possible sense-validations, on the basis of which descriptions of something as something are first possible, including descriptions of man. In speaking of the "human," the so-called noematic can never be separated from the noetic, for there is nothing noematic without the appertinent *noesis*, and no *noesis* is imaginable without a *noema*. From the outset, as in all investigations of this kind, including the anthropological, it must be pointed out that the meant *noema* can signify any unity of sense, and it is never restricted to signifying something given matter-of-coursely as an object. Even when, for example, anxiety as a so-called unintentional mental process does not encounter any mundane constituted thing, it has its sense: what matters is only to grasp it in the right attitude. The object of anxiety would then be, for instance, the act of calling-in-question! In anxiety there emerges what could be called the essence of calling-in-question. And so anxiety is, of course, not devoid of sense. *I am the one who appears* when called in question. Of course, anxiety need not refer to a segment of the world that is present-at-hand, as its object, but this has absolutely nothing to do with the question whether it does not mean something—whether it does not have its sense.

The *cogito* will bring all this to evidence.

In Husserlian phenomenology, when man appears, he is, like every phenomenon, an object of apprehension—thus, moreover, in this case, of a *self*-apprehension, which is not free of processing and inclusion in apprehensions that have become known to *others*. Self-apprehension and others' apprehensions condition the image of man as man. What being a man means can be detected nowhere else than by the achievements of understanding which the individual man performs with respect to himself and to others.[24] The dependence of one on the other remains a constitutive moment of self-apprehension.

The question of being can, however, be posed only when it is presupposed that this being can also be brought to appearance. In the question concerning man's being, man himself must be asked how he can become an object for himself from his own vantage point and in living together with other men. Some have seen in this very enterprise the "process of a universal objectification."[25] Universal phenomenological reflection depends just on what the object is in such reflection, and on nothing else. It wants to clarify sense, perhaps also the sense of being— but an un-understood being remains an absurdity.

The traditional statement now suggests that Husserl would have to stipulate the *sense of being* as *being-an-object*. And the critique that follows from this says that this approach would in each case ignore and fail to see the concrete "that" of being. This argument must be examined.

First, Husserl speaks of being as it comes to appearance, i.e., as the correlate of consciousness. And every being has a corresponding consciousness. The Husserlian statement of the problem is, in effect, abridged when it is argued that Husserl always asked how the performances of consciousness would have to appear so that a being of the kind *a* can be given according to its essence. Because man is an existent among other existents, Husserl, it is argued, applied the question completely analogously to man and so obtained the answer: man is the creature that in its being is understood in terms of its becoming the object of an appertinent consciousness. Abbreviated, this would mean: man's being consists in being an object of an appertinent consciousness. What is thus expressed holds good in general for man, and so it would be wrong to say that man is not a case or a specimen of his species and that he always deals only with his own experiences.

This line of argument sounds strange.

When one asks about the sense of being, in no case is one speaking about the being of an individual existent, but about the sense of being in general.[26] Even if every individual as a particular existent has to be being in its particular way, it surely does not thereby have a particular being. If one were to admit that every individual *Dasein* as *Dasein* also has its particular being, the question of the sense of being immediately becomes superfluous. For only the question of the sense of being *a*, of being *b*, of being *c*, etc., then remains meaningful. When something imposes itself on an actual existent as "this-there," and comes to his experience, compelling him to an encounter, then the way this taking of a position follows is either singularized or it is not singularized. If this mode of *Dasein* is singularized to *Dasein*, then there is no question about the sense of being at all, because no authority could be given from whose vantage point this question could be answered. Or else it is the way of taking a position, and not singularized; then there is a form of being that remains the same even when what stands in this form is different. One example may clarify this. If the being of an existent consisted in its free ability to take a position, the form of the position-taking would remain the same from one existent of this kind to the other, but the free position-taking as such would look different.

The Husserlian ego, too, is what it is as a unity of determinate appertinent performances of consciousness. How this ego appears in detail, what habits it develops, depends on the activated concrete experiences. But this remains the coinciding character: that this ego is the center of the experiences attributed to it. It is thus incomprehensible what the objection to the Husserlian doctrine of the *cogitationes*, of the *ego* and of the *cogito* really mean to say with the reproach of "objectivated thought."[27] Either one starts with the fact that "something" is grasped, that the "sense of being" should be grasped—then it is not a matter of experiencing this existent or that existent, nor of the existence of this *Dasein* or that *Dasein*; rather, what is sought is the sense of *Dasein*, the "sense of being"—a sense that is supposed to be expressed.

Even the form of life and existence to be fixed for the most concrete life, for the most decisive existence, is anything but life itself, anything but existence itself. Structures and ways of being are not just this being itself purely and simply.[28] The "that" of life, the "that" of existence is the presupposition for the objectivating detection of forms of life and existence. Metaphysics is the starting ground for epistemology; but epistemology is not adherence to metaphysics. Husserlian phenomenology reaches further than vitalism and existentialism, which claim to consider concrete life and full existence. For it is already an objectivating performance of consciousness when it is determined that being consists in an ability to be. On the other hand, the ability to be is one thing and the demonstration that the ability to be is the sense of being is a completely different thing.

Naturally, it is, for Husserl's phenomenology, quite clear that every concrete consciousness develops according to the self-activated experiences as a unity in multiplicity, and this unity will then in each case have to be a particular one. But that it is so holds good in general. According to the "principle of all principles," that what is imposed by evidence must be left standing as valid; which validations actually constitute it as "this-there" cannot be anticipated in any consciousness. Nor can it be anticipated that this consciousness is just the correlatively posited center for perceptions, intuitions, ideas from the area of the present-on-hand: it is always only the addressed individual consciousness itself that can decide about "what" comes to its consciousness and how this happens.

Every ascertainment that is partly categorial form, partly life-syntagma, partly existential structure, goes beyond what always already happens in a living along in these category-, life-, and existence-systems. In a categorially determined system no knowledge of these categorial determinations need be prevalent; in an operational context permeated by life-forms, no knowledge of these life-orders need be given; in a *Dasein* permeated by existentials as *Dasein*, no understanding of understanding *as* an existential structure will be found.

Transcendental phenomenology, person-anthropology, and fundamental ontology are and remain, as systems of knowledge, philosophy of consciousness. Even the exclusion of the term "consciousness" can change nothing about that.[29]

Every philosophy will strive for the existent to come to view in its *self*-givenness. Philosophy itself, and what it holds, is a phenomenon—a particular kind of phenomenon. It too, if it is to be grounded, needs a self-validation. Here too, neither a philosophy of life nor of existence is even possible as philosophy that wishes to communicate permanent sense without advertence on the part of consciousness. In life and in existence much can happen, but this one thing certainly does not happen: that life itself has always already developed knowledge of the form of life, or that existence has always already developed knowledge of the form of existing. That something is ascertained here transcends the present life and sheer existence; and only consciousness is the organ of such a "transcendence in immanence" that is fitted with a new sense and reflectively determined. The philosophy of subjectivity is proven in every philosophy of life and existence, even if it is proven only in the mode of the demand for the elimination and overcoming of such a philosophy of subjectivity.

Husserl reduces all phenomenal givens to pure consciousness freed from the natural thesis of being and from the naive apprehensions of life. And basically, of course, in him too this reduction is performed always on one thing, namely consciousness, until only the *solus ipse* is left. But this *solus ipse*, too, has an evidence, namely that of being evident to itself only as a member of a community of consciousness.

The ever-repeated objection to Husserl's universal reflection is this: Husserl goes back to constitutional performances, because of which alone a consciousness can apprehend itself as "this-there." With such reflection man comes into view only as object of his own consciousness—and not in any other way whatsoever.[30] Furthermore, actual *Dasein* thus becomes an intrinsically indifferent initial fact and remains only a starting point for the question of the modes of constitution which must start correlatively.

One must, however, ask whether the "life" chosen as concrete point of departure, whether decision-making *Dasein* with its respectively activated arrangement in life and existence, does not likewise remain completely indifferent, since in each case not a biography of this and only this particular life is written, and since it is not a matter of a "monodoxy" of the addressed existence, but in both cases always of "life" or "existence" in general, of which a concept is transmitted.

Even in *Dasein* it is not "the factical" that is ascertained in fundamental ontology, but rather what is discussed is only the "facticity" of *Dasein*. And the facticity of *Dasein* is something absolutely different from this "factical *Dasein*." Man in his historical situation is already something essentially universal that is accessible only to consciousness and to objectification by consciousness-philosophy.

The philosophy of life and existence is not concerned at all with any "factical" ego, with precisely "this" man; rather, it is concerned only with man as *Dasein*, as life: i.e., from a particular point of view. With the adoption of such a point of view, the unreflecting performance of life and existence is transcended. Of course, any philosophy can ascertain something only when guidelines for determination have been stipulated. It is wrong to assume that the philosophy of life and existence, insofar as it wants to ascertain anything at all, could do so without such leading points of view. Nor does it; and so it demands structural contexts of every kind, which life as life and existence as existence do not discover and make understandable—except in "existential reflection."[31]

To live and to exhaust oneself in life, to exist and to be completely absorbed in existence, leaves no possibility to transcend this individual life and existence: philosophy is itself not simply life, and philosophy is also not restless decisionistic existing. Only by rising above the individual living-along, only by transcending the present existence, does it become apparent that a form of life, a way of being is involved. That is reflective, regressive, reiterative elevation of consciousness.[32]

The philosophy of subjectity can, from the attitude of distance, make discoveries which a concrete life and existence, absorbed completely in the naive performance of life and existence, is incapable of making with respect to itself.

The Husserlian concept of "consciousness in general" seems distorted when it is interpreted as if it meant a totalizing all-encompassing consciousness. "Consciousness in general" probably means simply that there is a particular privileged mode of conscious attitude, which is: to understand all particular dogmatic, doxic experiences in which I can be absorbed directly in life *as* something. And for that I must transcend them as experiences and, in the attitude of distance, grasp them as standing in determinate form.

In the interpretation of the Husserl-Scheler-Heidegger line, it has become customary to point out that the ego is conceived too narrowly as the point of reference for grasping man's being.[33] Little effort, however, has been taken to explain or to found the reproach. One will not want to assume that a primitive confusion or misunderstanding is at the root of this view.

But what if it should be so that not enough attention has been paid to the distinction between giving performance and given thing (mediated object)?[34] This would of course be an example of bad work in the history of philosophy. Subjectity is, for Husserl, the aggregate of all presuppositions responsible for the constitution of something. The presupposition for something is not the same thing as what is to be explained by this presupposition. Subjectity as the aggregate of all performances which validate anything whatever in evidence thus coincides with none of the moments which become evident in these validations. Even if something corporeal may become evident, even if the meaning of sensuousness may be understood, still subjectity, in whose performances such evidences come to light, is not corporeal or sensuous. "Consciousness of" does not take on the character of what has become conscious. Thus subjectity, too, never coincides with the being of the objects which it brings to evidence. Consciousness, which is here always given, is consciousness of something intuited, perceived, felt, wanted, of anger or anxiety. Of course, anger and anxiety are something else than the consciousness that this is anger and that that is anxiety. But existentialism too is not based on anxiety, but on the fact that something is anxiety and as such anxiety has for man as *Dasein* this and that function—namely, it enables one to understand *Dasein*'s exposure to nothingness.

There can be no doubt that here too performances of consciousness are present when such ascertainments are made, and that anxiety merely as anxiety, life merely as life, and not as understood anxiety, as understood life, remain philosophically unproductive.

The polemic against "idealism" in philosophy falls short of the mark when it aims, with unsurpassable naiveté, to counter the performances of consciousness with the unobstructed, lived, concrete reality.[35] Of course, it is right that the possibilities of every constitutive analysis are co-posited by the fact (not the facticity) of the point of departure. But to comprehend the fact as "general mode of being," and hence to interpret the fact as the "facticity" of *Dasein* in its *Dasein* goes beyond the individual fact itself. And the talk of the facticity of *Dasein*" always goes beyond the factual, individual, engaged, decided, and enraged *Dasein*.

The historical horizons in which a determinate life stands, the frameworks in which *Dasein* can develop, are, of course, in their contents, not made by consciousness, but rather are understood and ascertained by consciousness *as* horizons and *as* framework, and to that extent constituted as such.

When it was said that even Husserl had not ultimately arrived at "a general essence of man and his consciousness at all, but rather at this man in his historical situation, his possibilities and his needs," no one can say who, then, this man is supposed to be. Even "this" man does not exist, unless a consciousness that ascertains universals has grasped him. This man, who is being spoken of here, is the correlate of a very determinate attitude of consciousness—namely, the one that tries to ascertain an essential concept for a determinate situation in time and epoch. But one should not persuade oneself that this man really existed somewhere.

Again, as soon as biographies and monographs do not mark the end of philosophical information, the concretely given is disregarded in some mode of understanding, since the posited points of view bring it into combination with something else.[36] As *factum brutum*, everything that is, is different from everything else: only from the point of view that one thing has this or that way of being in common with another does it combine with it into a form of being, of *Dasein*, of life.

Scientific philosophy is possible only in the form of the transcending of concrete facts. And if in the philosophy of life and existence certain forms of life, precisely distinguished ways of being, are designated as characteristic of man (constituting his essence), in each case the individual life and the individual man in his possibilities and hardships is transcended. This man really was totally exhausted in his hardships which were and are his particular ones; he did not discover forms of *Dasein* and existence—which presupposes a different way of being than the one which actually was his. One thing can be practiced by man as well as the other. But there is a great deal of difference. From the vantage point of consciousness, something can be discerned concerning the ways of being and of life. From the concrete absorption in life and existence, on the contrary, no access to consciousness which perceives universals is obtained—for it is totally exhausted in its particular concerns of the moment. This is the reason why even the philosophies of life and existence, if they are not to lead to absurdities, are possible only on the ground of a phenomenological philosophy of consciousness, which works with reflections and reiterative regresses, with reductions and surpassable processes of explanation. It discovers in each case something "as. . . ."[37]

Consciousness grasps the non-conscious; however, non-consciousness finds no access to consciousness. Philosophy seeks, controllably, to bring something to consciousness, i.e., it must make use of this very consciousness. When it steps forth as science, it proceeds methodically; and with its methodical critique, it puts a particular form of "metaphysics" to the test.

Notes

Introduction

1. With such a demanding theme as this, it would be well to remember an adage of Georg Christoph Lichtenberg's: "We all err, but each one errs differently."

2. By invitation, a report on the investigations was made to various Japanese universities in Tokyo and Kyoto in 1964 and 1965.

3. The trains of thought delineated have been discussed in the most varied contexts with students of the Mainz Philosophical Seminar. This elaboration owes numerous insights to participants in those discussions. The author is obligated especially to Dr. W. H. Müller (Neuwied), Dr. T. M. Seebohm (Bad Godesberg) and Dr. W. E. Orth (Mainz) for suggestions and a great deal of assistance.

Chapter One

1. From the very outset, however, the misunderstanding must be avoided that the title "What is Philosophy?" announces "an elementary introduction to philosophy which treats the entire complex of traditional philosophical questions in a superficial and simplified fashion," as Ortega y Gasset says in *What is Philosophy?* (New York, 1960), p. 18.

2. L. Landgrebe, *Was bedeutet uns heute Philosophie?* (Hamburg, 1954), esp. pp. 15 ff.

3. Cf. Gerhard Funke, rector's address: *Beantwortung der Frage, welchen Gegenstand die Philosophie habe oder ob sie gegenstandlos sei* (Mainz, 1966), esp. pp. 7 ff., which is largely followed here.

4. Cf. A. Diemer, *Was heisst Wissenschaft?* (Meisenheim, 1964), § 4, pp. 16 ff.

5. Cf. E. Husserl, *Logical Investigations*, trans. J. N. Findlay (New York, 1970), I, chap. 2: "Theoretical Disciplines as the Foundation of Normative Disciplines," pp. 74–89.

6. "The revolutions decisive for the progress of philosophy are those in which the claims of former philosophies to be scientific are discredited by a critique of their pretended scientific procedure. Then at the helm is the fully conscious will to establish philosophy in a radically new fashion in the sense of rigorous science, determining the order in which tasks are undertaken." E. Husserl, "Philosophy as Rigorous Science," trans. Quentin Lauer, in Husserl, *Shorter Works*, ed. Peter McCormick and Frederick A. Elliston (Notre Dame/Brighton, 1981), pp. 167–68.

7. In this sense, Kant's transcendental-philosophical reflections are also "naive," because they themselves are not questioned again concerning the conditions for their possibility. Cf. T. Litt, *Kant und Herder* (Heidelberg, 1949), p. 38.

8. Yet one constantly gives way to "metaphysics" at random, without checking or admitting that one does so and that one has thereby "decided" for a very specific metaphysics. Cf. Maurice Gex, *Initiation à la philosophie*, German trans.: *Einleitung in die Philosophie* (Vienna/Stuttgart, n.d.), pp. 27 ff.

9. In the *Theorie der phänomenologischen Reduktion (1923/24) Husserl demands precisely that. Cf. Erste Philosophie* II (Husserliana, Vol. VIII, The Hague, 1959), p. 22. [The Husserliana series will henceforth be indicated with the abbreviation Hua plus the volume number—*Trans.*]

10. Cf. Caspar Isenkrahe, *Zum Problem der Evidenz* (Kempten/Munich, 1917), pp. 36 ff.

11. Decisive arguments are found in J. E. Heyde, "Relativität der Wahrheit?" in *Grundwissenschaft*, 12 (1933), pp. 47–89, esp. pp. 49 ff., now in *Wege zur Klarheit* (Berlin, 1960), pp. 153–75, esp. pp. 163 ff.; and in Th. Litt, *Philosophie und Zeitgeist* (Leipzig, 1935), pp. 14 ff., 41 ff., 49 ff.

12. On the "state of philosophy" see Heinrich Rombach's essay by that name in *Philosophische Jahrbücher der Görresgesellschaft* 65 (Munich, 1957), pp. 309–41, esp. pp. 336 f.

13. H. Noack, *Die philosophischen Bemühungen des 20. Jahrhunderts: Die Philosophie Westeuropas* (Darmstadt, 1963), p. 10.

14. This is the image of philosophy drawn by Husserl's transcendental phenomenology, which seeks to fulfill the ideal of a philosophy as rigorous science. Cf. the attempt to portray a "new idea of the grounding of knowledge" in Husserl's *Cartesian Meditations*, trans. Dorion Cairns (The Hague, 1960), p. 27.

15. Very informative on this subject is Manfred Brelage's essay "Über das Begründungsproblem in Philosophie und Wissenschaft" in *Studien zur Transzendentalphilosophie* (Berlin, 1965); cf. pp. 45–62.

16. To forestall any misunderstandings in this context at least the

following shall be said: "We are now certain that the rationalism of the eighteenth century, the manner in which it sought to secure the necessary roots of European humanity, was *naive*. But in giving up this naive and (if carefully thought through) even absurd rationalism, is it necessary to sacrifice the *genuine* sense of rationalism? And what of the serious clarification of that naiveté, of that absurdity? And what of the rationality of that irrationalism which is so much vaunted and expected of us? Does it not have to convince us, if we are expected to listen to it, with rational considerations and reasons? Is its irrationality not finally rather a narrow-minded and bad rationality, worse than that of the old rationalism? Is it not rather the rationality of 'lazy reason,' which *evades* the struggle to clarify the ultimate data and the goals and directions which they alone can rationally and truthfully prescribe?" E. Husserl, *The Crisis of European Sciences and Transcendental Phenomenology*, trans. David Carr (Evanston: Northwestern U. Press, 1970), § 6, p. 16.

17. Doxic standpoints which may be mentioned are, among others: "more life" (Simmel), before World War I; "divine air is blowing everywhere" (Losskij), during the roaring twenties; "concentration of the unconnected individual sciences into a unified science" (Neurath, Carnap), before World War II; "dialectical materialism, the science of the all-comprehensive context," after the middle of the twentieth century.

18. On phenomenology as "originary positing of a philosophical radicalism," see *Erste Philosophie* II, Hua VIII, pp. 17 ff.

19. Cf. Max Weber's classical distinction between "science" and "salvational knowledge," teacher and leader, scholar and charismatic. See "Wissenschaft als Beruf" (1919), in *Gesammelte Aufsätze zur Wissenschaftslehre* (Tübingen, 1922), pp. 524–55, esp. pp. 533, 547, 551.

20. It is then *ktēsis epistēmēs*, acquisition of knowledge (Plato, *Euthydemos* 288 D).

21. M. Verworn, *Kausale oder konditionale Weltanschauung* (Jena, 1912): "Every occurrence or state is . . . identical with the sum of its conditions. Its conditions are its essence" (p. 20), and "the scientific investigation of all being and happening can consist only in the ascertainment of its conditions" (p. 17).

22. "Every good beginner is a sceptic, but every sceptic is only a beginner" (Herbart).

23. Noack, p. 10.

24. On "topics" as the "technique of thinking a problem," see (in another connection) T. Viehweg, *Topik und Jurisprudenz* (Munich, 1953) esp. § 3: "Analyse der Topik" (ps. 15 ff.).

25. Husserl, "Philosophy as Rigorous Science," in *Shorter Works*, p. 167.

26. Max Bense, in *Die Philosophie zwischen den beiden Kriegen* (Frankfurt a. M., 1951), p. 13.

27. So one can say: "Philosophy . . . is essentially a science of true beginnings, or origins, of *rizōmata pantōn*. The science concerned with what is radical must from every point of view be radical itself in its procedure"—Husserl, "Philosophy as Rigorous Science," p. 196. It is a matter, let it be noted, of a logical, not a metaphysical radicalism, i.e., of a radical grounding attempt.

28. Peter Wust, *Die Auferstehung der Metaphysik* (Leipzig, 1920), was giving expression to a trend of the times, but he was, of necessity, corrected by Dietrich Heinrich Kerler, who stood close to Husserl. Cf. Kerler, *Die auferstandene Metaphysik* (Ulm, 1921), p. 283 (where even Husserl is not exempt from criticism).

29. That the outcome always results from a dogmatically taken stance can, of course, not be denied. Cf. E. Rothacker, *Die dogmatische Denkform in den Geisteswissenschaften und das Problem des Historismus*, in *Mainzer Akademie der Wissenschaften: Abhandlungen der Geistes- und Sozialwissenschaftlichen Klasse* (1954), Nr. 6, pp. 243–98, esp. pp. 249 ff.: "Der Begriff der dogmatischen Denkform."

30. The above was said in altercation with Alwin Diemer's work "Was ist Philosophie?" in *Die medizinische Welt* 20 (Stuttgart, 1964), pp. 4 ff.

31. "Chaos and lack of direction seem to be the sign of the time," declares Fritz Heinemann, in *Neue Wege der Philosophie* (Frankfurt a. M., 1929), p. 1.

32. Cf. M. Brelage, pp. 179 ff.

33. On knowledge in the direct attitude, in turning-inward and double turning-inward, see T. Litt, *Einleitung in die Philosophie* (Leipzig, 1933), pp. 9, 12, 23 ff.

34. On the "general concept of philosophy," so conceived, cf. Robert Reininger, *Metaphysik der Wirklichkeit*, 2 vols. (Vienna, 1947), esp. I, pp. 1–17.

35. Max Bense, p. 22.

36. Ibid.

37. See B. Bolzano, *Was ist Philosophie?* in *Nachlass* (Vienna, 1849), new ed. (Darmstadt, 1964), p. 30.

38. Husserl, *Erste Philosophie* I, Hua VII (The Hague, 1956), p. 6.

39. The question as to what philosophy really is, has often been asked. On this subject, see: H. Barth, "Philosophie der Zukunft," in *Joel-Festschrift* (Basel, 1934); H. Bergson, "L'intuition philosophique," in *La Pensée et le Mouvant* (Paris, 1934); B. Bolzano, *Was ist Philosophie?* (1849) (Darmstadt, 1964); P. Caraballese, *Che cose è la*

Filosofia? (Rome, 1942); R. Carnap, *Scheinprobleme der Philosophie* (Berlin, 1928); A. Dempf, *Philosophie als Forschung und Synthese* (Munich, 1954); A. Diemer, "Was heisst Philosophie?" in *Die medizinische Welt* 20 (Stuttgart, 1964) and *Was heisst Wissenschaft* (Meisenheim, 1964); W. Dilthey, "Das Wesen der Philosophie," *Wirkendes Wort* V (Berlin/Leipzig, 1924); R. Frondizi, *Hay una Filosofia Iberoamericana?* (Buenos Aires, 1948); J. Gaos, *Filosofía de la Filosofía* (Mexico, 1947); M. Gentile, *Che cos' è il sapere?* (Brescia, 1948); P. Haeberlin, *Das Wesen der Philosophie* (Munich, 1934); N. Hartmann, *Der philosophische Gedanke und seine Geschichte* (Berlin, 1936) and "Zur Methode der Philosophiegeschichte," *Kantstudien* (1910); M. Heidegger, *What is Philosophy?* (New York, 1958); E. Husserl, "Philosophie als strenge Wissenschaft," *Logos* (1911), English trans: *Husserl: Shorter Works*, pp. 166–97; W. Illemann, *Wesen und Begriff der Philosophie* (Leipzig, 1910); K. Jaspers, *Existenzphilosophie* (Frankfurt a. M., 1937, 1956); K. Joel, *Die philosophische Krisis der Gegenwart* (Leipzig, 1914); L. Landgrebe, *Was bedeutet uns heute Philosophie?* (Hamburg, 1954); P. F. Linke, *Niedergangserscheinungen der Philosophie der Gegenwart* (Munich/Basel, 1961); H. Lipps, "Einleitung in die Philosophie," in *Die Wirklichkeit des Menschen* (Frankfurt a. M., 1954); T. Litt, *Einleitung in die Philosophie* (Leipzig, 1933); P. Natorp, *Philosophie—ihr Problem und ihre Probleme* (Göttingen, 1911); J. Ortega y Gasset, *Was ist Philosophie?* (1930, German trans.: Stuttgart, 1958); R. B. Perry, *Is there a North American Philosophy?* (Cambridge, Mass., 1949); H. Plessner, "Die Frage nach dem Wesen der Philosophie" (Zurich, 1934; Bern, 1953) (in *Zwischen Philosophie und Gesellschaft*), and *Gibt es einen Fortschritt in der Philosophie?* (Groningen, 1946; Basel, 1947); J. Rehmke, *Philosophie als Grundwissenschaft* (Leipzig, 1910); H. Rickert, "Vom Begriff der Philosophie," in *Logos* I (1910); A. Riehl, *Über Begriff und Form der Philosophie* (Berlin, 1872); E. Rothacker, "Philosophiegeschichte und Geistesgeschichte" (1940), in *Mensch und Geschichte* (Bonn, 1950); M. Scheler, "Vom Wesen der Philosophie," in *Vom Ewigen im Menschen* (Leipzig, 1921); N. P. Stallknecht/R. S. Brumbaugh, *The Compass of Philosophy* (New York, 1954); W. Szilasi, *Wissenschaft als Philosophie* (Zurich/New York, 1945); W. Windelband, "Was ist Philosophie?—Über Begriff und Geschichte der Philosophie," in *Präludien* I (Tübingen, 1884); L. Wittgenstein, "Logisch-philosophische Abhandlung," in *Ostwalds Annalen für Naturphilosophie* (1921); L. Zea, *En torno a una Filosofía americana* (Mexico, 1945); X. Zubiri, "Sobre el problema de la Filosofía," *Revista de Occidente* (Madrid, 1933).

Chapter Two

1. Cf. Erich Rothacker, *Die dogmatische Denkform in den Geisteswissenschaften und das Problem des Historismus,* in *Abhandlungen der Mainzer Akademie der Wissenschaften und der Literatur* (1954), Nr. 6, pp. 243–98. Also Husserl, *Crisis,* pp. 4–5 ff.

2. Fritz Heinemann, *Neue Wege der Philosophie* (Frankfurt a. M., 1929), p. x, and esp. pp. 315, 373.

3. Ibid., p. 373. On the repression of the spirit, cf. F. Heinemann, *Jenseits des Existentialismus* (Stuttgart, 1957), p. 13, esp. pp. 97 ff., and also his *Existenzphilosophie—lebendig oder tot?* (Stuttgart, 1954), pp. 11 ff.

4. On philosophy's own justification, see Hermann Noack, *Die Philosophie Westeuropas* (Darmstadt, 1962), pp. 30 ff.

5. Ludwig Landgrebe, *Der Weg der Philosophie* (Gütersloh, 1963), pp. 28 ff., esp. p. 30. (The essay in question in this volume—"Heideggers *Sein und Zeit* und das Problem einer Grenze der phänomenologische Methode"—is already to be found in Landgrebe's *Phänomenologie und Metaphysik [Hamburg, 1948]; see pp. 56 ff., esp. p. 83.*

6. Ibid., p. 28.

7. Hermann Lübbe treated of the link between positivism and phenomenology, especially of the "human" or the "natural world-concept" in "Positivismus und Phänomenologie (Mach oder Husserl)" in *Szilasi-Festschrift: Beiträge zur Philosophie und Wissenschaft* (Munich, 1960), pp. 161–84, esp. p. 171.

8. *Husserl: Shorter Works,* p. 176.

9. A. Meinong, "Gegenstände höherer Ordnung," *Zeitschrift für Psychologie und Physiologie der Sinnesorgane* 21 (1899), p. 188. Cf. also *Geschichtliche Abhandlungen* II (Leipzig, 1904), pp. 385 f.

10. Husserl, *Ideas Pertaining to a General Introduction to a Pure Phenomenological Philosophy* I, trans. F. Kersten (The Hague, 1982) § 24, p. 44.

11. Cf. Martin Heidegger, *Being and Time,* trans. John Macquarrie and Edward Robinson (New York, 1962), p. 58.

12. Emil Przywara, *Das Ringen der Gegenwart* (Augsburg, 1929), e.g., pp. 170, 178, 251, 260, 342, 564, 772, 930, esp. Vol. II, pp. 939, 955, studied the various "turnings of the spirit" around the year 1920, i.e., the turning to Hegel, Fichte, Schelling, the turning to St. Thomas, and the turning to metaphysics, viz., the turning to the object.

13. Peter Wust, in his book by that title—*Die Auferstehung der Metaphysik* (Leipzig, 1920)—studied the "resurrection of metaphysics." Dietrich Heinrich Kerler in his book, *Die Auferstandene Metaphysik*

(Ulm, 1921), referred to as a "settling of scores," subjected metaphysics to a sharp critique, especially as exemplified by Driesch (pp. 1 ff.), Bergson (p. 168), Keyserling (p. 135), etc., but also Husserl (pp. 283 ff.).

14. The "theology of crisis" or "dialectical theology" therefore speaks more and more of this "Completely Other." Cf. Kurt Stavenhagen, *Absolute Stellungnahmen: Eine ontologische Untersuchung über das Wesen der Religion* (Erlangen, 1925), p. 108, esp. pp. 207 ff. See also E. Przywara, II, pp. 552 ff. Cf. R. Otto, *Das Heilige* (Breslau, 1917; Munich, 1932), pp. 31 ff.

15. *Crisis*, Appendix IV, pp. 335–41; Hua VI (The Hague,1954), § 73, pp. 269–76.

16. Cf. the possibilities for a spiritual attitude shown in principle by T. Litt in his book *Kant und Herder* (Leipzig, 1930; Heidelberg, 1949), esp. chap. 3, "Das Erkennen des Erkennens" (pp. 30–43).

17. Likewise Heidegger in *Being and Time*, p. 62.

18. On the "apriorism of the emotional," see Max Scheler, *Der Formalismus in der Ethik und die materiale Wertethik* (Halle, 1913, 1927), p. 61. In the study "Ordo amoris," love is the spiritual basic act, cf. Scheler, *Schriften aus dem Nachlass* I (1933; Bern, 1957), p. 356.

19. *Being and Time*, pp. 67 ff.

20. Johannes Rehmke in his historical study of consciousness, *Das Bewusstsein* (Berlin, 1910), makes the statement that "consciousness is synonymous with the word spirit" (p. 244).

21. Cf. L. Landgrebe, *Major Problems in Contemporary European Philosophy*, trans. Kurt F. Reinhardt (New York, 1966), p. 8; but esp. Przywara, p. 749: "The fundamental word of liberation is 'reality.'"

22. L. Landgrebe, *Der Weg der Phänomenologie*, p. 38.

23. E. Husserl, *Formal and Transcendental Logic*, trans. Dorion Cairns (The Hague, 1969), p. 251.

24. Husserl, *Ideas* I, § 57, p. 133.

25. Besides Heinemann, Erich Przywara, in his book *Das Ringen der Gegenwart* (Augsburg, 1929), expressed himself in the same sense (Vol. I, p. 304, n. 17).

26. About the "philosophy of the object" see also Przywara, II, p. 898 and passim.

27. Thus Hans Leisegang, in *Deutsche Philosophie im 20. Jahrhundert* (Breslau, 1925), p. 118 ("the insatiable longing for reality").

28. Heidegger, *Being and Time*, § 6, pp. 41 ff.

29. On "problem-forgottenness" occasioned by "being-forgottenness," see M. Heidegger, § 1, p. 20, viz., § 6, p. 43.

30. E. Husserl, "Nachwort zu meinen *Ideen zu einer reinen Phänomenologie usw.*," in *Jahrbücher für Philosophie und phänome-*

nologische Forschung 11 (Halle, 1930,) pp. 561 ff. (now also Hua V, [The Hague, 1952] p. 152). [Cf. "Author's Preface to the English Edition of *Ideas*," trans. W. R. Boyce Gibson, now in *Husserl: Shorter Works*, p. 48. The German ed. cited by Funke is Husserl's revision, addressed to German readers, of the text he had sent Gibson in 1929— *Trans.*]

31. This must be said against Alwin Diemer, who would like to have phenomenology become almost a *"gnosis"*! Cf. his essay, "Die Phänomenologie und die Idee der Philosophie als strenge Wissenschaft," in *Zeitschrift für philosophische Forschung* 13: 2 (1959), p. 247.

32. Hegel, *Enzyklopädie.* § 93; cf. on this, W. Schulz, *Das Problem der absoluten Reflexion* (Frankfurt a. M., 1963), esp. pp. 18, pp. 26 ff.

33. *Jenaer Realphilosophie* I, pp. 195 ff.

34. Cf. W. Schulz, pp. 16 ff.

35. Wilhelm Szilasi called attention to this way in his new edition of Husserl's *Logos* essay "Philosophie als strenge Wissenschaft" (Frankfurt a. M., 1965) in the "Nachwort" (pp. 87–101, above all, pp. 91 ff.).

36. This would have to be said of the term "turn"; cf. M. Müller, *Existenzphilosophie im geistigen Leben der Gegenwart* (Heidelberg, 1949, 1958), esp. p. 12.

37. Johannes Rehmke, *Philosophie als Grundwissenschaft* (Leipzig, 1929), esp. pp. 4 ff.

38. M. Heidegger, *Being and Time*, pp. 67 ff.

39. See *Grundzüge einer Metaphysik der Erkenntnis* (Berlin, 1921, 1925), esp. p. 176: "But consciousness is also an existent, a kind of being."

40. Ernesto Grassi, *Die zweite Aufklärung* (Hamburg, 1958), p. 15.

41. Here the most various names could be mentioned, from Ludwig Klages, through Henri Bergson, Walter F. Otto, Karl Kerényi, and Mircea Eliade, all the way to Vladimir Jankélévitch and M. Heidegger. Cf. Gerhard Krüger's article "Mythisches Denken in der Gegenwart," in the *Gadamer-Festschrift* (Tübingen, 1960), pp. 117–22.

42. Cf. Wilhelm Szilasi, *Wissenschaft als Philosophie* (Zurich, 1945): it is a matter of the "philosophical character of the sciences" (p. 13).

43. In the *Cartesian Meditations*, Husserl consciously goes beyond Descartes, from whom he adopts only the approach of radical questioning, § 10, pp. 23–24. Cf. also *The Paris Lectures*, trans. by Peter Koestenbaum (The Hague, 1964), pp. 9–10.

44. Cf. Oskar Becker, "Die Absurdität des Pythagoräischen Gedankens," in *Die Gegenwart der Griechen im neueren Denken* (*Gadamer-Festschrift*) (Tübingen, 1960) pp. 7–30, esp. p. 30. Becker calls for "a wide-awake, attentive scepticism . . . , which is directed as much

against a certain 'new belief' in dogma and myth stemming from a wishful thinking as against a depth psychology as well as a sociological unmasking tendency, down to complete triviality" (p. 30).

45. *Crisis*, pp. 8, 21, 73 ff., but esp. pp. 75–76.

46. See Karl Kerényi's remarks on "Mythos in verbaler Form" in *Beiträge zur Philosophie und Wissenschaft (Szilasi-Festschrift)* (Munich, 1960), pp. 121–28, esp. p. 128.

47. Ludwig Schajowicz, *Mito y Existencia* (San Juan, 1962): "For modern man, the mythical world is the universe of ambiguities. Whoever decides to penetrate into that twilight realm must renounce, from the outset, the norms which orient him in the sphere of reason. Certainly, the study of myth does not constitute an avoidance of reality, but rather an effort to discover its foundation" (p. 11).

48. One can in this sense speak of a "transcendentally understood transcendence," as Gerhard Huber does in another context (in evaluating Heinrich Barth's philosophy). Cf. *Philosophie und christliche Existenz (Festschrift for Heinrich Barth)* (Basel, 1960), pp. 203 ff.

49. Cf. W. Schulz, *Der Gott der neuzeitlichen Metaphysik* (Pfullingen, 1957), pp. 33–58, esp. p. 40.

50. So M. Heidegger asserts in *What is Philosophy?* (New York, 1958), p. 20.

51. That is the "emergence of becoming-conscious," of which Heinrich Barth speaks in his *Philosophie der Erscheinung* II (Basel, 1959), p. 633.

52. He takes "phenomenology" expressly as a "methods-concept" and interprets it as a challenge to get "to the things themselves" (p. 50). The method consists in letting "that which shows itself be seen from itself in the very way in which it shows itself from itself" (*Being and Time*, p. 58).

53. Cf. Maximilian Beck's critique of Heidegger in *Philosophische Hefte* 1: 1 (1928), pp. 26 and passim.

54. Peter Wust indeed wants to explain his thesis from the year 1920 in the sense that the "resurrection of metaphysics" is a question of "metaphysics of particularization" (*Naivität und Pietät*, Tübingen, 1925, pp. v/vi), but he does not let it be superseded in principle.

55. L. Landgrebe, in his introductory work, *Was bedeutet uns heute Philosophie?* (Hamburg, 1954), esp. pp. 49 ff., describes "knowledge as a binding of man."

56. Cf. T. M. Seebohm, *Bedingungen der Möglichkeit einer Transzendentalphilosophie* (Bonn, 1962), pp. 1 ff.

57. Marx stated: "It is thus the task of history, once the beyond of truth has disappeared, to establish the truth of the this-earthly. It is primarily the task of philosophy which stands in the service of history, after the saintly figure of human self-alienation has been unmasked, to unmask

self-alienation in its unholy forms. The critique of heaven is thus transformed into critique of earth, the critique of religion into the critique of politics." *Marx-Engels-Gesamtausgabe*, Part I, Vol. I (1927), p. 608.

58. Cf. K. Löwith, *Von Hegel bis Nietzsche* (Stuttgart, 1939, 1958), esp. pp. 295 ff.

59. Litt, in his book *Mensch und Welt* (Munich, 1948), used this argument against Gehlen. Cf. esp. the Appendix, p. 293.

60. See W. Schulz, *Der Gott der neuzeitlichen Metaphysik*, pp. 25, 38.

61. "He may deceive however much he wills, but never will he succeed in making me be nothing, as long as I think myself to be something," so Descartes says in the *Meditationes de prima philosophia* (*Oeuvres*, ed. Adam-Tannery, Vol. VII, p. 18).

62. Descartes does not, of course, pose the question according to the "ontology of *Dasein*," to which Heidegger refers (*Being and Time*, p. 45), but this is an omission only from a dogmatic position.

63. "Even the problem solver cannot deal with phenomena and senses which have not yet become visible," says Erich Rothacker in the analysis of the history of philosophy in *Problemgeschichte und Geistesgeschichte*. Cf. also the essay "Philosophiegeschichte und Geistesgeschichte," in *DVj*. 18 (1940), now in *Mensch und Geschichte* (Bonn, 1950), pp. 84–102, esp. p. 97.

64. It is something quite different when Gerhard Krüger, in his numerous investigations on history, states: "History is today our greatest problem. It is so in the threefold sense that it is at the same time our most urgent, our most comprehensive, and our most difficult problem" (in *Freiheit und Weltverwaltung*, Freiburg i. Br./Munich, 1958): "Die Geschichte im Denken der Gegenwart," pp. 97–126, esp. p. 97 (previously Frankfurt a. M., 1947 and Tübingen, 1949). For it is *our* problem and it is so *today*—that is, in a topical (situative-contextual) respect, and thus precisely not absolutely.

65. Erich Rothacker has not tired of pointing out that this consciousness always has to be taken as historical-concrete reason. Cf. *Logik und Systematik der Geisteswissenschaften* (Munich/Berlin, 1927), p. 154; *Geschichtsphilosophie* (Munich/Berlin, 1934), pp. 49, 133; "Probleme der Kulturanthropologie," in *Systematische Philosophie*, ed. N. Hartmann (Berlin, 1942), pp. 140 (86), 174 (120).

66. L. Landgrebe, *Major Problems*, p. 13.

67. See Erich Rothacker, *Die dogmatische Denkform*, p. 264 (Cf. p. 26: "It is a certain mysterious but inviolable essential law that only the concrete can be real, but the real is always determinate; determinations, however, are explicable only dogmatically").

68. Kant, *Critique of Pure Reason*, B xxxv.

69. Erich Rothacker, pp. 243 f.

70. Ibid., p. 251.

71. Ibid., p. 253.

72. Ibid., p. 252.

73. Ibid., p. 254.

74. Ibid., p. 252.

75. *Being and Time*, § 32, esp. pp. 194 ff., previously § 2, p. 27 ff.

76. Alwin Diemer, *Die Phänomenologie und die Idee der Philosophie als strenge Wissenschaft*, p. 249.

77. Husserl, *Erste Philosophie* II, Hua VIII; cf. esp. pp. 182 ff.

78. *Erste Philosophie* II, p. 181.

79. On the connection between universal critique, universal reflection, and universal *epochē*, see ibid., pp. 154 ff.

80. "The way of philosophy [is that] of the most radical liberation from prejudices" (E. Husserl, Appendix XXX., p. 479).

81. Cf. Husserl, ibid., Appendix XXXIII, p. 506.

82. "History is the grand fact of absolute being"—Husserl, ibid., p. 506.

83. Of course: "The will to final responsibility, in which the universe of possible knowledge is supposed to emerge, leads to knowledge of the fundamental inadequacy of all 'rigorous science' in positivity"—E. Husserl, *Phänomenologische Psychologie*, Hua IX (The Hague, 1962), p. 345, n. 1. [Supplementary texts, "Amsterdamer Vorträge," not in English translation—*Trans.*]

84. On the critique of critique in reiterated steps of reflection, see T. M. Seebohm, pp. 130 ff.

Chapter Three

1. This must be said against a recent interpretation which restricts the scientific character of philosophy in an unwarranted fashion. See A. Diemer, *Was heisst Wissenschaft?* (Meisenheim, 1964), esp. pp. 80 ff.

2. Accordingly, one can in no way speak of "consciousness as doom" (cf. A. Seidel's book, 1927).

3. It is the problem of the "beginning," of the "radical approach," the "revolution," constantly discussed by E. Husserl; cf. *Cartesian Meditations*, pp. 7 ff.; *Crisis*, pp. 78 ff.; *Erste Philosophie* I, pp. 5 ff. and II, pp. 3 ff.; "Phenomenology," *Encyclopedia Britannica* article, *Shorter Works*, pp. 21–35.

4. The very last starting basis may be some mysticism or other that knows everything but explains nothing. Cf. E. Underhill, *Mysticism, a Study on the Nature and Development of Man's Spiritual Consciousness* (London, 1911).

5. It is science on the basis of the occurrence of newly appearing syntheses which consciousness undertakes by applying hitherto unknown points of view. This event, of course, represents a particular kind of phenomenon. Cf. Gerhard Funke, "Geschichte als Phänomen," in *Zeitschrift für philosophische Forschung*, 11: 2 (1957), pp. 188–234.

6. That is the phenomenological meaning of "problematicism." Cf. A. Banfi, *L'uomo copernicano* (Milan, 1950), pp. 267 ff.; U. Spirito, *Significato del nostro tempo* (Florence, 1955), pp. 227 ff. The term first occurs in U. Spirito, *Il problematicismo* (Florence, 1948).

7. Among the "complementary texts" to Husserl's *Erste Philosophie* is the treatise "Weg in die transzendentale Phänomenologie als absolute und universale Ontologie durch die positiven Ontologien und die positive Erste Philosophie," Hua VIII, pp. 219–28.

8. The "formal logic" of natural consciousness then persisted in a "naiveté" of a higher level. Cf. E. Husserl, *Formal and Transcendental Logic*, pp. 2, 153, 226.

9. The attempt at a "transcendental logic" must thereby always take into consideration Kant, Fichte, and Husserl, who systematized it in principle. Cf. recently H. Krings, *Transzendentale Logik* (Munich, 1964), pp. 26 ff.

10. There is no going beyond the historicity of consciousness. L. von Renthe-Fink has made it clear that the term "historicity" probably leads back to Hegel and from him reached Dilthey and the Heidegger school via Haym. In any case, here a Hegelian moment is found. Cf. *Geschichtlichkeit* (Göttingen, 1965), esp. Part II.

11. Cf. Landgrebe, "Husserl's Departure from Cartesianism," trans. R. O. Elveton, in *The Phenomenology of Edmund Husserl: Six Essays*, ed. Donn Welton (Ithaca/ London, 1981), pp. 66–121.

12. It is, as a continual critique of the dogmatically and naively accepted foundations, a science of crises; and sociology is not that, as Francisco Ayala declares. Cf. *Tratado de Sociologia* I (Buenos Aires, 1947), pp. 20 ff.

13. "Consciousness of the world is consciousness in the mode of certainty of belief," says Husserl in *Experience and Judgment*, trans. James S. Churchill and Karl Ameriks (Evanston, 1973), p. 30. And phenomenology investigates precisely the certainties of belief.

14. Husserl does not remain in the natural or quasi-natural certainties of belief. He therefore does not link up directly with Hume and his "belief," as A. de Waelhens states in *Phénoménologie et Vérité* (Paris, 1953), p. 50, or as Gaston Berger could suggest in "Husserl et Hume," *Revue internationale de Philosophie* 2 (1939), pp. 342 ff.

15. Here the sentence which Jean Hyppolite once used with respect to

Hegel applies: "The absolute is reflection, that is, philosophical knowledge is for Hegel both self-knowledge and knowledge of the existent"— *Logique et Existence* (Paris, 1953), p. 88.

16. That is the meaning of continual "phenomenological reduction as absolute justification." Cf. E. Husserl, *Erste Philosophie* II, pp. 497 ff.

17. It can be regarded as the attempt to become "the unprejudiced science of the prejudices concerning the underlying most general things," as Johannes Erich Heyde demands for "philosophy as basic science." Cf. J. E. Heyde, *Grundwissenschaftliche Philosophie* (Leipzig, 1924), p. 26.

18. Husserl speaks of the *telos* of reason only where the sudden change of theoretical reason into the apodictic-rational attitude is treated, in the closing paragraph of *Crisis*, Appendix IV, pp. 335–41.

19. Cf. P. K. Schneider, *Die wissenschaftbegründende Funktion der Transzendentalphilosophie* (Freiburg/Munich, 1965), who treats especially Descartes, Kant, Fichte, Hegel, and Husserl (pp. 134 ff.), without forgetting logistics (pp. 37 ff.) and cybernetics (pp. 150 ff.).

20. Hans Wagner, *Philosophie und Reflexion* (Munich, 1958), under Hönigwald's influence, elaborated a "philosophy of reflection upon scientific principles." Cf. also his arguments against Husserl in "Critical Observations Concerning Husserl's Posthumous Writings," in R. O. Elveton, ed. and trans., *The Phenomenology of Husserl: Selected Critical Readings* (Chicago, 1970), pp. 204–58.

21. On this topic, see the methodically clear development of "transcendental idealism" in Robert Reininger, *Metaphysik der Wirklichkeit*, 2 vols. (Vienna, 1931, 1947), esp. "Das Bewusstsein und seine Stufen," pp. 21 ff.

22. The ideal of the most possible freedom from prejudice which is striven for with the "method of proximity to reality" is now supposed to be attained. So states W. Stegmuller on Robert Reininger in *Hauptströmungen der Gegenwartsphilosophie* (Vienna/Stuttgart, 1952), pp. 278 ff.

23. T. Litt saw the relation between direct turning-toward and turning-inward in this sense. Cf. *Kant und Herder* (Heidelberg, 1949), esp. pp. 30 ff.: "Erkennen des Erkennens" and "Einleitung in die Philosophie," pp. 12 ff.

24. *Kant und Herder*, p. 40.

25. Th. Litt, *Denken und Sein* (Stuttgart, 1948) made this clear, especially through chap. VI, "Sein, Denken, Sichselbstdenken" (pp. 144–66). Cf. *Mensch und Welt* (Heidelberg, 1948), esp. p. 293.

26. Cf. Litt, *Denken und Sein*, pp. 147 ff., and *Philosophie und Zeitgeist* (Leipzig, 1935), pp. 24 ff.

27. There is, then, in philosophy no "state of forgottenness," unless

philosophy ceases to be philosophy. Cf. M. F. Sciacca, *Akt und Sein* (Freiburg/Munich, 1964), pp. 11 ff.

28. The "first of all philosophies" is for Husserl the "science of method in general." Cf. *Ideas* I, Introduction, p. xxii, and *Erste Philosophie* II, Hua VIII, p. 249.

29. Preface to Hegel's *Philosophy of Right*, trans. T. M. Knox (London, 1952), p. 11.

30. "That is the performance of thinking, which is called the 'refutation' of the earlier philosophy by the subsequent one. But this refutation does not consist in simply rejecting the refuted principle, cancelling it as 'error.' For the 'refutation' is nothing else but the enunciation of the contradiction which, though in the 'refuted' system it does not arrive at self-consciousness, was nonetheless already contained in it"—so says Litt in *Philosophie und Zeitgeist*, p. 38.

31. Formally, it is always transcendental philosophy—namely, asking back concerning the ultimate conditions for the possibility of knowledge. Cf. E. Husserl, *Crisis*, § 26, pp. 97 ff.

32. Philosophy is, then, not one science among others, but as transcendental experience it presents horizons of being and thought within which the sciences work. Cf. H. Hohl, *Lebenswelt und Geschichte* (Freiburg/Munich, 1962), p. 20.

33. On this subject, see T. Litt's investigations of "knowledge of knowledge" in his book *Kant und Herder* (1930; Heidelberg, 1949), pp. 30 ff., but esp. his *Einleitung in die Philosophie* (Leipzig, 1933), pp. 9, 12 ff.

34. Ibid., pp. 33 ff.; viz. pp. 12 and 23 ff.

35. Cf. the comments on the "two-spheres theorem" in Hans Wagner, "Critical Observations Concerning Husserl's Posthumous Writings," in Elveton, ed. and trans., *The Phenomenology of Husserl*, esp. pp. 220 ff., 224 ff.

36. In such views it is a question of "naivetés of a higher level," as Husserl says in *Formal and Transcendental Logic*, p. 2.

37. Cf. P. K. Schneider's remarks on "the understanding of the world and the objective sciences of being as project of transcendental meaning-giving" in *Die wissenschaftsbegründende Funktion der Transzendental-philosophie* (Freiburg/Munich, 1965), pp. 134–46, esp. pp. 137 ff.

38. The distinctive essence of philosophy as theory of science is and remains that it demands "radical reflection." Cf. R. Lauth, "J. G. Fichtes Gesamtidee der Philosophie," manuscript, p. 2, cited in P. K. Schneider, p. 173.

39. The individual sciences developed "methods, not indeed with the everyday man's naiveté, but still with a *naiveté of a higher level, which*

abandoned the appeal to the pure idea, the justifying of method by pure principles, according to ultimate apriori possibilities and necessities," as Husserl states in *Formal and Transcendental Logic*, p. 2.

40. Husserl also speaks of the "naiveté of an externally appended and *ex post facto* theory of cognition," ibid., p. 13.

41. Caspar Isenkrahe makes it clear that such "documentary evidences accepted without proof" must always be posited. Cf. *Zum Problem der Evidenz* (Kempten/Munich, 1917), p. 34, esp. pp. 36 ff.

42. Cf. Husserl's MS. E III 5 with the title "Universale Teleologie," presented in *Tempo e Intenzionalità* (Archivo di Filosofia, Padua, 1960), pp. 9–12, (Italian version, pp. 13–16).

43. Again: there is for philosophy absolutely no "state of forgottenness." Cf. Michele Federico Sciacca *Akt und Sein* (Freiburg/Munich, 1964), p. 11.

44. The term "problematicism" was, as stated above, coined by Ugo Spirito, *Il problematicismo* (Florence, 1948). The anti-dogmatic, critical aspect of the philosophical investigations of foundations finds expression in it. Cf. A. Banfi, *L'uomo copernicano* (Milan, 1950), pp. 267–76, and U. Spirito, *Significato del nostro tempo* (Florence, 1955), pp. 227 ff.

45. This is the non-positional consciousness given in reflection, of which Sartre, for instance, speaks. Cf. *The Transcendence of the Ego* (New York, 1957), esp. pp. 45 ff.

46. In the *Symposium sobre la noción Husserliana de la Lebenswelt*, at the 13th World Congress for Philosophy in Mexico (Sept., 1963), José Gaos pointed out in his article "La Lebenswelt de Husserl" that "progressive analysis" is the key word for a "purely phenomenological, anti-metaphysical philosophy." Cf. *Symposium*, Publications of the Congress (Mexico, 1963), pp. 17–24, esp. p. 24.

47. All this has nothing to do with "philosophies of history calculated out only historically," of which Heidegger speaks in *Holzwege* (Frankfurt, 1950). Cf. therein the "Spruch des Anaximander" (p. 300).

48. Its task is something else than that of the "fetishistic objectivity," which Enzo Paci treats of. Cf. Paci's essay "Die Lebensweltwissenschaft," in *Symposium*, pp. 51–75, esp. p. 63.

49. Cf. Enzo Paci, "Tempo e relazione intenzionale in Husserl," in the anthology *Tempo e Intenzionalità* (Padua, 1960), pp. 23–48, esp. p. 48.

50. Cf. *Crisis*, p. 340.

51. In his essay "Kant et Husserl," *Kantstudien*, 46: 1 (1954/55), pp. 44–67, Paul Ricoeur explains what transcendental experience is for Husserl: "In short, it is the very theme of Kantian phenomenology, the theme which the Copernican revolution brings out; when it is not reduced to the axiomatization of Newtonian physics, this revolution is

nothing else but the reduction of existents to their appearance in the mind" (p. 49).

52. Oskar Becker discusses the "questionableness of the philosopher" in his article "Von der Abenteuerlichkeit des Künstlers und der vorsichtigen Verwegenheit des Philosophen," in *Konkrete Vernunft*, commemorative volume for Erich Rothacker, ed. G. Funke (Bonn, 1958), pp. 25–38, esp. p. 34; now also in Becker's *Gesammelte philosophische Aufsätze* (Pfullingen, 1963), pp. 103–26, esp. p. 120.

53. This also belongs to "metaphysics as history of being," of which Heidegger speaks in his *Nietzsche* II (Pfullingen, 1961), II, pp. 399 ff.

54. Enzo Paci, in the essay "Die Lebensweltwissenschaft" cited above, states as follows: "The subjects act on the basis of a 'purely passive possession of the world': they transform passivity into activity. In the last analysis, that is a fundamental conquest; it is quite specifically the theoretical disinterestedness that allows philosophy to become active transformation of the world, which reverses passiveness into activity 'on the basis of a passive possession of the world'" (p. 56).

55. Husserl, *Ideas* I, § 1, p. 45.

56. Husserl can therefore, also in *Ideas* I, characterize the "natural attitude" in terms of the scienticized views which have become natural; cf. § 30, pp. 56 f.

57. Cf. Husserl's remarks in *Crisis*, § 9, pp. 23–59.

58. There is no such thing as "phenomenology practiced with straight-forward naiveté," no "phenomenological groping around," if the method of the fundamental clarification of foundations is understood correctly. Cf. W. H. Müller, *Die Philosophie Edmund Husserls* (Bonn, 1956), pp. 35 ff.

59. Landgrebe, in his book *Der Weg der Phänomenologie* (Gütersloh, 1963), p. 100, speaks of "perspectives of phenomenological metaphysics."

60. Phenomenology took a turn toward the speculative with Eugen Fink. Cf. "L'analyse intentionelle et le problème de la pensée spécula-tive," in H. L van Breda, ed., *Problèmes actuels de la phénoménologie* (Paris, 1952), pp. 53–87, esp. pp. 84 ff.

61. Cf. G. Funke, *Beantwortung der Frage, welchen Gegenstand die Philosophie habe oder ob sie gegenstandslos sei* (Mainz Rector's Speech) (Mainz, 1966), esp. pp. 14 ff.

62. Cf. T. Litt, *Mensch und Welt* (Heidelberg, 1948), p. 293; *Philosophie und Zeitgeist* (Leipzig, 1935), p. 23.

Chapter Four

1. An overall view is presented in Herbert Spiegelberg's compendious description in *The Phenomenological Movement*, 2 vols. (The Hague,

1960), though some individual gaps are left. Spiegelberg overemphasizes Brentano's predecessorship (I, pp. 27 ff.) at the expense of an adequate exposition of Husserl (I, pp. 73–163). He draws Heidegger (I, pp. 271 ff.) as well as N. Hartmann (I, 358) into his interpretation. In unexpected detail, the greatest part of Volume II is dedicated to the "French Phase of the Movement" (II, pp. 396–592). Cursory prospects (II, pp. 595–650) round out the information. On the whole, the proportions seem misdrawn, the significances leveled out, and the accents arbitrarily placed. The basic tenor of his view of Husserl is that "the establishment of a new transcendental philosophy should have led him to a dead end" (I, p. 163).

2. Erich Przywara, S.J., in the two volumes *Ringen der Gegenwart* (Augsburg, 1929), more than once pointed out the difference of positions within phenomenology and, for instance, distinguished a methodological from a systematic, i.e., a descriptive from a transcendental-idealistic "trend" (I, p. 290). Cf. then also E. Przywara, "Drei Richtungen der Phänomenologie," *Stimmen der Zeit* 115 (1927–1928), pp. 252 ff.

3. Spiegelberg, I, pp. 168 ff.

4. Ibid., I, pp. 171 ff.

5. Ibid., I, pp. 228 ff.

6. Ibid., I, p. 271, esp I, p. 353.

7. Cf. Franz Josef Brecht's description, written from an extreme Heideggerian standpoint, in *Bewusstsein und Existenz—Wesen und Weg der Phänomenologie* (Bremen, 1948), esp. pp. 161 ff.

8. One manages by then having phenomenology be the precursor for any genuine philosophy appearing later; e.g., F. J. Brecht in *Einführung in die Philosophie der Existenz* (Heidelberg, 1948) pp. 43–50; and L. Landgrebe in *Major Problems of Contemporary European Philosophy*, esp. pp. 38f, 76, 100, 118, 131, 156, 170.

9. *Neue Wege der Philosophie* (Frankfurt a. M., 1929), pp. 334 ff.

10. Oskar Becker, "The Philosophy of Edmund Husserl," in, R. O. Elveton, ed. and trans., *The Phenomenology of Husserl: Selected Critical Readings* (Chicago, 1970), pp. 40–72, esp. pp. 44 ff.

11. Cf. Wilhelm Szilasi, op. cit., pp. 7, 51, 92.

12. Walter Biemel, "The Decisive Phases in the Development of Husserl's Philosophy," in Elveton, *The Phenomenology of Husserl*, pp. 148–73.

13. Husserl speaks of a "genetic phenomenology" already in the *Cartesian Meditations*, § 34, p. 69; cf. also *Crisis*, esp. pp. 9 ff, 11 ff., 15 ff.

14. See Husserl, *Crisis*, § 7, pp. 16 ff.

15. The following exposition is based on Biemel's arguments (p. 149 ff.), but then takes a different turn.

16. Biemel, pp. 150 f.

17. Ibid., p. 153.

18. Ibid., p. 155.

19. Ibid., p. 154.

20. Ms. F I 36 (1925), cited by Biemel, pp. 155–59.

21. Ibid., pp. 155 f.

22. Cf. *Wissenschaftslehre* (Sulzbach, 1837; new edition, Leipzig, 1914), esp. Vol. I, §§ 19–31, "Vom Dasein der Wahrheiten an sich," and II, §§ 121–94, "Von den Sätzen an sich."

23. Phenomenology deals with this connection, and "the great confusion then begins when one resorts to Husserlian phenomenology and on the whole construes it as something it is not, namely as a method for as precise as possible a clarification of the so-called facts of any field." Hermann Drüe, in his commendable portrayal of *Edmund Husserls System der phänomenologischen Psychologie* (Berlin, 1963), brought this to unmistakable expression.

24. This results in a "transcendental theory of transcendent cognition." Cf. Husserl, *Formal and Transcendental Logic*, p. 253.

25. On the method of reflection, see first F. Weidauer, *Kritik der Transzendental-Phänomenologie Husserls* (Leipzig, 1933) esp. §§ 16–17, and then T. M. Seebohm's statements in his analysis *Die Bedingungen der Möglichkeit der Transzendentalphilosophie. Edmund Husserls transzendentalphänomenologischer Ansatz, dargestellt in Anschluss an seine Kant-Kritik* (Bonn, 1962), esp. pp. 51 ff.

26. On the "historicity of consciousness," see Seebohm, pp. 142 ff.; cf. first the paragraph "Reflexion und Zeitbewusstsein" (§ 26, pp. 123 ff.) as well as the paragraph on "Die absolute Wissenschaft" (§ 27, pp. 130 ff.).

27. Husserl, *The Phenomenology of Internal Time-Consciousness*, ed. M. Heidegger, trans. James S. Churchill (Bloomington, 1964), § 36, p. 100.

28. Cf. G. Funke, *Zur transzendentalen Phänomenologie* (Bonn, 1958), esp. pp. 7–15 ("Akt, Genesis, Habitus").

29. Cf. H. Drüe, pp. 302 ff.

30. Already in the *Lectures on the Phenomenology of Inner Time-Consciousness*, Husserl says: "A distinction must thus be drawn between the prephenomenal being of the experiences, their being prior to the reflective turning toward them, and their being as phenomenon"— Appendix XII; p. 118 cf. English trans., pp. 178–79.

31. Cf. in addition *Crisis*, Appendix IV, pp. 335 ff.

32. This can already be seen from the lectures on *The Idea of Phenomenology* (1907), trans. William P. Alston and George Nakhnikian (The Hague, 1964), esp. Lecture V, pp. 52–60, esp. pp. 59 f.

33. *Husserl: Shorter Works*, p. 166.

34. Ibid., p. 195.

35. Cf. W. Szilasi's remarks in the Afterword to the new German edition of this essay. *Die Idee der Phänomenologie* (Frankfurt a. M., 1965), pp. 87–101, esp. pp. 91, 97.

36. *Formal and Transcendental Logic*, pp. 209–10.

37. *Cartesian Meditations*, § 42, p. 89 f.

38. Ibid., § 64, p. 156.

39. Ibid.

40. Ibid.

41. Cf. Alwin Diemer's comments on "Die Phänomenologie und die Idee der Philosophie als strenge Wissenschaft," *Zeitschrift für philosophische Forschung* 13: 2 (1959), pp. 243–62, esp. on the "metaphysical *epoché*," p. 256. One cannot agree with Diemer's paralleling of phenomenology with late-antique Gnosis, i.e., with his sociology-of-knowledge simplification (p. 249).

42. Phenomenology designs no project, not even an "axiomatic of possible metaphysics," but rather it maintains a critical relationship toward the respectively present position, whose secret metaphysics it unmasks hypothetically as implicitly operative presupposition. Cf. Diemer, p. 261.

43. Husserl, "Philosophy as Rigorous Science," *Shorter Works*, p. 195.

44. *Cartesian Meditations*, § 64, p. 156.

45. Ibid.

46. Ibid.

47. § 86, pp. 208 ff: "The evidence of pre-predicative experience."

48. Cf. *Crisis*, § 28, pp. 103 ff: "Kant's unexpressed 'presupposition': the surrounding world of life, taken for granted as valid"; § 29, pp. 111 ff.: "The life-world can be disclosed as a realm of subjective phenomena which have remained 'anonymous'"; § 33, pp. 121 ff.: "The problem of the 'life-world' as a partial problem within the general problem of objective science."

49. A "theory of prepredicative experience as the first part of the *genetic* theory of judgment" (italics added) is presented in *Experience and Judgment*, § 6, pp. 27 ff.

50. Already in *Formal and Transcendental Logic*, § 60, pp. 159 ff., esp. p. 161.

51. *Crisis*, Appendix IV, p. 340.

52. In *Experience and Judgment*, the "retrogression to the self-evidence of experience" is portrayed "as retrogression to the life-world" (§ 10, pp. 41–46). Accordingly, there is also talk of a "genealogy of logic" (§ 11, pp. 47 ff.).

53. *Crisis*, § 7, pp. 16–18, esp. p. 17.

54. *Formal and Transcendental Logic*, § 86, pp. 208–12, esp. p. 211.

55. Biemel, in Elveton, ed., *The Phenomenology of Husserl*, p. 170.

56. Landgrebe seems to be undertaking such an attempt when, in the treatise "The Problem of a Transcendental Science of the A Priori of the Life-World," in *The Phenomenology of Edmund Husserl: Six Essays*, ed. Donn Welton (Ithaca, 1981), he states the following: "*Doxa* can no longer be circumvented by philosophy. It itself must be accounted for in its necessity and truth through a 'return to the naiveté of life'—but in a reflection which rises above this naiveté" (p. 185). This means, however, that phenomenology, with its return to the life-world and the constitutive achievements which make it possible, moves on a terrain which is no longer that of the metaphysical thinking of tradition. Husserl thus, in his own way, is confronted with a task which Heidegger had characterized at approximately the same time as that of the "return to the ground of metaphysics."

57. Cf. W. Schulz, *Das Problem der absoluten Reflexion* (Frankfurt a. M., 1963), esp. pp. 13, 27 ff.

58. On the "problem of the beginning," see Diemer's book on Husserl (Meisenheim, 1956) pp. 270 ff., as well as on the "*Limesproblematik*," pp. 271, 272, 278, 279.

59. But actually it involves "the systematic unfolding of the all-embracing Apriori innate in the essence of a transcendental subjectivity" or "the universal logos of all conceivable being"— Husserl, *Cartesian Meditations*, § 64, p. 155.

60. *Crisis*, Appendix I, "The Vienna Lecture," p. 286.

61. "There arises, then, a particular humanity and a particular life-vocation correlative to the accomplishment of a new culture," says Husserl in the *Crisis*, Appendix I, "The Vienna Lecture," p. 287.

62. Husserl thus demands "that apriori science must not be naive; on the contrary, it must have originated from ultimate transcendental-phenomenological sources"—*Cartesian Meditations*, § 64, p. 155.

63. Landgrebe, *The Phenomenology of Edmund Husserl*, pp. 189 f.

64. Cf. Husserl's treatise on "The Attitude of Natural Science and the Attitude of Humanistic Science," in *Crisis*, Appendix III, pp. 315–34, esp. p. 323.

65. Cf. *Krisis*, Appendix XXV, Hua VI, p. 500 [not in Carr's translation of *Crisis*—Trans.]. "All possible worlds are variants of the one that is valid for us."

66. A "hermeneutic difference" always exists insofar as one must "inquire from what is said to what is meant." Cf. Josef Derbolav's essay "Was Plato sagte und was er gemeint hat," in *Beispiele, Festschrift für*

Eugen Fink (The Hague, 1965), pp. 161–87. The treatise bears the subtitle "Erörterungen einer hermeneutisch bedeutsamen Differenz" (pp. 161, 187).

67. *Crisis*, Appendix VI, "The Origin of Geometry," pp. 353–78, esp. pp. 370 ff.

68. Ibid., p. 369.

69. Husserl, in setting the theme in the *Crisis*, asks, "Can reason and that-which-is be separated, where reason, as knowing, determines what is?" (§ 5, p. 11).

70. Cf. *Crisis*, p. 370: "Certainly theory of knowledge has never been seen as a peculiarly historical task. But this is precisely what we object to in the past."

71. Landgrebe, *The Phenomenology of Edmund Husserl*, p. 198.

72. Nor has the problem been essentially clarified by Orlando Pugliese's book on *Vermittlung und Kehre* (Freiburg/Munich, 1965), esp. Part II, pp. 91 ff.

73. Landgrebe, pp. 198f.

74. Ibid., p. 198.

75. The "new phenomenology" which A. Diemer speaks of in his essay on "Phänomenologie und die Idee der Philosophie als strenge Wissenschaft" has always achieved this as transcendental-phenomenological idealism. Cf. Diemer, p. 261.

76. Cf. Seebohm's comments in his book *Die Bedingungen der Möglichkeit der Transcendentalphilosophie*, § 29, pp. 155–65, esp. p. 164, where he treats of transcendental phenomenology and metaphysics.

77. Husserl, in the treatise "Idee der vollen Ontologie" (ca. 1924), says the following: "The difficulty here is to follow the stages of naiveté and finally to characterize the naiveté of naiveté, i.e., to bring out the at first hidden meaning of the transcendental with which the idea of a transcendental science arises"—*Erste Philosophie* II, Hua VIII, pp. 212–18, esp. pp. 212/13.

78. Therefore it is already stated early in Husserl: "Basically, phenomenological reduction, rightly understood, already points the way to transcendental idealism, since all phenomenology is nothing but the strictly scientific form of this idealism" (ibid., p. 181).

Chapter Five

1. Hubert Hohl in his portrayal of the "basic features of Edmund Husserl's late philosophy" under the title *Lebenswelt und Geschichte* (Freiburg/Munich, 1962) devoted a special study to horizon-structure. Cf. § 13, "Horizont und kosmologische Differenz," pp. 39–42.

2. Accordingly, in phenomenological investigation of foundations an *epochē* is made with respect to the scienticized world and a return to the so-called life-world, and this life-world is, furthermore, reduced to the appertinent subjectivity. Cf. Husserl, *Experience and Judgment*, § 11, pp. 47 ff. and *Crisis*, §§ 39–40, pp. 148 ff.

3. Cf. Husserl, *Crisis*, § 5, pp. 11–14, esp. p. 12.

4. This becomes clear when Husserl says "that the proper return to the naiveté of life—but in a reflection which rises above this naiveté—is the only possible way to overcome the philosophical naiveté which lies in the [supposedly] 'scientific' character of traditional objectivistic philosophy. This will open the gates to the new dimension we have repeatedly referred to in advance"—*Crisis* § 9, p. 59.

5. And even a consistently applied formal logic persists in a "naiveté at a higher level." Cf. Husserl, *Formal and Transcendental Logic*, esp. pp. 2, 13, 153, 176, 226, 265, 272 f., introduced as an "attempt at a critique of logical reason." Indeed, "the whole of phenomenology is nothing more than scientific self-examination on the part of transcendental subjectivity, an examination that at first proceeds straightforwardly and therefore with a certain naiveté of its own, but later becomes critically intent on its own logos" (§ 104, p. 273).

6. An example of Husserl's makes the phenomenological intention clear. Husserl says: "The whole of 'exact' physics operates with such 'idealities'; thus, beneath actually experienced Nature, beneath the Nature dealt with in actual living, it places a Nature as idea, as a regulative ideal norm, as the logos, in a higher sense, belonging to actually experienced Nature. What that signifies, what it can do for the cognition and control of Nature, every undergraduate 'understands' with naive positiveness. But, for a radical self-understanding and a transcendental criticism of 'exact' cognition of Nature, vast problems are implicit here" (ibid., pp. 292 f.).

7. That is the much-cited "self-explication on the part of subjectivity, as it investigates the sense of its own transcendental functions"; cf. ibid., § 104, p. 274.

8. See "Philosophy as Rigorous Science," *Husserl: Shorter Works*, p. 167.

9. Thus transcendental logic becomes the theory of science purely and simply (vide Kant, Fichte, Husserl). Cf. H. Krings, *Transzendentale Logik* (Munich, 1964), esp. Vorrede 3, pp. 26–37, above all, p. 36.

10. Stephan Strasser, in his book *Phänomenologie und Erfahrungswissenschaft vom Menschen* (Berlin, 1964), drew the picture of phenomenological efforts at the foundations as follows: "The phenomenological philosopher sees the phenomenon 'science' in a different light than the

nineteenth century 'scienticist.' According to him, scientific thinking is just one phase in the process of mankind's becoming conscious" (p. 283).

11. Cf. H. Krings, p. 48: "Transcendental logic . . . asks about the immanent possibility of the fact; it is the depiction of the transcendental 'genesis' of the fact, as Fichte says."

12. Accordingly, Strasser, in the fundamental second of three investigations in his book *Phänomenologie und Erfahrungswissenschaft vom Menschen*, discusses precisely "the nature and change of form of objectivity" (pp. 61–220), starting with the Husserlian connection of life-world and world of science (p. 61 ff.).

13. Diemer, in his essay on "Die Phänomenologie und die Idee der Philosophie als strenge Wissenschaft," pp. 245 f.

14. Consciousness must obviously "make its history itself," as W. Szilasi says in *Einführung in die Phänomenologie Edmund Husserls* (Tübingen, 1959), p. 142.

15. To that extent it is right to say that philosophy is "by its origin and essence the explicitly carried out turning back of human cognition into itself, not just with respect to its transcendental constitution as its ground of possibility, but also with respect to its ground of reality and truth"—H. Krings, p. 56.

16. Cf. Husserl, *Logical Investigations* II, pp. 535 f.

17. *Ideas*, § 78, p. 180.

18. *Cartesianische Meditationen* (The Hague, 1950), p. 192. [Not in Cairns' translation—Trans.].

19. *Crisis*, §§ 8 ff., pp. 21 ff.

20. Ibid., § 9, p. 51.

21. Ibid., § 9, p. 52.

22. *Ideas* I, § 24, pp. 44 f.

23. *Ideas* I, § 78, p. 181.

24. *Experience and Judgment*, § 4, pp. 19 ff.

25. W. Szilasi therefore also does better to speak of a "transcendental positivism" of Husserl's. Cf. his book on Husserl, § 47, pp. 116 ff.

26. *Ideas*, § 20, p. 39.

27. Cf. *Ideas* I, § 20, p. 38 [on "standpoint-philosophers— Trans.].

28. *Ideas* I, § 78, pp. 177–81, esp. pp. 177 f.

29. Cf. T. Litt, *Einleitung in die Philosophie* (Leipzig/Berlin, 1933) p. 9.

30. *Ideas* I, § 3, p. 8: essential insight (*Wesensschauung* = ideation).

31. *Ideas* I, § 79, p. 188, esp. n. 8.

32. *Ideas* I, § 79, p. 188, n. 18.

33. Diemer exaggerates this point in his essay on Husserl cited above (p. 247).

34. Reflection discovers that for every basic kind of objectivity, there is a basic form of experience, of evidence. Cf. *Formal and Transcendental Logic*, § 60, p. 161.

35. *Ideas* I, § 77 "Reflection as a Fundamental Peculiarity of the Sphere of Mental Processes. Studies in Reflection" pp. 174–77.

36. Ibid., p. 174.

37. E.g., A. Diemer, p. 247.

38. That in a wholly parallel view, e.g., Gaston Bachelard in his writings aims to make the "self-evidencing of reality in reason" become transparent is clarified excellently by Joachim Kopper and must be added here. Cf. "Das gedoppelte Wesen des Wissens um Wahrheit," *Zeitschrift für philosophische Forschung* 18: 2 (1964) pp. 297–309, esp. p. 298.

39. *Crisis*, Appendix IV, pp. 335–41.

40. Even in reflection the "evident-making activity of consciousness," or, "stated more pregnantly, the primally institutive constitution, of ideal objectivities of the sort with which logic is concerned" shows up; cf. *Formal and Transcendental Logic*, § 63, p. 168.

41. Cf. Diemer's remarks, p. 249/250.

42. That is *also* "life-history of consciousness" (cf. Szilasi, p. 142).

43. Whether phenomenology in its procedure should consequently be qualified as "dialectical phenomenology," as Stephan Strasser does, may be left undecided (cf. *Phänomenologie und Erfahrungswissenschaft vom Menschen*, pp. 223 ff., esp. pp. 226, 232, 254).

44. Although "positive" is a term that originated in the language of the Enlightenment, since Hegel it has denoted primarily, as the word suggests, something "posited, given" (*Philosophie der Religion* III, 1, p. 23), i.e., something added to man from the outside and deriving its authority from there (cf. P. Henrici, *Hegel und Blondel* [Pullach, near Munich, 1958], p. 13, n. 17).

45. On "positivism and phenomenology" from a historical point of view, see H. Lübbe's essay in the *Szilasi-Festschrift* (Munich, 1960), pp. 161–84.

46. On the "legitimating basis for the distinction between the actual and the ideal," see K. H. Volkmann-Schluck in the essay "Die Idealität der Bedeutung nach Husserl," in *Husserl und das Denken der Neuzeit* (The Hague, 1959), pp.d 230–41, esp. pp. 232 ff.

47. Husserl, *Formal and Transcendental Logic*, § 99, p. 250, esp. p. 251.

48. An example that this is still not seen even in the most recent studies on phenomenology is Alois Roth's commentary on the "phenom-

enological method" in his book on *Husserls ethische Untersuchungen* (The Hague, 1960), pp. 3 ff.

49. From here, then, ultimately all phenomena can actually be brought into connection with the life-world problems. Cf. H. Blumenberg, "Lebenswelt und Technisierung unter Aspekten der Phänomenologie, in *Sguardi su la Filsofia contemporanea* 51 (Turin, 1953), esp. pp. 9 ff.

50. Husserl, *Cartesian Meditations*, § 41, pp. 83 ff.

51. Cf. Manfred Brelage's valuable comments on "the phenomenological theory of pure and of transcendental consciousness," now in *Studien zur Transzendentalphilosophie* (Berlin, 1965) esp. pp. 115–19.

52. Diemer, p. 254.

53. And when criticism says that "nothing can be thought independently of thought," one can add "but [it can be thought] as independent of thought"—as was done by Richard Hönigswald in his inscription in Bruno Bauch's works (quoted in Brelage, p. 135).

54. On various interpretions of "immanence" and "transcendence," see Husserl, *The Idea of Phenomenology*, pp. 27 ff.

55. "Transcendental phenomenology does not deal with the 'experiencing' of the existent by a subjectivity, but with the constitution of all existents as such in the consciousness"— Brelage, p. 108.

56. On this topic, Eugen Fink's interpretation, authorized by Husserl in 1933, says the following: "*Being shut off* from the dimension of the 'transcendental' belongs to the essence of the imprisonment within the world which defines the natural attitude." "Die phänomenologische Philosophie E. Husserls in der gegenwärtigen Kritik," *Kant-Studien*, 38 (1933), p. 347; trans. R. O. Elveton, in Elveton, ed., *The Phenomenology of Husserl*, p. 105.

57. This opinion can be found, in a weakened form, even in the otherwise so subtle Brelage (p. 119).

58. "World" is then an "idea correlative to a perfect experiential evidence," says Husserl in *Cartesian Meditations*, § 28, pp. 61 ff.

59. "There is no conceivable place where the life of consciousness is broken through, or could be broken through, and we might come upon a transcendency that possibly had any sense other than that of an intentional unity making its appearance in the subjectivity itself of consciousness," Husserl declares in *Formal and Transcendental Logic*. § 94, p. 236.

60. The "temptations of the natural modes of thought and judgment" are thereby avoided. Cf. Husserl, *The Idea of Phenomenology*, p. 32.

61. It is avoided where the "reiterated reflexive bearing [of transcendental phenomenology] upon itself" is maintained—*Formal and Transcendental Logic*, § 101, p. 268.

62. This would have to be said against Diemer (p. 261).

63. See *Ideas* I, § 30, pp. 56–57.

64. To this extent one can, indeed, speak of phenomenological "Enlightenment": cf. Manfred Brelage, p. 114.

65. It is solely a matter of the "correlation between world and world-consciousness"—*Crisis*, § 41, p. 151.

66. On these clues, see *Formal and Transcendental Logic*, § 97, p. 245 and § 102, p. 269, etc.

67. Phenomenology, as epistemology and correlational research, is prior to any metaphysics which assumes a definitive position. Cf. already Husserl, *Logical Investigations* II, p. 265.

68. In a classic statement, Husserl says: ". . . experience is not an opening through which a world existing, prior to all experience, shines into a room of consciousness; it is not a mere taking of something alien to consciousness into consciousness. For how could I make a rational statement to that effect, without seeing such a state-of-affairs and therefore seeing not only consciousness but also the something alien to consciousness—that is: *experiencing* the alien affair?" See *Formal and Transcendental Logic*, § 94, pp. 232–36, esp. pp. 232/233.

69. "No being nor being-thus for me, whether as actuality or as possibility, but as accepted by me [*mir geltend*]"—ibid., p. 234.

70. "Phenomenological idealism does not deny the real existence of the real world. . . . Its only task and achievement is to elucidate the meaning of this world, precisely the meaning in which everyone considers it to be really existing"—Cf. Hua V. p. 152; cf. *Husserl: Shorter Works*, p. 48.

71. Cf. Hua V, p. 153 (*Husserl: Shorter Works*, p. 48).

72. The "new idea of foundation, namely a transcendental foundation" is discussed by Husserl in the *Paris Lectures*, p. 11.

Chapter Six

1. Husserl, on the occasion of the Kant celebration of May 1, 1924, in Freiburg i. Breisgau, went beyond Kant in his delineation of the fundamental task of transcendental philosophy. Cf. "Kant und die Idee der Transzendentalphilosophie," in *Erste Philosophie* I (1923/24), Hua VII, pp. 230–87; "Kant and the Idea of Transcendental Philosophy," trans. Ted E. Klein and William E. Pohl, *The Southwestern Journal of Philosophy* 5: 3 (Fall 1974), pp. 9–56.

2. Cf. Husserl, pp. 22–23: "The 'unquestionableness' of what goes without question in the natural cognition of what is be valid in its naive evidence, is, says transcendental philosophy, not the understandableness of the insight developed through the most radical lines of inquiries and

clarifications, is not that highest and ultimately necessary indubitability which leaves remaining no unasked and therefore unsettled questions of that fundamental sort which belong inseparably, because essentially, to every theme of cognition whatsoever. The whole aim of transcendental philosophy goes back ultimately to those fundamental matters that are unquestioned . . . , of which we spoke earlier. In them it sees the most profound and most difficult problems of the world and of world-cognition. . . ."

3. In the "Afterword" to his *Ideen*, Husserl clearly distinguished his phenomenology from all more or less thought through further developments. Cf. *Jahrbuch für Philosophie und phänomenologische Forschung.* 11 (1930), pp. 549 ff. (cf Husserl: Shorter Works, pp 43 ff.) L. Landgrebe has studied the "motives for its transformation" first in *Phänomenologie und Metaphysik* (Hamburg, 1948), now in *Der Weg der Phänomenologie* (Gütersloh, 1963), pp. 9–39, esp. pp. 18–27).

4. Cf. *Ideas* I, §§ 31–33, pp. 57 ff., esp. p. 63: "the world as *Eidos.*"

5. *Cartesian Meditations*, esp. § 8, p. 20.

6. Cf. *Crisis*, § 42, pp. 152 ff.

7. In the *Cartesian Meditations*, Husserl had discovered "Descartes' failure to make the transcendental turn." Cf. § 10, pp. 23–25.

8. Cf. *Cartesian Meditations*, § 22, pp. 53 ff.

9. *Crisis*, § 34e, pp. 129 ff.

10. Ibid., p. 129.

11. Phenomenology is "a method and an attitude of mind" (cf. *The Idea of Phenomenology*, p. 19). "Metaphysics of nature" and "metaphysics of all forms of mental life" must be seen only in connection with a "critique of cognition" (ibid., p. 46). This must be said against H. Hohl's speculations on metaphysics—cf. *Lebenswelt und Geschichte* (Freiburg/Munich, 1962), first p. 15, then mainly pp. 54 ff.

12. In the treatise on "Kant and the Idea of Transcendental Philosophy," the following is stated (p. 11): "The world took on an infinite wideness as soon as the actual life-world, the world in the 'how' of the givenness of [lived experience], was observed. It took on the whole range of the manifold subjective appearances, modes of consciousness, modes of possible position-taking; for it was, for the subject, never given otherwise than in this milieu" [trans. altered] On the term "life-world," cf. otherwise H. Hohl, § 7, pp. 23 ff., esp. p. 24/25, note.

13. "La Noción Husserliana de la 'Lebenswelt,'" in *Symposium* (Mexico, 1963). As José Gaos rightly formulates it, "analysis" is the task—the task for the purpose of "explanation" (p. 7).

14. Husserl's clear statement in *Formal and Transcendental Logic* (§ 102, p. 269) can serve as documentation: "Truth, at least in the

province of the most fundamental—the 'purely egological'—phenomenology . . . is no longer '*truth in itself* in any normal sense, not even in a sense that has a relation to a *transcendental* 'everyone.'"

15. "Science in naive positivity" will be one thing; "genuine science, which is nothing other than philosophy," another. Cf. *Formal and Transcendental Logic*, § 103, p. 272. Even a "life-world science" posited in principle as "final" (Paci) would in that respect still be science in comparatively naive positivity.

16. Cf. on this, the section on "Matters of the World That Are Taken for Granted and the Life of Consciousness," in "Kant and the Idea of Transcendental Philosophy," from which it can be seen that "absolutely no damage of any kind is to be supposed done . . . to the proper *legitimacy* of this life"—see pp. 19–24, esp. 22.

17. Walter Schulz, in *Das Problem der absoluten Reflexion* (Frankfurt a. M., 1963), p. 30.

18. One must simply take seriously the sentence which Husserl brings in this context: "Metaphysics in the common sense of the word, referring to transcendences in principle trans-subjective, is an infinite realm, but a realm contrary to sense, as must be made evident"—"Kant and the Idea of Transcendental Philosophy," p. 14.

19. The historical genesis of the modern view of science and scientific-objective cognition becomes the theme of Husserlian reflection after World War I. Cf. Eugen Fink in the preliminary remark to Husserl's "Entwurf einer 'Vorrede' zu den 'Logischen Untersuchungen'" (1913) *Tijdschrift voor Philosophie*, 1939, p. 106; Husserl, *Introduction to the Logical Investigations*, trans. Philip J. Bossert and Curtis H. Peters (The Hague, 1975), p. 13.

20. *Crisis*, § 28, p. 109.

21. Ibid., Appendix IV, p. 338.

22. Ibid.

23. *Ideas* I, § 27, p. 51.

24. F. J. Brecht, *Bewusstsein und Existenz* (Hamburg, 1948), p. 11; L. Landgrebe, *Major Problems in Contemporary European Philosophy*, p. 34; also M. Brelage, *Studien zur Transzendentalphilosophie* (Berlin, 1965), pp. 118 ff.

25. L. Landgrebe, "A Transcendental Science of the A Priori of the Life-World," in Landgrebe, *The Phenomenology of Edmund Husserl*, p. 198.

26. On "transcendental philosophy and metaphysics" according to Heidegger, see O. Pöggeler, *Der Denkweg Martin Heideggers* (Pfullingen, 1963) esp. pp. 80–87.

27. In this respect, Husserl speaks of a "turn predelineated in the

essential sense of philosophy itself in its development from the natural to
the transcendental method of cognition, from the positive or dogmatic to
the transcendental cognition and science of the world; the turn . . . from
the naive positive stage of world-cognition to world-cognition through
ultimate self-consciousness of cognition . . ." ("Kant and the Idea of
Transcendental Philosophy," I, p. 55).

28. See *Erste Philosophie* II, Hua VIII, pp. 69–77.

29. Ibid., pp. 160/61.

30. Ibid., p. 162.

31. Ibid., p. 164.

32. Cf. *Crisis*, § 54, pp. 184 ff.

33. *Crisis*, § 55, pp. 186 ff.

34. The critique by Celms, Ingarden, and Fink must be rejected:
Husserl most certainly did not go over to a speculative metaphysics.
Against this, see M. Brelage, p. 119.

35. It is, indeed, a question of the "original founding of all sciences"
and nothing else. See *Formal and Transcendental Logic*, pp. 116, 272 f.

36. Cf. *Erste Philosophie* II, p. 78.

37. Ibid., p. 79.

38. Ibid.

39. That is: "Contrary to the false ideal of an absolute existent and the
absolute trueness of an absolute existent, every existent is ultimately
relative; not only everything that is relative in any usual sense, but *every
existent is relative to transcendental subjectivity*"—*Formal and Transcendental Logic*, § 103, pp. 272 f.

40. Walter Schulz, pp. 24–25.

41. *Erste Philosophie* II, p. 79.

42. Ibid., p. 80.

43. Ibid.

44. Ibid.

45. The second of the Vienna Lectures on *The Crisis of European
Mankind and Philosophy* (10. V. 1935) says: "Only when the spirit returns
from its naive external orientation to itself, and remains with itself and
purely with itself, can it be sufficient unto itself"—*Crisis*, Appendix I, p.
297. The "radical self-comprehension of the spirit" is, however, something handed down historically.

46. The "original grounding of all the sciences" results just from the
"one transcendental subjectivity" (*Formal and Transcendental Logic*,
§ 103, p. 272).

47. L. Landgrebe, *The Phenomenology of Edmund Husserl*, p. 178.

48. On historical reflection, tradition, and philosophy, see *Crisis*, Appendix IX, pp. 389–95, esp. pp. 391 f.

49. *Crisis*, § 9, pp. 23–59.

50. In this regard one can speak of a "world given in 'pure experience'" and of an "Objective worldly being," each having its own right. See the "conclusion" to *Formal and Transcendental Logic*, p. 292.

51. Landgrebe, *The Phenomenology of Edmund Husserl*, p. 182.

52. Ibid.

53. Ibid., p. 183.

54. Hua VI, Appendix XVIII to § 34, pp. 463, 465, esp. p. 465. [Not in Carr's translation of *Crisis—Trans.*]

55. *Crisis*, § 52, p. 175.

56. *Crisis*, § 33, pp. 121-23: "The problem of the 'life-world' as a partial problem within the general problem of objective science." In § 51 (pp. 173-74) "The task of an 'ontology of the life-world'" is developed.

57. Hua VI, Appendix XIII to the entire Part III A, pp. 435–45, esp. 441. [Not in Carr's translation of *Crisis—Trans.*]

58. *Crisis*, § 9h, p. 51.

59. For "ontology is cognition, carried out straightforwardly, of a world in general as such" and transcendental philosophy is "not straightforward ontology," but the study of the "manner of cognition of a possible world, and purely as such, in pure immanence." This also applies to the "life-world," and to that extent phenomenology should be called "radical epistemological theory." Cf. *Erste Philosophie* II, pp. 497–506, esp. pp. 502 and 498.

60. As if transcendental phenomenology were a doctrine, that is, a "pretended already present philosophy" and did not first become by continued "elimination of prejudices." Cf. Appendix XIII to *Krisis* III A, Hua VI, pp. 438–39.

61. Husserl quite saw that neometaphysical interpretations are here quickly resorted to, for he says "so one orients oneself by the interpretations and critiques of Scheler, Heidegger, and others, and spares oneself this indeed very difficult study of my writings." Cf. Hua VI, p. 439.

62. *Crisis*, § 9, p. 59.

63. Landgrebe, *The Phenomenology of Edmund Husserl*, p. 185.

64. See M. Heidegger, *What is Philosophy?*, trans. William Kluback and Jean T. Wilde (New York, 1958), esp. p. 45: "Through the audible Greek word we are directly in the presence of the thing itself, not first in the presence of a mere word sign."

65. Accordingly such expressions as the "becoming-word of being," the "original saying," *aletheia* as "legend" and "language-event" are used. Werner Marx emphasizes the turn directed against "tradition." See *Heidegger und die Tradition*, esp. Main Division V, 3: "Das Wesen der Sprache," p. 203.

66. In the foreword to the third edition of his treatise *Vom Wesen des Grundes* (Frankfurt a. M., 1949), p. 5, Heidegger states: "The 'nothing' is the 'not' of the existent and so being experienced from the perspective of the existent. The ontological difference is not between being and the existent"—an expression which was not yet contained in the version dedicated to Husserl (Halle, 1929). The neo-Kantian Emil Lask in his work *Die Logik der Philosophie und die Kategorienlehre* (1911) expressly distinguished the moment of "objectivity" from the "objects," the moment of "thingliness" from the "thing," the moment of "being" from the "existent," and asked directly about the "being of the existent." Cf. Emil Lask, *Gesammelte Schriften* II (Tübingen, 1923), pp. 31, 46, 69. One must agree with M. Brelage when he says—in Lask's logic—"the grounds, the conditions of possibility for Heidegger's concept of the ontological difference lie" here (Brelage, pp. 42/43).

67. On "the universal attitude of critique," see *Erste Philosophie* II, pp. 284 ff.

68. In the text on the "meaning of a successorship to Kant," precisely such a task is discussed. Cf. *Erste Philosophie* I, pp. 284 ff.

69. *Crisis*, § 52, p. 175.

70. On the world-relatedness of traditional logic and the problem of an "ultimate logic" to surpass it, see *Formal and Transcendental Logic*, § 92a, pp. 223 ff., and § 102, pp. 268 ff.; also *Experience and Judgment*, § 9, pp. 39 ff.

71. *Crisis*, § 52, p. 176.

72. On the meaning of the reflective method in the "transcendental-phenomenological and transcendental-logical grounding of cognition," see Manfred Brelage, p. 121.

73. Thus, this is constantly required: "retrogression to a hidden subjectivity—hidden because it is not capable of being exhibited as present [*aktuell*] in reflection in its intentional activity"—*Experience and Judgment*, § 11, p. 48.

74. On the "'wholly optional' Anything Whatever" and its correlation-character, see *Formal and Transcendental Logic*, § 98, p. 249.

75. On Husserl's approximation to Fichte, see Brelage, p. 121.

76. Therefore, the "universal science" is not—as Enzo Paci claims—"the science of the prescientific, of prescientific world-life." Cf. his remarks on the "life-world science" in *Symposium* (Mexico, 1963), pp. 51–75, esp. p. 65.

77. Historically, however, even that is the "first germination" of the "idea of a philosophical culture," which remains absolutely "rationalism." Cf. the supplementary text on "Die Idee einer philosophischen Kultur," in *Erste Philosophie* II, pp. 203–7.

78. The right to life of "matter-of-course" convictions, of the implicit "presuppositions" of all metaphysical positions, however qualified, is nowhere contested. Transcendental philosophy is then also not "dissolution" of the world into "merely subjective appearances" and "illusion"; it is, rather, the "radicalism of pure contemplation of consciousness." Cf. "Kant and the Idea of Transcendental Philosophy," pp. 21 ff.

79. In this regard, it is historical through and through, and "stages of historicity" have rightly been called the foundation of the historical forms of philosophy. Cf. Hua VI, Appendix XXVI, pp. 502–3. [Not in Carr's translation of *Crisis—Trans.*]

80. "Scientific life, life as a scientist in a horizon of fellow scientists, signifies a new kind of historicity"—cf. Husserl, Hua VI, Appendix XXVII, p. 507. [Not in Carr's translation of *Crisis—Trans.*]

81. If in an appendix to the *Crisis* it is stated purportedly in closing: "Philosophy as science, as serious, rigorous, indeed apodictically rigorous science—*the dream is over*," then a few things must be said about this often cited passage. Obviously, this passage does *not* mean that the systematic thought of a philosophy as a strict science is an impossibility! It means only that actually (precisely in the mid-thirties of this century) the idea of such a scientific philosophy finds no supporters: "A powerful and constantly growing current of philosophy which renounces scientific discipline, like the current of religious disbelief, is inundating European humanity"—*Crisis*, Appendix IX, pp. 389, 390. Here one should be able to draw the distinction between the *quaestio iuris* and the *quaestio facti*.

Chapter Seven

1. "Philosophy as Rigorous Science," trans. Quentin Lauer, in *Husserl: Shorter Works*, ed. Peter McCormick and Frederick A. Elliston (Notre Dame, 1981), pp. 166–97, esp. p. 167.

2. Husserl in describing the "purpose of the investigations," in the *Crisis* states the following: "Gradually, at first unnoticed but growing more and more pressing, possibilities for a complete reorientation of view will make themselves felt, pointing to new dimensions. Questions never before asked will arise; fields of endeavor never before entered, correlations never before grasped or radically understood, will show themselves. In the end they will require that the total sense of philosophy, accepted as 'obvious' throughout all its historical forms, be basically and essentially transformed. Together with the new task and its universal apodictic ground, the *practical* possibility of a new philosophy will prove itself through its execution"— *Crisis*, § 7, p. 18. Phenomenology wishes to be such an implementation as rigorous science.

3. *Crisis*, § 9, p. 23.

4. Ibid., pp. 23–24.

5. Husserl, in describing what a philosophy as a strict science would have to achieve, opposes both "naturalistic philosophy" and "historicism and *Weltanschauung* philosophy," i.e., mainly the "naturalization of consciousness" and the "epistemological confusion" of historicism. Cf. "Philosophy as Rigorous Science," in *Husserl: Shorter Works*, p. 168 ff. and pp. 185 ff.

6. To be sure, Husserl denies the character of scientificity to so-called "*Weltanschauung* philosophy." But *Weltanschauung* philosophy does not claim to be scientific. Moreover, even the "scientific fanaticism" of the age should have its limits. Science is just one value among others. See ibid., p. 194.

7. This question of whether "science" can be conceived "as philosophy" is raised by Wilhelm Szilasi in his Zurich lecture of the same name (1945), based directly on Husserl. Cf. *Wissenschaft als Philosophie* (Zurich/New York, 1945), pp. 17, 99 ff.

8. Here belongs all historically developed science, which Husserl calls "science in naive positivity" and which represents a stage preliminary to "genuine science" "grounded by virtue of original sources in transcendental subjectivity." Cf. *Formal and Transcendental Logic*, § 103, p. 272.

9. See *Symposium* (Mexico, 1963), pp. 51–75, esp. p. 64.

10. In principle a "*reduction of truths*, of the truths belonging to a higher level to those belonging on the *lowest level*" is considered possible. *Formal and Transcendental Logic*, § 83, p. 204.

11. *Crisis* § 34, p. 125.

12. Husserl, therefore, quite rightly discusses the "difference between objective science and science in general"—namely, in the sense that the transcendental reflections must claim no less "scientificity" for themselves than do the experiential objects of segments of the world apprehended in the *intentio recta*. Cf. *Crisis* § 34, pp. 123 f.

13. Here too we would have to cite J. E. Heyde's explanation in his excellent treatise *Relativität der Wahrheit* (1933). Cf. now *Wege zur Klarheit* (Berlin, 1960), pp. 153–75, esp. pp. 162/169.

14. Enzo Paci, p. 64.

15. If there are "levels of validity" and "cognition of cognition," then also an investigation of the "validity of a cognition that is turned back upon its own activity," says Theodor Litt while sketching the relationship between *Kant and Herder* (Leipzig, Berlin, 1930), pp. 23 ff, 30 ff, 42).

16. Helmuth Plessner's incidentally quite problematic Husserl-evaluation (1938) allows only the motif of "permanent revision of founda-

tions" to stand. See *Zwischen Philosophie und Gesellschaft* (Bern, 1953), the chapter titled "Phänomenologie. Das Werk Edmund Husserls," pp. 39–59, esp. p. 57.

17. This statement applies to philosophy, and genuine "philosophizing is characterized by its constancy, which is manifested in all events in which man calls himself to account concerning his own possibilities"—W. Szilasi, pp. 93 ff.

18. Cf. Heyde, *mutatis mutandis*, p. 170.

19. *Crisis*, § 34, p. 124.

20. Ibid., § 28, p. 110.

21. Ibid., § 28, p. 108.

22. *Being and Time*, § 9, p. 67.

23. Cf., however, Landgrebe's essay "Heideggers *Sein und Zeit* und das Problem einer Grenze der Phänomenologischen Methode," now in *Weg der Phänomenologie* (Gütersloh, 1963), pp. 28–39, esp. pp. 32, 34.

24. The "things" to which philosophy wishes to penetrate are not identical with "empirical facts." Cf. "Philosophy as Rigorous Science," in *Husserl: Shorter Works*, p. 196.

25. Cf. *Crisis*, pp. 244 ff., esp p. 251.

26. Husserl explains, for instance: ". . . the phenomenologist and phenomenology themselves stand in this historicity. Appearing in worldly form like everything transcendental, it proclaims a level of development of transcendental subjectivity itself, of transcendental pan-subjectivity." Cf. MS. A V 10, p. 27, cited by Hohl, p. 79.

27. This reflection too brings knowledge, but not natural-scientific knowledge. Actually Husserl announces a new scientificity without being able to make it quite clear. Cf. Hohl, p. 80.

28. Enzo Paci, *Die Lebensweltwissenschaft*, p. 55.

29. Ibid., p. 55.

30. Ibid., p. 56.

31. Cf. the "conclusion" which J. P. Sartre draws from his attempt at a phenomenological description of the transcendency of the ego. Cf. *The Transcendence of the Ego* (1936), pp. 93–106.

32. This applies also to transcendental-phenomenological idealism, if it seeks to grasp "subjectivity as subjectivity." Cf. *Crisis*, Appendix IV, p. 337.

33. Paci, p. 63.

34. Eugen Fink expressed himself on this kind of problem: "Zum Problem ontologischer Erfahrung," in *Actas del Primer Congreso Nacional de Filosofía* II (Mendoza, 1949), pp. 733–47. Philosophy is ontological reflection, Fink declares (p. 736), namely when it reverses the self-evident into the questionable; but "it is not its affair to cause only a

greater clarity of the performance of life. It has only the task of thinking being. Such thinking, however, is something else than merely to bring preconceptual knowledge into the concept. Philosophy thinks being insofar as it designs the fundamental concepts which henceforth comprise the scaffolding of the world; it is design of the ontological basic thoughts" (p. 738). Here philosophy is, thus, obviously speculative.

35. On the grasping of scientificity, cf. Hua VI, Appendix X to § 21, esp. p. 428; furthermore, Hua VI, Appendix IX, esp. pp. 390 ff. [Not in Carr's translation of *Crisis—Trans.*]

36. *Crisis*, § 34a, p. 124.

37. On the world-doubling theorem, cf. H. Wagner, "Critical Observations Concerning Husserl's Writings," in R. O. Elveton, ed. and trans., *The Phenomenology of Husserl: Selected Critical Readings* (Chicago, 1970), pp. 221 ff.; also, M. Brelage, "Transzendentalphilosophie und konkrete Subjektivität," in *Studien zur Transzendentalphilosophie* (Berlin, 1935), pp. 19 ff., esp. p. 125.

38. *Crisis*, § 34b, p. 126.

39. *Crisis*, § 34a, pp. 123f.

40. In the lectures on "Philosophy and the Crisis of European Mankind" (Vienna, 1935), Husserl expressly speaks of "the universal critique of all life and all life-goals," and he believes that "a philosophy is universal knowledge" only through "constant reflexivity." See the treatise in *Crisis*, "The Vienna Lecture," pp. 265–299, esp. pp. 283 and 291.

41. There is no basis for concluding that "Husserl lost confidence in the phenomenological method," as T. W. Adorno asserts flatly in a misunderstanding of anti-metaphysical, i.e., precisely transcendental-phenomenological, idealism. See *Zur Metakritik der Erkenntnistheorie. Studien über Husserl und die phänomenologischen Antinomien* (Stuttgart, 1956); moreover, Adorno indulges in an emotional attack on "obsolete philosophy of consciousness" (p. 242).

42. *Crisis*, § 36, pp. 137 ff.

43. Ibid., p. 139.

44. Ibid.

45. Ibid., p. 140.

46. Ibid., § 37, pp. 142f.

47. W. H. Müller states rightly: "Transcendental-phenomenological interest does not focus on the content of the life-world, but on the manner of pregivenness of something for communalized subjects. This something is the thematicized life-world, and we are the subjects"—*Die Philosophie Edmund Husserls* (Bonn, 1956), p. 80.

48. Phenomenology thus, as a theory of the clarification of cognition, is always "prior to all metaphysics"; cf. Husserl, *Logische Untersuchungen*

II (1900/1, 1928), p. 80. [This phrase could not be located in the English version.—*Trans.*]

49. In any genuine or purported evidence, the constitutive conditions must be disclosed, and Husserl expressly names the "always again" and the question of the clarification of its evidence. See *Formal and Transcendental Logic*, § 44, pp. 120 f; § 107, p. 285.

50. Precisely such a decision which, being irrational, can turn out one way or the other and does not permit revisability would be a sign for the crisis of consciousness. Cf. on this topic Enzo Paci, *The Function of the Sciences and the Meaning of Man*, trans. Paul Piccone and James E. Hansen (Evanston, 1972), esp. Part I, chap. 1: "The Crisis of Science as the Crisis of the Meaning of Science for Man," pp. 3–17.

51. We must realize "that there is neither an absolute reflection, nor a man who, existing independently of reflection, is what is originally given and therefore the genuine existent." Cf. W. Schulz, *Das Problem der absoluten Reflexion* (Frankfurt a. M., 1963), p. 30.

52. From here it can, biographically, come to the establishment of the habitual life-form of the developing philosopher with "a new, really radical cognitive life." Cf. *Erste Philosophie* II, Hua VIII, p. 10 ff., esp. p. 11.

53. *Crisis*, § 34d, p. 127.

54. Ibid., p. 128.

55. Enzo Paci, "Die Lebensweltwissenschaft," p. 66.

56. Cf. "Author's Preface to the English Edition of *Ideas*," in *Husserl: Shorter Works*, pp. 43–53, esp. p. 48.

57. Paci, p. 67.

58. The actual "origin of theories" refers to the "need to clarify the dogmatic sciences"—*Ideas* III, trans. Ted E. Klein and William E. Pohl (The Hague, 1980), § 18, pp. 81 ff.

59. For "only a science clarified and justified transcendentally . . . can be an ultimate science; only a transcendentally-phenomenologically clarified world can be an ultimately understood world; only a transcendental logic can be an ultimate theory of science . . . [a universal] theory of the principles and norms of all the sciences." Cf. *Formal and Transcendental Logic*, Introduction, p. 16.

60. The problem is that the "system-constitutive act of reflection" is not "raised to consciousness." With these words, P. K. Schneider has, in quite a different context, characterized the naiveté of Scholz's book *Metaphysik als strenge Wissenschaft* as well as the more definite "mathematical logics" and "cybernetics." See *Die wissenschaftsbegründende Funktion der Transzendentalphilosophie* (Freiburg-Munich, 1965), esp. pp. 12 ff.

61. Although the "metacritique" given there in each case does itself start with a determinate operation, in transcendental philosophy it does not dogmatize this operation over again. In that respect, Adorno's attempt is inappropriate when he intends to discuss "Husserl's pure phenomenology in the spirit of dialectics" and thus remains "naive" as regards the history of philosophy. Cf. *Zur Metakritik der Erkenntnistheorie*, p. 12.

62. It is a matter of a "cognition of cognition" in the radical sense. Cf. *Erste Philosophie* II, Appendix XXXII, pp. 497–506, esp. p. 498, and also elsewhere in Husserl.

63. *Crisis*, § 34f, p. 133.

64. Ibid., p. 133.

65. Every metaphysics, including the one "in the busy routine of the 'resurrected metaphysics' that has become so vocal and so bewitching of late," must in principle be stripped of its naiveté; and this holds true, furthermore, for life-world metaphysics. Cf. *Crisis*, § 34, p. 133.

66. The article "Philosophy as Rigorous Science" already demands this. For "the science concerned with what is radical must from every point of view be radical itself in its procedure. Above all it must not rest until it has attained its own absolutely clear beginnings"—*Husserl: Shorter Works*, p. 196.

67. Cf. *Formal and Transcendental Logic*, § 106, p. 280.

68. Paci, "Die Lebensweltwissenschaft", p. 73.

69. *Crisis*, § 36, p. 141.

70. *Crisis*, § 34, pp. 128, 133.

71. Ibid., pp. 127–128.

72. E. Paci, "Die Lebensweltwissenschaft," p. 74.

73. Cf. the text "Idee der vollen Ontologie" (1924), in *Erste Philosophie* II, pp. 212 ff.

74. Ibid., pp. 10–17, esp. p. 11.

75. E. Paci, p. 71.

76. There is, rightly, talk of a "first theory of science." Cf. *Erste Philosophie* II, Appendix III, pp. 320 ff., esp. p. 323.

77. "To recast the conjectures of profundity into unequivocal rational forms—that is the essential process in constituting anew the rigorous sciences"—so it is said at the end of "Philosophy as Rigorous Science," *Husserl: Shorter Works*, p. 195.

Chapter Eight

1. Subject and object in their basic relation to each other are the theme of the fundamental science, and it in turn must, according to

Husserl, be understood as "radical epistemological theory." Cf. *Erste Philosophie* II, Hua VIII, Appendix XXXII, p. 498.

2. On this topic, cf. Ludwig Landgrebe's essay on "Die Methode der Phänomenologie Edmund Husserls," in *Neue Jahrbücher für Wissenschaft und Jugendbildung* 9:5 (Leipzig-Berlin, 1933).

3. In *Erste Philosophie* I, Husserl treats of the "preparation of a future genuine metaphysics that is hampered by the lack of a transcendental basic science," Hua VII, pp. 182 ff.

4. Heinrich Barth calls attention to this when in an essay on the "Philosophie der Existenz" (1942) he says: "Out of the need for a critical grounding of cognition in its transcendental unity, the philosophy of existence becomes transcendental philosophy" and "Existence is appearance in its entering-into-appearance." Cf. *Jahrbücher der Schweizerischen Philosophischen Gesellschaft*. II (Basel, 1942), pp. 22–46, esp. pp. 40 ff., 31.

5. The "principle of all principles: that every originary presentive intuition is a legitimizing source of cognition" or that "each [theory] can only again draw its truth itself from originary data" (*Ideas* I, § 24, p. 44) surely holds true *mutatis mutandis* also for the evidence of reflection.

6. Cf. the entire beginning of Landgrebe's essay quoted above.

7. *The Paris Lectures*, esp. p. 32.

8. The *Theory of Phenomenological Reduction* is no doubt precisely this radicalization. Cf. the pre-meditation or the apodictic beginning of philosophy with the introduction "Die Motivation des anfangenden Philosophen in der absoluten Situation," where it is stated: "Philosophy should be . . . knowledge out of a thoroughly highest and ultimate self-reflection, self-comprehension, self-responsibility of the knower for his acts of cognition, or what amounts to the same thing, it should be an absolutely self-legitimating science, and moreover universal science"— *Erste Philosophie* II, p. 3.

9. *Erste Philosophie* II, Appendix III, pp. 320 ff.

10. Husserl's relation to Kant is subject to great vacillations. The "Kritische Ideengeschichte" judges very negatively, especially Appendix XV to the 25th Lecture (*Erste Philosophie* I, Hua VII, pp. 350–56, esp. p. 356); the text "Kant and the Idea of Transcendental Philosophy" (ibid., pp. 230–87) is more positive.

11. Cf. T. M. Seebohm's fundamental description in *Die Bedingungen der Möglichkeit der Transzendentalphilosophie* (Bonn, 1962), esp. pp. 21–38.

12. Landgrebe, "Die Methode der Phänomenologie Edmund Husserls"; see the entire introduction.

13. If the natural, mundane consciousness apprehends the world as

objective world, as a world existing-in-itself and transcendent, then this apprehension is not affected by the phenomenological effort, and absolutely not denied; rather, such an apprehension is clarified in its possibility. For it is not a question of the world independent of consciousness but of the world meant as existing in itself, which as such presupposes consciousness. Cf. M. Brelage, *Studien zur Transzendentalphilosophie*, p. 109.

14. *Formal and Transcendental Logic*, § 94, pp. 232–36, esp. p. 233, where the particular meaning "transcendent being" is under discussion.

15. Cf. the treatises which were added to *Erste Philosophie* II: 1) "Die Idee der vollen Ontologie" (Hua VIII, pp. 212–18, esp. pp. 213, 215); 2) "Der Weg in die transzendentale Phänomenologie als absolute und universale Ontologie durch die positiven Ontologien und die positive Erste Philosophie" (Hua VIII, pp. 219–28, esp. p. 225).

16. Thus "inclusion of the ontologies within phenomenology" is the starting point. Cf. *Ideas* III, §§ 14, 15, pp. 66–72 (cf. p. 68 on "ontology as dogmatic science").

17. Cf. *Erste Philosophie* II: Appendix XV: "All being presupposes subjectivity" (p. 408)—"Subjectivity, however, is consciousness" (p. 408).

18. This also holds good for any consciousness which, dedicated to the existent, apprehends itself as immediately existing with the existent. What H. Plessner, *Die Stufen des Organischen und der Mensch* (Berlin, 1928), has called the "eccentric positionality of the spirit" means for the explanation of cognition "mediated immediacy": the immediate attitude toward the existent (the intentionality of consciousness) is itself mediated by the spontaneity of consciousness. Cf. N. Hartmann, *Das Problem des geistigen Seins* (Berlin, 1933), p. 121, where the "mediated immediacy of self-consciousness" is discussed.

19. But as objective consciousness, as mundane consciousness, consciousness attains self-consciousness. Cf. M. Brelage's investigations on the controversy between N. Hartmann and phenomenology in *Studien zur Transzendentalphilosophie*, p. 176, esp. n. 218.

20. On the method of intentional analysis and the method of clues, see Landgrebe, *Der Weg der Phänomenologie*, p. 35.

21. Cf., on this topic, the entire Fifth Meditation of the *Cartesian Meditations* (pp. 89–151); see also D. Sinn, *Die transzendentale Intersubjektivität mit ihren Seinshorizonten bei Edmund Husserl* (Diss. Heidelberg, 1958).

22. If "phenomenological reduction and absolute validation" is under discussion, then I want to "become phenomenologically familiar with the act of cognition as such . . . according to its kinds, forms, essential possibilities, and to illuminate from all sides and bring to my understand-

ing the essence of rational consciousness." Cf. *Erste Philosophie* II, Appendix XXXII, p. 498.

23. In the treatise "Kant and the Idea of Transcendental Philosophy," pp. 14. 55, Husserl speaks of "science" and "scientific basic" (*grundwissenschaftlich*) understanding, indeed precisely with respect to transcendental-phenomenological idealism.

24. See *Erste Philosophie* I, Appendix XX, p. 394.

25. For "of essential necessity . . . , to every 'truly existing' object there corresponds the idea of a possible consciousness" (see *Ideas* I, § 142, p. 341). Of course, being is not an existent of a mundane sort, but does it thereby cease to be sense-determined, i.e., ultimately still a sense-construct for a correlatively appertinent consciousness?

26. Cf. *Erste Philosophie* II, Appendix XXXII, p. 502, where the relation between ontology and phenomenology is clarified.

27. Husserl says expressly: "Thus all ontologies lie within the field of phenomenology—but as correlates of knowledge" (*Erste Philosophie* II, p. 504).

28. On the problematic of "living-through," and of "inner being" see Roman Ingarden's "Kritische Bemerkungen" [critical remarks] on the *Cartesian Meditations* in Hua I (The Hague, 1950), pp. 203–18, esp. p. 216.

29. This may be said in a variation of Heyde's well-known analysis on the "Relativity of Truth?" Cf. *Wege zur Klarheit* (Berlin, 1960), esp. pp. 157, 168.

30. *Erste Philosophie* II, p. 504.

31. On the turning around of the "straightforward" attitude into the "transcendental" one, see ibid., p. 504.

32. At the beginning stands the "absolutely evident insight . . . , that all being is related back intentionally to the being of egos" (ibid., p. 505).

33. On the two possibilities of aprioristic rationalism—of going back in knowledge to ontology and function-theory or to essences and categories—see H. Plessner, *Die Einheit der Sinne* (Bonn, 1923), p. 31.

34. L. Landgrebe expressly raised the question in the essay "Heideggers *Sein und Zeit* und das Problem einer Grenze der phänomenologischen Methode." Cf. *Der Weg der Phänomenologie*, pp. 28–39.

35. On this subject, see the discussions of Husserl, N. Hartmann and Hönigswald in M. Brelage, *Studien zur Transzendentalphilosophie*, pp. 179 ff., esp. pp. 185 ff.

36. This is the case with P. K. Schneider, *Die wissenschaftsbegründende Funktion der Transzendentalphilosophie* (Freiburg-Munich, 1965). See there esp. pp. 159 ff.

37. *Formal and Transcendental Logic*, § 6, p. 29.

38. See *Erste Philosophie* II, pp. 203 ff.

39. Hermann Drüe in his important book on *Edmund Husserls System der phänomenologischen Psychologie* (Berlin, 1963) § 49, p. 260.

40. Cf. *Erste Philosophie* II, Appendix XVI, pp. 408–410, esp. p. 409.

41. Ibid., Appendix XXI, pp. 439 ff.

42. Ibid., Appendix XXXII, pp. 498 ff.

43. Here a radicalism and a universality of pure contemplation of consciousness must be demanded (*Erste Philosophie* I, p. 254).

44. See ibid., *Erste Philosophie* II, Appendix XXIX, p. 475.

45. Ibid., p. 473.

46. Ibid., p. 476.

47. Cf. *Cartesian Meditations*, pp. 89 ff.; *Erste Philosophie* II, p. 64.

48. Cf. the whole of Part E in A. Diemer's book on Husserl (Meisenheim, 1956), esp. "Von der Primordialität zur Intersubjektivität," pp. 269–373, esp. pp. 283 ff.

49. On reduction as intersubjective reduction, cf. Landgrebe, *Der Weg der Phänomenologie*, pp. 89–97.

50. On "*Intentionalia*," see Husserl's *Ideas* I, §§ 77, 78, pp. 177 ff.; also Diemer, *Edmund Husserl*, p. 48, n. 114; and Hohl, *Lebenswelt und Geschichte*, p. 57.

51. The problem of intersubjective communities can also be approached from here. Cf. Husserl, *Ideas* II (The Hague, 1952) § 51, p. 142; and *Cartesian Meditations*, § 56, pp. 128 ff.

52. On the "concept of world" and the problematic of the "present-on-hand," see L. Landgrebe, *Major Problems*, pp. 56–82, esp. p. 65, and also pp. 83 ff, "The World as Nature."

53. To be sure, "no one ever thinks about the predications and truths which precede science, about the 'logic' which provides norms within this sphere of relativity, or about the possibility, even in the case of these logical structures conforming purely descriptively to the life-world, of inquiring into the system of principles that give them their norms a priori"—*Crisis*, § 34, p. 135.

54. Method of reflection and method of regression, meditation on the beginnings and reduction belong together. On reflection of the first and the second levels, cf. *Erste Philosophie* II, pp. 86–92, and pp. 92–97.

55. Ibid., p. 3.

56. "Meditation on the idea of an individual and communal life in absolute self-responsibility"—ibid., pp. 193–202, esp. p. 194.

57. Cf. Husserl's treatise "The Attitude of Natural Science- and the Attitude of [Human] Science," in *Crisis*, Appendix III, pp. 315– 34.

58. Ibid., p. 334.

59. Thus "world-science" is discussed—ibid., p. 333.

60. What matters is "the correlation between world and world-consciousness" (cf. *Crisis*, § 41, pp. 151 ff.) and the "iteration" of the explanation by reflective-regressive "reduction." Cf. *Erste Philosophie* II, pp. 132 ff.

61. Various reductions have the task of creating clarity here. On their necessity in the psychological field, cf. H. Drüe, *Edmund Husserls System der phänomenologischen Psychologie*, p. 191.

62. If recently a "phenomenology as experiental science of man" is announced, as in Stephan Strasser's book *Phänomenologie als Erfahrungswissenschaft vom Menschen* (Berlin, 1962), and if then precisely this transcendental turn is not accomplished (p. 223), such a "doctrine" really remains stuck in scientific naivité.

63. Cf. *Erste Philosophie* II, pp. 112 ff.

64. Husserl, *Cartesian Meditations*, § 64, p. 155.

65. In such *cogitationes*, "philosophy as systematic self-development of transcendental subjectivity" also gives itself "in the form of systematic transcendental self-theoretization on the ground of transcendental self-experience," according to Husserl in *Erste Philosophie* II, pp. 164 ff.

66. See Husserl, *Experience and Judgment*, § 4, pp. 19 ff.

67. Husserl, *Erste Philosophie* II, p. 6; *Paris Lectures*, p. 38; *Cartesian Meditations*, § 64, p. 155.

68. *Erste Philosophie* I, pp. 78 ff., where the term occurs; see also MS. C 3 I, p. 27.

69. *Erste Philosophie* II, p. 7.

70. Ibid.

71. Husserl speaks of "archeology" in MS. C 16 VI (see Diemer, p. 19, n. 33), of "phansiology" in MS. F I 23, p. 150 (cf. Diemer, p. 83, Note 36).

72. *Erste Philosophie* II, p. 11, "Leben aus Berufung."

73. *Cartesian Meditations*, § 55, pp. 120 ff.

74. The question of the scientificity of transcendental-reflective statements at all is connected with this. Cf. *Erste Philosophie* II, Appendix XXIX, pp. 472 ff.

75. *Cartesian Meditations*, § 55, pp. 120 ff.

76. He says: "The only absolute being, however, is to be a subject, as being constituted originally for oneself alone." See *Erste Philosophie* II, p. 190.

77. For "the primary mode of appearing . . . is therefore the appearance of determinate form"—cf. *Erste Philosophie* II, Appendix XVI, p. 412.

78. See T. Litt, *Denken und Sein* (Stuttgart, 1948), p. 146: "Das Sichselbstdenken."

79. Cf. *Erste Philosophie* II, Appendix I, pp. 7, and 302 ff.

80. This rationalism consists in the progressive escalation of the reflections. Cf. *Erste Philosophie* I, pp. 262 ff.

Chapter Nine

1. Cf. on the contrary L. Landgrebe, *Major Problems in Contemporary European Philosophy*, pp. 17–55.

2. Ibid., p. 21.

3. The reproach of "forgottenness" is fashionable; cf. "world-forgottenness" in Nietzsche, "problem-forgottenness" in Nicolai Hartmann, "history-forgottenness" in Litt.

4. *Being and Time*, § 3, "The ontological priority of the question of being" (p. 28); § 4, "The ontic priority of the question of being" (p. 32); § 4 also contains statements on the ontico-ontological priority of the question of being.

5. It is then the "fundamental science" that aims "at a radical new grounding of a scientific philosophy." Cf. the "Encyclopedia Britannica article" in *Phänomenologische Psychologie*, Hua IX, p. 237 (cf. *Husserl: Shorter Works*, pp. 21–35, esp. p. 22).

6. *Being and Time*, § 7, p. 62.

7. What Husserl means by object can be seen most succinctly in *Formal and Transcendental Logic* (Halle, 1929) § 99, pp. 250 ff.

8. *Ideas* I, §§ 47, 49, pp. 105, 109.

9. So it is said: "The 'essence' of this entity consists in its 'to be' [*Zu-sein*]" and "The 'essence' of *Dasein* lies in its existence" (*Being and Time*, § 9, p. 42).

10. *Formal and Transcendental Logic*, p. 251.

11. *Being and Time*, § 2, p. 24.

12. Landgrebe, *Major Problems*, pp. 18 ff.

13. W. Schulz, *Der Gott der neuzeitlichen Metaphysik* (Pfullingen, 1957), pp. 33f.

14. *Oeuvres*, ed. Adam-Tannery, VII, p. 25.

15. See Husserl's reflections in *Crisis*, Appendix A I, "Philosophy and the Crisis of European Humanity" (The Vienna Lecture), pp. 269–99, esp. p. 297.

16. On this topic, see the book *Geschichtlichkeit. Wege und Irrwege eines Begriffes* (Berlin, 1963) by Gerhard Bauer, but especially the accurate review by E. W. Orth in the *Hist. Zeitschrift* 200:2, pp. 347–55.

17. Cf. Eugen Fink, "Das Problem der ontologischen Erfahrung," in *Actas del primero congreso nacional de filosofia* (Mendoza, 1949), pp. 733–41, esp. p. 740; "L'analyse intentionnelle et le problème de la pensée spéculative," in H. L. van Breda, ed., *Problèmes actuels de la*

phénoménologie (Paris, 1952) pp. 53–87, esp. p. 58; *Nachdenkliches zur ontologischen Frühgeschichte von Raum-Zeit-Bewegung* (The Hague, 1957), esp. pp. 9 ff; *Sein, Wahrheit, Welt* (The Hague, 1958), pp. 20 ff.

18. Cf. F. Heinemann, *Neue Wege der Philosophie* (Frankfurt a. M., 1929), Afterword as Foreword, pp. xi ff.

19. Its history is long, but still remains to be written. Cf. W. Schulz, p. 14.

20. *Crisis*, Appendix IV, p. 338: "Thus philosophy is nothing other than [rationalism] through and through."

21. In *Ideas* I, § 27, p. 57, Husserl speaks of the "world of the natural attitude"; in *Crisis*, esp. § 9, p. 59, of the "life-world" and the "return to the naiveté of life."

22. Landgrebe, *Major Problems*, p. 29.

23. It can then first be treated "descriptively," as in F. J. J. Buytendijk, *Das Menschliche* (Stuttgart, 1958)—see foreword, p. ix.

24. Cf. *Cartesian Meditations*, § 42, pp. 89 ff.

25. The real "unscientific" thinking of being would be lost over this; philosophy thus appears under the aspect of after-the-factness. Cf. E. Fink, *Zur ontologischen Frühgeschichte von Raum-Zeit-Bewegung*, p. 16.

26. Cf. Maximilian Beck's critique of Heidegger's *Being and Time* in *Philosophische Hefte* I (Berlin, 1928), §§ 2 ff.

27. Eugen Fink, in his later writings, rejects as inadequate the whole "approach of modern phenomenology." Cf. *Sein, Wahrheit, Welt*, p. 88.

28. The "question of the fundamental structures of world-experiencing life" is therefore placed at the beginning. Cf. G. Brand, *Welt, Ich und Zeit* (The Hague, 1955), esp. § 10, pp. 54 ff.

29. Even "speculation" must bring to evidence what it means in a given case. To experience the "essence of the appearance of an entity" is still an achievement of consciousness. Cf. E. Fink, *Zur ontologischen Frühgeschichte von Raum-Zeit-Bewegung*, pp. 131 f.

30. When it is a matter of clearings, obviously a "living through" and a mere "being aware" is not sufficient. What is needed is "a radical reconstruction which will satisfy the ideal of philosophy as being the universal unity of knowledge by means of a unitary and absolutely rational foundation," as Husserl says at the beginning of the *Paris Lectures*, p. 3.

31. Even a "knowledge of existence" can stand completely "under the sign of transcendental philosophy" if existence should mean decision in the appearance of knowledge, namely by its entering into appearance. Cf. Heinrich Barth, *Erkenntnis der Existenz* (Basel/Stuttgart, 1965), p. 9.

32. What lies at the basis of the course of all science can be called "existential knowledge." Cf. H. Barth, p. 168.

33. There was quite unwarranted talk of the "solitariness of the

transcendental self" in Husserl, e. g., by F. Heinemann in *Existenz-philosophie—lebendig oder tot?* (Stuttgart, 1954), pp. 48–60.

34. A distinction must be made between the "nonscientific world" and "nonscientific level" of an insight! Cf. S. Strasser, *Phänomenologie und Erfahrungswissenschaft vom Menschen* (Berlin, 1962), pp. 66–67.

35. Also known is the "respondeo, ergo sum," which Fritz Heinemann, in *Jenseits des Existentialismus* (Stuttgart, 1957) pp. 153–78, places at the beginning as the starting point of philosophy and complements with the principle which is valid for nature "non respondet, sed est" (p. 178).

36. In terms of individual psychology as well as of transcendental philosophy, one can speak of the "undermining of the matter-of-course." Cf. F. Copei, *Der fruchtbare Moment im Bildungsprozess* (Heidelberg, 1950), p. 61, and the reference to the undoubtedness of the natural world-experience in Husserl, *Phenomenological Psychology*, trans. John Scanlon (The Hague, 1977), p. 46.

37. Concerning "being-as as an existential that determines the being-structure of being human and is just as originary as being-oneself," see W. Maihofer, *Recht und Sein* (Frankfurt a. M., 1954), Foreword.

Index of Names

Index of Topics

47; oblique 49, ontic 151;
philosophical 51;
prejudgmental 87;
prescientific 126; pure 85,
174, 203 n. 51;
quasi-natural 48; rational
51, 53, 54, 59, 93, 96, 142
166–8; reflective 41ff., 71,
121, 130, 136, 166;
scientific 12, 46, 105;
subjective 67; technical
167; topical 101ff., 104;
topical-doxic 101, 117;
totalizing 175;
transcendental 58, 71, 96,
104, 137, 203 n. 51;
transcendentally structured
55; variable 69; absolutism
of 21; achievement of 222
n. 29; act of 29; advertence
of 173; circle of 35;
community of 174; concept
of 85; constitution of 106;
correlate of 36, 164;
context of 37; disclosures of
33; expansion of 68;
framework of 94; historicity
of 196 n. 26; horizon of 38,
64; life of 26, 102, 111,
114; metaphysics of 38,
44–5, 63, 70, 102, 121;
modes of 205 n. 12;
performance of 21–2, 28,
47, 92, 171, 173, 176;
phenomenon of 167;
philosophy of 22, 24–5, 30,
47, 83, 161ff., 163, 173,
Cartesian 32,
phenomenological 26, 37f.,
45–6, 51, 95, 129;
positions of 77; process of
144; project of 28; pure

contemplation, attitude of
18. 167, 176, 210 n. 78,
219 n. 43; regressive steps
of 168; reiterative elevation
of 175; room for 204 n. 68;
situation of 36; state of 37,
38, 52, 64, 68–9, 72–3,
75–7, 103, 105, 108, 116,
124, 129, 132–3, 136,
concrete 140, critical 74,
disinterested 129,
existential 140, static 77,
subjective 128,
transcendental 73;
structure of 46, 54, 57,
111; system of 94; theory of
145; world of 69; in general
131, 175; as doom 189;
alien to 204 n. 68; of
something 26, 144, 175;
conscious-unconscious 115
consensus, general 82
constitution 25–6, 30–1, 41, 45,
53, 63, 67–70, 74–5, 86,
92–3, 94, 96–7, 99, 101–2,
104, 116–9, 121, 124, 144,
146, 149–53, 154– 6, 158,
171, 173–4, 198 n. 56, 203
n. 55; group-subjective
154; individual-subjective
114; intentional 158;
life-world 103;
phenomenological 164;
primarily institutive 202 n.
40; subjective 127;
transcendental 30, 53, 151;
transcendental idealist 63;
analysis 90, 104, 107, 121,
125–7, 132–2; condition
41, 53, 92, 101, 118, 120,
214 n. 49; connection 53,
75, 79, 92, 96, 97, 110,

institution 35
intellectus divinus 140, 159, 167
intensive 56
intentionality 26–7, 36, 49, 55,
   67–8, 78, 82, 96, 98, 102,
   106, 108, 118, 144–5, 149,
   151–4, 158, 165, 167, 203
   n. 59, 109 n. 73, 218 n. 35;
   of consciousness 26;
   intentio 64, 67, 71, 92,
   102; what it intends 88;
   intentional analysis 144–5,
   147–8, 150, 152, 159, 217
   n. 20
intentio recta 25, 36, 50, 52, 56,
   149, 154; obliqua 149;
intentum 64, 67, 71, 92, 93, 102
interest 55, 65, 129, 139–40;
   fetishized 131; historical-
   teleological 131;
   practical-political 19;
   transcendental
   phenomenological 213 n.
   47; raised to a higher level
   129; direction of 130
interior 155
interiority 9, 155
interpretation 16, 20–1, 27–8,
   31–2, 33–4, 36, 58–9, 78,
   92, 124, 125, 130, 132,
   138, 144, 166, 176;
   contentually dogmatized
   166;
   fundamental-ontological
   169; natural-scientific, of
   the world 115; vitalist 169;
   of Husserl, Scheler, and
   Heidegger 169; of
   philosophy 12; design
   124–5; horizon of 94; states
   of 37; system of 37
interrelation 112

intersubjectivity 56, 71, 85, 102,
   105, 139, 141, 150, 152–4,
   158, 169, 219 n. 48, n. 49,
   n. 51; monadic 158;
   transcendental 70
intuition 22, 66, 86–9, 132, 137,
   141, 173; originary 20, 86;
   subjective-relative 127;
   form of 140; mode of 138;
   typology of 133
invariable 93, 106, 134; system of
   invariants 96
invention 168
inversion 92
inward turning 48–9, 52, 83, 84,
   182 n. 33, 191 n. 23;
   double 182 n. 33; oblique
   16
irrational 30, 65, 214 n. 50
irrationalism 1, 19, 115, 169
irreal 68, 94, 148; irreality 67, 109

judgment 66, 144, 145; apodictic
   15; original 74; predicative
   149; evidence 87; genetic
   theory of 107 n. 49; natural
   modes of 203 n. 60

Kantianism 1, 21, 92, 101, 128,
   145; crypto- 145; latent 95;
   Kant interpretation 92
kinesthetic 129, 134–5
knowledge 2, 3, 6, 8, 16, 27, 44,
   46, 49, 52, 56, 75–7,
   79–81, 84, 86, 90, 113,
   117–9, 121, 123, 126–8,
   138–40, 148, 169, 173–4,
   181 n. 20, 182 n. 33, 187
   n. 55, 189 n. 83, 216 n. 8,
   222 n. 31; absolute 77,
   144, of the intellectus
   divinus 167; acquired by

-factor 156; formation 15,
102, 146, 147–9, 151,
154–6, 159–60,
constitutive 102, 157;
intentional 158, fulfilment
of 170; horizons 143;
implications of 92, 147,
152, 159; moment of 154;
philosophy of 146;
phenomenological -analysis
164, regressive 164;
problematic of, hidden 170;
question of 148, 163–4;
research 148, universal
146, 150; structure of 114;
system of 35; unity of 17,
24, 30, 64, 67– 8, 93–4,
128, 144, 153, 171; of
being 33, 99, 116, 146–8,
158, 164, 171–2; of *Dasein*
172; of object 146; of
objectivity 147, 152–3
shell, stabilization in one's own 9
sheltering standpoints 10
significancy, principle of 152, 208
signs, system of 65
situation 9, 14, 26, 33, 37, 157,
159; concrete 57; historical
174, 176; lived 91;
situative-contextual 188 n.
64
size 124
society 166; unstratified,
pragmatically oriented 5;
sociohistorical 169
socio-economic unity 168
sociology 187 n. 44, 190 n. 12; of
knowledge 197 n. 41
solipsism, problematic of 153;
solus ipse 174
soul 155–6; dogmatism of 44
space 63, 106, 140

space-time form 124, 140;
spatio-temporal 134
speaking, of the *logos* 91
speculation 5, 7, 59, 132, 139, 221
n. 17, 194 n. 60, 207 n. 34,
213 n. 34, 222 n. 29;
idealistic 86; metaphysical
90
spirit 25, 132, 167, 184 n. 3, n.
12, 185 n. 20, 207 n 45,
217 n. 18; of nations 169;
spiritual 185 n. 16, n. 18;
spirituality 213
spontaneous 64, 217 n. 18
stage 106
standpoint-philosophies 87
state 147, 166; of affairs 86, 145;
of mind 27, 50, 55, 56
statements in themselves 66
static 51, 56, 68, 89, 91
starting basis 102, 105, 119, 126;
starting point 92, 174;
metaphysical 140; starting
position 26; subjective
dogmatic 29; point of
departure, ultimately valid
69; apparently
insurmountable 70; initial
fact 174; initial level 7
stratum 19, 28, 123; stratification
20
structure 30, 53, 71, 73, 78, 83,
139–41, 155, 173; animal-
social 168; aprioristic 27,
134; cogitative 96;
constituted 116, 158;
correlative 67; existential
30, 150; ideal 67, 68; inner
28; intentional 96; irreal
68; logical 66–7; mental 66;
noematic 96; objective 46;
sociohistorical 169;